Interpreting LGBT History at Museums and Historic Sites

INTERPRETING HISTORY

SERIES EDITOR
Russell Lewis, Chicago History Museum

EDITORIAL ADVISORY BOARD
Eloise Batic, Indiana Historical Society
Jessica Dorman, The Historic New Orleans Collection
W. Eric Emerson, South Carolina Department of Archives and History
Tim Grove, National Air and Space Museum
Lorraine McConaghy, Museum of History and Industry, Seattle, Washington
Sandra Smith, Heinz History Center
Ellen Spear, Heritage Museums & Gardens
Larry Wagenaar, Historical Society of Michigan

STAFF
Bob Beatty, AASLH
Charles Harmon, Rowman & Littlefield Publishers

About the Series

The American Association for State and Local History publishes the *Interpreting History* series in order to provide expert, in-depth guidance in interpretation for history professionals at museums and historic sites. The books are intended to help practitioners expand their interpretation to be more inclusive of the range of American history.

Books in this series help readers:
- quickly learn about the questions surrounding a specific topic,
- introduce them to the challenges of interpreting this part of history, and
- highlight best-practice examples of how interpretation has been done by different organizations.

They enable institutions to place their interpretative efforts into a larger context, despite each having a specific and often localized mission. These books serve as quick references to practical considerations, further research, and historical information.

Titles in the Series

Interpreting Native American History and Culture at Museums and Historic Sites by Raney Bench
Interpreting the Prohibition Era at Museums and Historic Sites by Jason D. Lantzer
Interpreting African American History and Culture at Museums and Historic Sites by Max van Balgooy
Interpreting LGBT History at Museums and Historic Sites by Susan Ferentinos
Interpreting Slavery at Museums and Historic Sites by Kristin L. Gallas and James DeWolf Perry

Interpreting LGBT History at Museums and Historic Sites

By Susan Ferentinos

ROWMAN & LITTLEFIELD
Lanham • Boulder • New York • London

Published by Rowman & Littlefield
A wholly owned subsidiary of The Rowman & Littlefield Publishing Group, Inc.
4501 Forbes Boulevard, Suite 200, Lanham, Maryland 20706
www.rowman.com

Unit A, Whitacre Mews, 26-34 Stannary Street, London SE11 4AB

Copyright © 2015 by Rowman & Littlefield

All rights reserved. No part of this book may be reproduced in any form or by any electronic or mechanical means, including information storage and retrieval systems, without written permission from the publisher, except by a reviewer who may quote passages in a review.

British Library Cataloguing in Publication Information Available

Library of Congress Cataloging-in-Publication Data Available
ISBN 978-0-7591-2372-4 (cloth : alk. paper)
ISBN 978-0-7591-2373-1 (pbk. : alk. paper)
ISBN 978-0-7591-2374-8 (electronic)

∞™ The paper used in this publication meets the minimum requirements of American National Standard for Information Sciences—Permanence of Paper for Printed Library Materials, ANSI/NISO Z39.48-1992.

Printed in the United States of America

For Danielle,
My Sunshine

Contents

Acknowledgments ix

PART I **INTRODUCTION**

CHAPTER 1 **Introduction** 3

CHAPTER 2 **A Pep Talk for the Faint of Heart** 9

PART II **HISTORICAL OVERVIEW**

CHAPTER 3 **Approaching LGBT History** 21

CHAPTER 4 **"The Abominable Sin": European Contact to the Late Nineteenth Century** 29

CHAPTER 5 **Creating Communities: Late Nineteenth Century to the Mid-1960s** 49

CHAPTER 6 **We're Here, We're Queer, Get Used to It: Mid-1960s to *United States v. Windsor* (2013)** 75

CHAPTER 7 **History Coda: What a Strange Year It's Been** 103

PART III INTERPRETING LGBT HISTORY

CHAPTER 8 **Trends in LGBT Historical Interpretation** 109

CHAPTER 9 **Case Study—Displaying Queer History at the Chicago History Museum: Lessons from the Curators of *Out in Chicago*** 119

Jill Austin and Jennifer Brier

CHAPTER 10 **Case Study—The Varied Telling of Queer History at Historic New England Sites** 131

Kenneth C. Turino

CHAPTER 11 **Case Study—Interpreting for the Next Generation: The Summer History Immersion Program (Minnesota)** 141

Kyle Parsons and Stewart Van Cleve

CHAPTER 12 **Issues to Consider When Interpreting LGBT History** 151

CHAPTER 13 **Conclusion: Some Suggestions** 161

APPENDICES

APPENDIX 1 **Timeline of Key Events in LGBT United States History** 171

APPENDIX 2 **Recommended Reading** 175

APPENDIX 3 **Bibliography** 181

Index 197

About the Authors 207

Acknowledgments

THE FIRST time I ever spoke with Bob Beatty, I was on vacation in the LGBT tourist town of Provincetown, Massachusetts. He called to discuss a business matter, but we soon became dear friends. A few years later, Bob once again intersected with my love of the queer past, when he called to suggest I write a book on interpreting LGBT history for museums and historic sites. He has been a wonderful colleague since the day I met him, and it is only fitting that I begin my acknowledgments with him.

Bob gave me the idea for this project, but it was Lois H. Silverman who convinced me to do it. Her enthusiasm for the project at its conceptual stage shifted my thinking from a scarcity of time to an abundance of possibility, and I am very grateful, because this effort became a labor of love for me. Likewise, encouragement from Barbara J. Howe, Heather Huyck, and Margaret (Peg) Strobel in the book's early stages set me on a steady path of exploration and productivity.

At key stages of the research and writing, I had the privilege of presenting my work and participating in conversations with audience members. I thank the Indiana University Department of History, the University of Michigan Eisenberg Institute for Historical Studies, the American Association for State and Local History Annual Meeting, and the American Alliance of Museums Annual Meeting for hosting me, and I thank those who attended these talks for their feedback and questions. I also thank Mary Rizzo and the rest of the editorial staff at the *Public Historian* for inviting me to reflect on this topic as part of the journal's blog.

To me, research often feels like detective work, and that was certainly true when locating examples of LGBT historical interpretation and its related literature. I am grateful to Donna Graves, Stacy Klingler, Laura A. Miller, and Stephanie Lehner Rowe for pointing me toward sources I would not have found otherwise. Bob Beatty again proved indispensable in this regard, sending me everything of relevance that he found in his wide travels of the museum world.

This book has benefited from the expertise of those who guided its progress. Wendy Gamber has patiently guided my professional development for nearly twenty years, and most recently this mentoring has expanded to include book writing. Charles Harmon, my editor at Rowman & Littlefield, filled a similar role, walking me through the more mysterious parts of the publishing process.

In the same vein, the authors of this volume's case studies—Jill Austin, Jennifer Brier, Kyle Parsons, Kenneth C. Turino, and Stewart Van Cleve—made significant contributions, both to the manuscript and to my thinking on the topic. I thank them for their willingness to share their experiences so that others might learn from them. Numerous others—Erin Bailey, Wesley Chenault, David Jobin, Stacia Kuceyeski, Janice Monger, Nicole Robert, and Elizabeth Tucker—were kind enough to share their insights on interpreting LGBT history. Nearly all of these folks, plus Melissa Bingmann, Michelle McClellan, Marla R. Miller, Lori Osborne, Margaret Puskar-Pasewicz, and John Spurlock, reviewed parts of the manuscript and offered useful feedback.

Any author is fortunate who has a band of dedicated friends who will cook good food and happily provide an antidote to the solitude of writing while at the same time being flexible if inspiration should happen to strike shortly before a planned rendezvous. For conviviality and support, I thank Beth Applegate, Tracy Bee, Joe Donnelly, Robert Downey, Lori Garraghty, Gabrielle Goodwin, Matthew Hicks, Jennifer Hottell, Trish Kerlé, Pam MacLaughlin, Rebecca Stanze, Harvey Stark, Julia Valiant, and Jennifer Wagelie. I thank Oscar Hicksbee for offering me the sweet escape of baby love and Mora MacLaughlin for allowing me to simply be an adult fixture of her life, no questions asked.

While I immersed myself in these explorations, real life was happening all around me. I am profoundly grateful to my parents, Joan Romano Ferentinos and Spero Ferentinos, and my siblings and their spouses, Ann Ferentinos, Peter Ferentinos, Joann Zaloga, and Paul Zaloga, for granting me the space to complete this project. Each of them shouldered a heavier burden of family responsibility so that I could write this book, and I thank them all for their willingness to do so.

I have saved my biggest debts for last. In addition to Bob Beatty, there are three other people without whom this book would not exist. Margaret Puskar-Pasewicz is a stalwart friend and colleague who kept me on track during a tight deadline, checked in nearly daily, and enthusiastically celebrated my every achievement, no matter how small. Kenneth C. Turino's contributions to this book go far beyond the case study he authored. An article Ken and I wrote for the fall 2012 issue of *AASLH History News* inspired me to delve further into this topic, and our subsequent conversations consistently gave me something new to think about. Ken is one of the most generous scholars I know. He has been researching LGBT interpretation in museums far longer than I have, and he kindly shared the results of his efforts in the hopes that his work could help other organizations move into this territory. His kindness not only saved me a great deal of legwork but also provided me with an example of professional collegiality that I can only hope to emulate.

Finally, I would like to extend my deepest thanks to my partner, Danielle McClelland. Danielle is that rare breed: a big dreamer who also has the commitment and stamina to make her dreams a reality. Watching her work her magic all these years, I have learned to question my own assumptions about what is and is not possible. One result of that tutelage is the book you hold before you. For that reason alone she deserves praise. However, she has also done more than her fair share of chores and errands; read every word of this manuscript (twice!); and accompanied me to an untold number of museums while cheerfully agreeing to call these treks "vacation." I am so lucky to share my life with her, and I thank her with all my heart.

PART I

INTRODUCTION

CHAPTER 1

Introduction

IN 1991, as a college senior, I set out to write a history paper on the impact of lesbian feminism on the wider women's movement of the 1960s and 1970s. As I recall, I found three books on lesbianism in my university's entire card catalog, one of which was published in the 1930s and titled *Female Sex Perversion*.[1] Having recently come out as queer, this experience gave me pause. Surely, more history than this existed. Where were the stories of my predecessors?

The prospects for learning about alternative sexuality are much improved today. Most libraries now offer many books on the topic; representations of same-sex desire and gender variance are relatively common in popular culture; and issues facing lesbian, gay, bisexual, and transgender (LGBT) communities are a regular topic on the nightly news. Yet the rapid rate at which queer topics have entered the mainstream, plus the emphasis on current events, could conceivably give the impression that LGBT people have only quite recently begun to form communities, advocate for civil rights, and contribute to US culture. Indeed, we could hardly blame someone not particularly informed about the past for assuming that same-sex desire itself is a product of the late twentieth century.

Clearly, the current situation calls for some historical context, and museums are well suited to respond to such a call. Plenty of books have been written on the subject, but these tend to appeal to a specialized audience. A few feature films have considered the lives of gays and lesbians in earlier eras, and a documentary on gay and lesbian AIDS activism was nominated for an Academy Award in 2013.[2] Museums, however, generally seem to be lagging behind in efforts to present the lives of LGBT people in the past. This is particularly troubling when we consider the respect given to museums as arbiters of history.[3] An important opportunity is being missed.

With this book, I hope to make a small contribution to rectifying the situation by providing a starting point for museums and historic sites interested in interpreting LGBT history. Written for museum professionals and focusing primarily on interpretation, this volume offers an introduction to the rewards and challenges of telling the stories of same-sex love and desire. The book is part of a larger series on "Interpreting History," a joint effort by the American Association for State and Local History (AASLH) and Rowman & Littlefield.

As with other books in the series, *Interpreting LGBT History at Museums and Historic Sites* provides a basic outline of the field with plenty of suggestions for further investigation.

Layout of the Book

Interpreting LGBT History, as one of the first monographs dealing specifically with LGBT history in museum settings, serves primarily as an introduction to the topic. In the chapters that follow, I seek to provide a broad synthesis of historical scholarship related to the LGBT past, a glimpse of some of the unique issues involved in interpreting this topic, a few case studies, and some guidance on where readers can learn more. We begin with this introductory part, which offers an orientation to the book's organization and premise. In the following chapter, also introductory, I advocate for the importance of organizations undertaking this work despite its potential challenges.

The second part of the book consists of a historical overview. Its introductory chapter explores some of the special considerations involved in researching people in the past whose lives were marked by secrecy and circumspection. The three main chapters of this part, followed by a short coda, explore the full sweep of variant sexuality and gender in US history, from colonization to the first decades of the twenty-first century. It is a fascinating story, and the limited space in this volume can hardly do it justice. I urge readers to keep in mind that these chapters tell only the highlights of an intricate tale. My endnotes and the annotated bibliography that appears in the back of this book will guide those who are interested to more detailed information.

We then move from the past to the present—from the history to the business of interpreting this history. The third part of this book considers some real-world examples of museums and historic sites that have included LGBT people in their telling of the past. The part begins with a chapter considering the current state of LGBT historical interpretation in an effort to tease out trends and alert readers to other organizations that may be able to provide guidance on new initiatives. After this overview, three case studies provide in-depth examples. These chapters—written by museum professionals with firsthand experience of the efforts they describe—include a major exhibit at a city history museum, a series of interpretive decisions at historic house museums, and LGBT history programming aimed specifically at high school students. The authors share not only their successes but also the questions and challenges the creation process posed for each one. After the case studies, we explore some issues all organizations must consider when planning interpretive efforts in this area. This part, and the book as a whole, concludes with an encapsulated discussion of suggestions made by others with experience interpreting LGBT history. Through this summary, perhaps future efforts can avoid some of the pitfalls of earlier projects and instead create increasingly nuanced and sophisticated interpretations of this part of the American past.

In addition to the narrative, this volume also offers a few appendices. One is a timeline of significant events in LGBT history. The timeline is followed by recommendations for further reading as well as a comprehensive bibliography of sources consulted in the course of writing this book.

Figure 1.1. Members of the Sisters of Perpetual Indulgence, a street performance troupe raising awareness about queer sexuality, New York City.
Courtesy of David Shankbone

Terminology and Theoretical Framework

One of the most difficult parts of this project has been deciding what terminology to use. The words used to describe variant gender expression and sexuality are by no means universally agreed upon, nor do they even necessarily carry the same connotation from one region of the country to another. Readers should be aware that the words I choose to employ throughout this book may well raise concern with others who work in this field. Interpreters should approach the task of determining appropriate terminology with care and in consultation with stakeholders. Nevertheless, I offer here an explanation of the choices I have made, in order to avoid confusion.

Throughout the volume, I employ the acronym LGBT, which stands for lesbian, gay, bisexual, and transgender. It replaces the term GLBT, which was in use for at least a decade; GLBT stands for the same words, just in a different order. Both of these terms—along with the alternative LGBTQ, where the Q stands for either "queer" or (in educational settings) "questioning"—are contemporary constructions, having been in use only since about the 1990s. As such, I am not entirely at peace with my decision to apply this term, LGBT, to the past. These four distinct groups of people have not always understood themselves to be part of one community—nor do they necessarily agree with that premise now. In addition, these terms are often employed as a gesture at inclusivity to bisexual and transgender people, when in reality the "community" is assumed to be gay and lesbian, and the inclusion of others is in name only. In an effort to be both more historically accurate and more specific, I often employ the term "gays and lesbians" or "homosexuals" when discussing historical events or controversies that involved these groups specifically, rather than the larger conglomeration that would be associated together in our own era. However, readers should be aware that in the contemporary era, the use of "homosexual" as a noun has potentially negative connotations. It refers to a specific medical construction, which equated same-sex desire with deviance and mental illness. I have chosen to use the word when discussing the past because it does describe the dominant framework for much of the twentieth century; however, I mark it here as a historical term, along the lines of "invert" or "sodomite."[4]

The term "transgender," like the phrase "LGBT," entered common parlance only a few decades ago and describes a range of gender expressions that do not match a person's physical sex. The word—or its more recent counterpart, "trans"—largely replaces the word "transsexual," which now, if used at all, specifically refers to people who have also undergone surgical modification to reassign their physical sex. Some people who do not strongly identify with their assigned gender but who reject the idea of binary gender roles (which demand a choice between only two options, man and woman) have more recently adopted the term "genderqueer" as a more comfortable description of their identity. Courtesy demands that transgender people be referred to by their chosen gender identity. Thus, the phrase "trans man" refers to someone who identifies as a man though born with a female body; masculine pronouns are most appropriate for such a person. (Genderqueer people often prefer gender-neutral pronouns.) In my historical discussions, I have adhered to these conventions when referring to people who chose to live full-time as the gender opposite of their sex. For people who temporarily chose to gender-cross, I employ the terms that match their physical sex.[5]

Though often representing itself to the larger culture as a united community, the LGBT umbrella in fact uneasily lumps together specific concepts, political agendas, and social experiences of distinct groups, and these do not always make easy bedfellows. While the labels lesbian, gay, and bisexual all refer to sexual orientation, transgender instead refers to gender identity. Although often misinterpreted by the general public as the same, one's gender identity and one's sexual orientation are separate considerations. Lesbians, gays, and bisexuals may challenge traditional ideas about gender, it is true, but they may also adhere pretty comfortably to their assigned gender roles. Likewise, transgender people may identify as homosexual, heterosexual, or bisexual. The groups share some common concerns regarding discrimination and the challenges of living in a world that defines them as deviating from the norm, but in other ways, their experiences of these categories differ. For instance, for the past ten years, a major focus of the ostensible LGBT movement has been securing the legal right for same-sex couples to marry, and this is an issue of minimal relevance to transgender people. They, on the other hand, have been advocating for the ability to change their "official" sex in order to have their identification papers (so important in the post-9/11 world) align with their gender presentation. Important political victories for lesbians, gays, and bisexuals have failed to protect those with transgender identity, and bisexuals and transfolk continue to struggle against prejudice both within the LGBT movement and within the larger culture of the United States. The conflation of sexual orientation and gender identity becomes even more complicated as we turn our gaze to the past, since people of different eras understood the relation between the two differently than we do in our own era.[6]

Furthermore, even within one category—gay, for instance—no uniform experience or agenda exists. Different identities—race, class, gender, religion, region, sexual orientation—all intersect to create often competing interests. Thus, a white, middle-class, gay Mormon from the Mountain West will experience his homosexuality quite differently from a Latino gay migrant worker in the Southeast, even though they both share an attraction to men. For all these reasons, the notion of a single "LGBT community" is problematic; I have rarely employed it, and when I have, it is specifically in the context of civil rights protections, which (at least ideally) apply equally to all members of a protected class.[7]

In any event, there are those who find the "alphabet soup" approach to identity a bit tedious and who instead employ the word "queer" as an umbrella term meant to encompass the full range of nonnormative sexual and gender expression. I employ this word quite liberally throughout the text, and when I do, I intend it essentially as a synonym for "LGBT" rather than as the more complicated signifier it is within the world of academic queer studies.

While the language is ever changing, the overarching topic of this book is same-sex love, desire, and sexual activity, with an accompanying interest in gender variance. As such, I employ these terms frequently, particularly when discussing an era before more modern labels had come into being. To avoid the redundancy of "same-sex sexual behavior" and "same-sex sexual activity," I have more commonly shortened these phrases to "same-sex behavior" and "same-sex activity."

The study of sexuality has flourished from a rich engagement with cultural theory, and in particular, the study of nonnormative sexuality has launched an entire academic discipline, "queer studies." While theoreticians provide useful frameworks with which to order our understanding of societies, I feel that these are conversations best left to the world of academic scholarship. I am not convinced that a solid grounding in queer theory is essential to the on-the-ground task of interpreting LGBT history to the public. As such, I have chosen to limit my discussion of theory. Nevertheless, two theoretical premises inform the discussion that follows, and I would like to state them explicitly before proceeding.[8]

Interpreting LGBT History begins from the assumption that sexual understanding and expression are, to a large extent, socially constructed. In other words, the ways in which people make sense of their sexual desires and act on them are determined in large part by the culture and time period in which they live. As such, historians of sexuality need to be vigilant about studying evidence within the context of the time in which it was created rather than simply applying modern categories to behavior in the past.[9]

My other starting point (which is also a starting point of queer studies) is the premise that presenting LGBT history is not simply an exercise in inclusion. Rather, a focus on outsiders has the potential to reveal a great deal about the society as a whole. Various eras and cultures have defined the boundaries of what is considered "normal" differently, and by exploring those differences—and the experiences of those who were considered "abnormal"—we can catch a glimpse of the assumptions and priorities of the larger group. In this way, the study of cultural outsiders permits us all to learn about ourselves. By incorporating "the other" into our historical understanding, we get closer to understanding where we as a society have come from and how the cultural diversity of the US past has contributed to making us the nation we are today.[10]

Notes

1. Maurice Chideckel, *Female Sex Perversion: The Sexually Aberrated Woman as She Is* (New York: Eugenics, 1938).
2. For feature films, see, for example, *Capote*, directed by Bennett Miller (2005; Culver City, CA: Sony Pictures Home Entertainment, 2006), DVD; *Milk*, directed by Gus Van Sant (2008; Universal City, CA: Universal Studios Home Entertainment, 2009), DVD; and *A Single Man*, directed by Tom Ford (2009; Culver City, CA: Sony Pictures Home Entertainment, 2010), DVD. The documentary is *How to Survive a Plague*, directed by David France (2012; Orland Park, IL: MPI Home Video, 2013), DVD.
3. Roy Rosenzweig and David Thelen, *The Presence of the Past: Popular Uses of History in American Life* (New York: Columbia University Press, 1998), 15–36; José-Marie Griffiths and Donald W. King, *Interconnections: The IMLS National Study on the Use of Libraries, Museums and the Internet: Conclusions Summary* (Washington, DC: Institute of Museums and Library Services, 2008), 3, http://interconnectionsreport.org/reports/ConclusionsSummaryFinalB.pdf.
4. Paul Gabriel, "Why Grapple with Queer When You Can Fondle It? Embracing Our Erotic Intelligence," in *Gender, Sexuality and Museums: A Routledge Reader*, ed. Amy K. Levin (New York: Routledge, 2010), 71–79; Marc Stein, *Rethinking the Gay and Lesbian Movement* (New York: Routledge, 2012), 5–9; Vicki Lynn Eaklor, *Queer America: A GLBT History of the 20th Century* (Westport, CT: Greenwood, 2008), 2; Jeremy W. Peters, "Decline and Fall of the 'H' Word," *New York Times*, March 21, 2014, http://www.nytimes.com/2014/03/23/fashion/gays-lesbians-the-term-homosexual.html.
5. Leslie Feinberg, *Transgender Warriors: Making History from Joan of Arc to RuPaul* (Boston: Beacon, 1996), ix–xiii; Susan Stryker, *Transgender History* (Berkeley: Seal, 2008), 1–29. Stryker includes a particularly useful glossary of words related to gender variance.
6. Gabriel, "Why Grapple with Queer?"; Stryker, *Transgender History*, 150–53.
7. Cornelia H. Dayton and Lisa Levenstein, "The Big Tent of U.S. Women's and Gender History: A State of the Field," *Journal of American History* 99, no. 3 (December 1, 2012): 793–817; Mieke Verloo, "Intersectional and Cross-Movement Politics and Policies: Reflections on Current Practices and Debates," *Signs* 38, no. 4 (June 1, 2013): 893–915; Nan Alamilla Boyd, "Same-Sex Sexuality in Western Women's History," *Frontiers: A Journal of Women Studies* 22, no. 3 (September 2001): 13.
8. Those interested in learning more about queer studies can start with Sharon Marcus, "Queer Theory for Everyone: A Review Essay," *Signs: Journal of Women in Culture & Society* 31, no. 1 (September 2005): 191–218; Larry Gross, "The Past and the Future of Gay, Lesbian, Bisexual, and Transgender Studies," *Journal of Communication* 55, no. 3 (September 2005): 508–28. For examples of queer studies applied to the museum world, see Deborah Bright and Erica Rand, "Queer Plymouth," *GLQ: A Journal of Lesbian & Gay Studies* 12, no. 2 (April 2006): 259–77; Erica Rand, *The Ellis Island Snow Globe* (Durham: Duke University Press, 2005).
9. David M. Halperin, *How to Do the History of Homosexuality* (Chicago: University of Chicago Press, 2002), 1–23; Leila J. Rupp, *A Desired Past: A Short History of Same-Sex Love in America* (Chicago: University of Chicago Press, 1999), 1–11.
10. Victoria Harris, "Sex on the Margins: New Directions in the Historiography of Sexuality and Gender," *Historical Journal* 53, no. 4 (December 2010): 1085–1104; Leila J. Rupp, "What's Queer Got to Do with It?," *Reviews in American History* 38, no. 2 (June 2010): 189–98; Marcus, "Queer Theory for Everyone."

CHAPTER 2

A Pep Talk for the Faint of Heart

WE LIVE in interesting times. The past five years have brought such a flood of change under the law that it seems like barely a day goes by without a breaking news story related to LGBT communities. At the same time, some parts of the United States are bitterly polarized over the issue of LGBT civil rights; violence against queer people—particularly those who are gender variant—continues; and LGBT activists debate among themselves whether the focus of their movement has drifted too much to middle-class concerns at the expense of addressing the realities of job discrimination, unequal access to medical treatment, and transphobia. This rapidly changing cultural landscape begs for a forum in which citizens can ponder the issues and gain a wider historical context for the questions of their own era.

The subject of LGBT history offers a perfect opportunity for museums to inhabit their roles as sites of conscience, education, and dialogue. Yet for many institutions, interpreting the queer past means moving into new terrain. *Interpreting LGBT History* provides a road map for this journey, one that I hope museum professionals will find useful as they consider new interpretive efforts. As we begin this exploration, I would like to discuss what I see as the four most compelling reasons for museums to undertake interpretation in the history of same-sex love and desire. The first involves the role of museums as sites of public dialogue. Related to this is the second issue, the responsibility of historical organizations to strive for a full and accurate presentation of the American past. Third, LGBT historical interpretation is likely to diversify and expand both audiences and collections. And finally, there is the powerful experience museums can offer by restoring visibility to a group of people who have been consistently marginalized or erased in the larger culture.

Creating Public Dialogue

Public attitudes about same-sex relationships have changed drastically in recent years. A recent *Washington Post*-ABC poll found that 59 percent of Americans now favor same-sex marriage, the highest percentage yet. What's more, this represents a 75 percent increase of support in just ten years.[1] At the same time, LGBT struggles for acceptance continue. The same poll found deep differences in opinion based on respondents' age, religion, and geographic region. To some, the political gains of the LGBT community represent losses for sexual morality, and these citizens are fighting back, as demonstrated by recent debates in state legislatures. Even those who profess acceptance of expressions of variant sexuality may be more comfortable with same-sex affection as represented by marriage than by other, more "queer" demonstrations of desire (such as nonmonogamous arrangements or leather fetishism). And acceptance of same-sex love and desire does not necessarily equal ease with the concept of gender crossing, as many transgender people will attest.

The rapidly changing cultural landscape begs for a wider historical perspective in which to understand the context and precursors of current debates. Museums provide a perfect setting for such exploration; they have become, in the words of Robert R. Archibald, "The New Town Square." The museum, he says, "is a place to discuss what we have done well, where we have fallen short, and how we can do better. It is a place for coming together and appreciating how we differ and examining how very much we share." Graham Black concurs, offering an ideal vision of museums that understand "the museum visit as a conversation between the collections, the users and the museum rather than viewing users as empty vessels to be filled with didactic content."[2]

The idea of museums as sites of public dialogue is not a new concept for anyone working in this profession; however, the means for engaging in meaningful dialogue can be extremely challenging. In previous centuries, museums served a more edifying function, reflecting on national accomplishments and schooling the uneducated masses in the lessons of "civilization." But that role has evolved in recent decades. Rather than simply imparting knowledge, museums now facilitate a process by which visitors participate in the construction of meaning. This meaning making quite often involves a conversation among visitors and between museum staff and the wider community. In this way, museums have become sites of intellectual exchange during a time when other physical spaces of public interaction have diminished. In the words of Nina Simon, "By designing explicit opportunities for interpersonal dialogue, cultural institutions can distinguish themselves as desirable real-world venues for discussion about important issues related to the content presented."[3]

To truly embrace their identity as town squares, however, museums must face the possibility of controversy. As thoughtful and meaningful intellectual exchange becomes more rare in American culture, some institutions have come to equate public debate about an exhibit with public relations failure rather than as a successful execution of the mission to create community dialogue. Yet if everyone agrees from the outset, a dialogue has not been achieved. As an example, one of the most thought-provoking exhibits of the 1990s, Fred Wilson's *Mining the Museum*, generated mixed reactions on the part of its fifty-five thousand visitors at the same time that it greatly influenced the museum field and the way that museum professionals view collections. The exhibit was revolutionary precisely *because* it sparked discussion and demanded audience members consider questions of race and power in society. In doing so, it illustrated the potential of museums to foster meaningful conversation with their visitors.[4]

Although it seems entirely appropriate that public dialogue occasionally erupt into spirited debate, the interpretation of LGBT history is no longer the lightning rod that it once was, at least in many parts of the country. In fact, in the course of writing this book, I discovered that many institutions interpreting the LGBT past received overwhelming support from their constituencies. This is particularly true of efforts undertaken in the past five years. As Kenneth C. Turino recounts later in this volume, Historic New England changed its interpretation at one of its historic house museums to acknowledge the homosexuality of Henry Davis Sleeper, a prominent turn-of-the-twentieth-century interior designer, and received only positive feedback. Similarly, when the Jane Addams Hull-House Museum introduced visitors to the fact that an American icon that was Jane Addams shared her life with a woman, the majority of visitor responses "revealed a hunger" for more information.[5]

Even interpretation that pushes further has prompted little controversy. LGBT historical programming for high school students at the Minnesota Historical Society also rendered no complaints, as the case study by Kyle Parsons and Stewart Van Cleve later in this volume attests. Likewise, the federally funded Rosie the Riveter/National World War II Home Front National Historical Park received only positive responses when it issued a call for firsthand LGBT stories of World War II. Even the tiny Morrison County (MN) Historical Society was able to include the story of a transgender county resident in its *What It's Like . . . in Morrison County* exhibit without outcry. Such examples suggest a public acknowledgment of the reality of sexual and gender variance and a desire to learn more, regardless of one's particular stand on current events. Museums represent a safe place in which the public can gain knowledge and consider the issues.[6]

Seeking an Inclusive National Past

Part of the shift from museums as conveyors of knowledge to museums as facilitators of meaning making stems from a larger acceptance of the United States as a multicultural society. The monolithic national narrative no longer holds the same respect it once did. In its place is a general acknowledgment—tacit or explicit—on the part of the public that American culture draws from many influences. The inclusion of LGBT stories within that larger historical tapestry aids in providing a richer and more accurate telling of the national past.

Museums' role as conveyors of cultural values and, by extension, relations of power, is well established within the field. In recent decades, the awareness of this role has led cultural organizations to expand their interpretive focus in an effort to reveal and interrogate standard social hierarchies. LGBT historical interpretation falls under this larger professional effort. It provides a means of telling a fuller story of the American past, introducing questions of power in society, and conveying welcome to a segment of society that has traditionally experienced exclusion.[7]

In 2008, Reach Advisors conducted a survey of visitors to outdoor history museums and found that 95 percent of respondents thought it important for the sites to include stories of different races and cultures in their interpretation. Even more revealing, a full 69 percent of respondents said it was "extremely important" to do so.[8] Museums and historic sites are generally responding to that desire, but there is still ample work to be done with regard to sexual minorities.

Even within the groundswell of inclusivity within the field, numerous scholars have noted that museums continue to enforce heteronormativity, the assumption that opposite-sex desire and adherence to dominant gender roles are the standard (that is, "normal") experience and other desires or expressions are the exception (or "abnormal"). By doing so, according to Kevin Coffee, museums promote "in-group/out-group stratification through their curatorial judgments, definitions of stakeholders, or specific treatments of visitors." Likewise, Stuart Frost argues that by choosing not to display homoerotic content, museums send a message that the experience of same-sex desire is shameful and something to be hidden. This tendency becomes even more worrisome when we consider the struggles of LGBT youth to find role models as they develop their sexual identity. In 2000, Klaus Muller conducted a survey of LGBT adolescents ages fourteen to nineteen and found that only *4 percent* of them had learned about LGBT history in a museum setting.[9]

The experiences of gays and lesbians, of bisexuals, and of transgender people are part of the multicultural fabric of the United States. If museums are to truly engage with a holistic telling of the American past, LGBT history must be included in the narrative.

Growth in Visitation and Collections

Telling an inclusive history has potential beyond simply achieving a more accurate portrayal of the past. In addition, inclusive interpretation can lead to audiences and collections that are also more representative of the modern United States. Indeed, Erin Bailey, curator of the *Revealing Queer* exhibit (2014) at Seattle's Museum of History and Industry (MOHAI), cited expanding audiences and collections growth as two of the greatest achievements of this interpretive effort.[10]

If the demographics of your museum visitors do not match the demographics of the community in which it resides, then there is room for improvement, and expanding interpretive topics is one avenue toward diversifying visitation. A preliminary study of lesbian, gay, and bisexual visitation to museums, whose results were published in 2008, found that LGB people (no transgender visitors participated in the study) decide to visit museums based primarily on three factors: "the ability to be demonstrative, feeling represented within the content, and feeling accepted with the context." Furthermore, the study found that "the overall atmosphere of the venues is less influential than the content or offerings of the venue."[11]

The United States Holocaust Memorial Museum (USHMM) in Washington, DC, offers one example of the interrelationship between interpretation and audiences. From its founding, USHMM committed itself to telling the history of all of the victims of the Holocaust, including homosexuals, but because of limited space and limited artifacts, this particular story was only "briefly told" in the museum's permanent exhibit. However, many LGBT people fundamentally understood the museum's relevance to their history. USHMM's opening coincided with the 1993 March on Washington for Gay, Lesbian, and Bisexual Rights and Liberation, and LGBT marchers flocked to the museum, creating a "huge and unexpected audience."[12] In recognition of this portion of their visitors, in 1996 the museum began to develop its exhibit *The Nazi Persecution of Homosexuals, 1933–1945*, which opened at the museum in 2002 and eventually became a traveling exhibit. In reflecting on his work with the exhibit, curator Edward Phillips has said, "The GLBT audience is everywhere. Let that audience know they will see and learn something about themselves/ourselves and their/our communities in our museum exhibitions, public programs, and outreach, and they will be at our doors."[13]

With regard to collections, chances are that the outreach involved in interpreting the history of same-sex desire will lead to donations of LGBT-related material to the collection, which in turn will ensure that these items are preserved for future generations. In truth, some examples of interpretation in this area actually began primarily as collecting efforts. The Brooklyn Historical Society began planning its exhibit *AIDS/Brooklyn* after executive director David Kahn noted that people who had lost loved ones to AIDS sometimes chose to destroy all material that reminded them of that loss. "I felt this was an understandable response," said Kahn, "but after hearing of this phenomenon several times, the historian in me became alarmed. How would future generations know what this crisis had been like? Who would preserve the material culture of AIDS?" The Brooklyn Historical Society responded to that question, opening its *AIDS* exhibit in 1993.[14]

Collecting is often an integral part of interpreting LGBT history, and this can be an added benefit to organizations that lack substantial holdings in this area. However, Stacia Kuceyeski, director of outreach at the Ohio History Connection (formerly the Ohio Historical Society) and staff liaison to the Gay Ohio History Initiative (GOHI), argues that collecting is not enough on its own. GOHI's initial purpose was to collect and preserve the material culture of Ohio's LGBT communities; it did not have an immediate plan to present the materials to the public. In retrospect, however, Kuceyeski realized that the momentum generated by the project might have been better sustained had GOHI's strategic plan included the display of some of the items collected.[15]

The Power of Revealing Lost History

Discussing LGBT history can be part of a larger mission of inclusivity. It can allow museums to reach new audiences and educate the public about the larger society in which they live. In addition to these benefits, there is also the simple power of providing a group of people with a past. Unlike ethnic minorities, queer people generally do not grow up among others like them. Many identify as LGBT only as adults or near-adults, and the act of adopting this identity quite often means abandoning other communities to which they have formerly belonged (such as families of origin, hometowns, and religious denominations). For people who have experienced this kind of displacement, history can heal. Unmoored people can find a sense of belonging in learning about the experiences of others like them who have come before. To offer roots to those who have at one time or another found themselves without any is a powerful gift indeed. And perhaps this is the most compelling reason of all to consider interpreting the LGBT past.

The absence of variant sexuality and gender expression in standard depictions of the past might surprise those accustomed to seeing people like themselves represented. Indeed, I suspect that many LGBT visitors have become so accustomed to this invisibility that they do not fully comprehend its negative effect until they encounter the opposite. Kelly Farrell, an interpreter based in Arkansas, recounts the experience of encountering the *Gay Liberation* monument, a memorial to the Stonewall riots in New York City (figure 2.1). Moved to tears, she told her companion:

> I'm a professional interpreter.... The work I do is about real people and real places and real purpose. I've traveled the world. I've seen thousands of interpretive exhibits and commemorative sculptures. But this ... is the only time I've encountered public interpretation of this story.[16]

This realization had an important impact on Farrell, who identifies as a lesbian. In her words, "I've found I work harder at fostering a sense of belonging for visitors. I am more conscious about relating to their lives, helping them to have firsthand experiences [that connect] with their minds and hearts."[17]

Figure 2.1. The Stonewall Riots of 1969 are memorialized in Christopher Park, New York City, with this statue, *Gay Liberation*, by George Segal. Courtesy of Ted Eytan

Independent curator Gregory Hinton, founder of the *Out West* programming effort, would agree. Begun at the Autry National Center of the American West, *Out West* has now spread to museums and libraries throughout the mountain states and as far east as Indiana. It has combined a variety of efforts—exhibits, collecting, public presentations, special tours—in the service of interpreting the experiences of lesbian, gay, bisexual, transgender, and Two-Spirit people in the American West. For Hinton, a gay Wyoming native, *Out West* is an act of reclamation and healing:

> Born in rural western towns, many of us feel forced to leave our families behind and move to the city in search of safety, community, and companionship. . . . I wanted to come home to the West, but I wanted to come home as who I am. The dignity a museum, a library or a university lends to our community by preserving and sharing LGBT western history and culture is reassuring, esteeming, and therefore immeasurable.[18]

Other observers agree, noting the power of LGBT history to provide "validation" to LGBT communities and assist in "constructing a sense of selfhood for many queer women and men."[19] One visitor to *Becoming Visible: The Legacy of Stonewall* (1994) at the New York Public Library cried as he walked through the exhibition, saying that the show made him feel he had "a place, a legitimate place, in the fabric of this country."[20] Aren't we striving to make all our visitors welcome and feel they have a place in our country's history?

The moment has arrived. Incorporating LGBT experiences into museum interpretation holds the potential to embody museums' higher purposes. LGBT historical interpretation can foster public dialogue, enrich the full telling of US history, expand audiences and collections, and provide a sense of belonging to a group whose contributions to the nation have been largely unrecognized.

Notes

1. Peyton M. Craighill and Scott Clement, "Support for Same-Sex Marriage Hits New High; Half Say Constitution Guarantees Right," *WP Politics*, March 5, 2014, http://www.washingtonpost.com/politics/support-for-same-sex-marriage-hits-new-high-half-say-constitution-guarantees-right/2014/03/04/f737e87e-a3e5-11e3-a5fa-55f0c77bf39c_story.html.
2. Robert R. Archibald, *The New Town Square: Museums and Communities in Transition* (Walnut Creek, CA: Alta Mira, 2004), 78; Graham Black, *Transforming Museums in the 21st Century: Developing Museums for Visitor Involvement* (Hoboken, NJ: Taylor & Francis, 2011), 143. Black goes on to offer specific suggestions for encouraging dialogue in museums, 143–65.
3. Nina Simon, *The Participatory Museum* (Santa Cruz, CA: Museum 2.0, 2010), preface; Jennifer Barrett, *Museums and the Public Sphere* (Malden, MA: Wiley-Blackwell, 2011), 1–9; Teresa Bergman, *Exhibiting Patriotism: Creating and Contesting Interpretations of American Historic Sites* (Walnut Creek, CA: Left Coast, 2013), 18–23; Archibald, *New Town Square*, 61–75; Bill Adair, Benjamin Filene, and Laura Koloski, eds., *Letting Go? Sharing Historical Authority in a User-Generated World* (Philadelphia: Pew Center for Arts & Heritage, 2011); Anne Clark and Geoffrey Wexler, "Queer Collections Appear: Oregon's Wedding Album," *Museums & Social Issues* 3, no. 1 (April 1, 2008): 115–24.

4. Contemporary Museum, Baltimore, and Maryland Historical Society, *Mining the Museum: An Installation by Fred Wilson*, ed. Lisa G. Corrin (Baltimore, New York: The Contemporary, in cooperation with the New Press, 1994); Fred Wilson, Paula Marincola, and Marjorie Schwartzer, "Mining the Museum Revisited: A Conversation," in Adair, Filene, and Koloski, *Letting Go?*, 230–41. For more on controversy in museums, see Ken Yellis, "Concerning the Telling of Painful Tales: The Case of Masks of the Sacred Bush," *Curator* 55, no. 2 (April 2012): 139–51; Stephanie Lehner, "Becoming Visible: Mainstream Cultural Institutions and the Successful Presentation of LGBTQ History Exhibitions" (MA thesis, State University of New York College at Oneonta, Cooperstown Graduate Program, 2008), 7.

5. Lisa Yun Lee, "Peering into the Bedroom: Restorative Justice at the Jane Addams Hull House Museum," in *Routledge Companion to Museum Ethics: Redefining Ethics for the Twenty-First Century Museum*, ed. Janet Marstine (New York: Routledge, 2011), 174–88, quotation from 181.

6. Elizabeth Tucker, lead park ranger, Rosie the Riveter/World War II Home Front National Historical Park, phone interview with Susan Ferentinos, April 29, 2014; Mary Warner, "Fighting Homophobia in Stealth Mode," *AASLH Small Museums Online Community* (blog), June 1, 2012, http://blogs.aaslh.org/fighting-homophobia-in-stealth-mode/.

7. Kevin Coffee, "Cultural Inclusion, Exclusion and the Formative Roles of Museums," *Museum Management & Curatorship* 23, no. 3 (September 2008): 261–79; Darryl McIntyre, "What to Collect? Museums and Lesbian, Gay, Bisexual and Transgender Collecting," *International Journal of Art & Design Education* 26, no. 1 (February 2007): 48–53; Bergman, *Exhibiting Patriotism*.

8. Reach Advisors, "Difficult Issues, Inclusive History," *Museum Audience Insight* (blog), July 8, 2008, http://reachadvisors.typepad.com/museum_audience_insight/2008/07/difficult-issues-inclusive-history.html.

9. Coffee, "Cultural Inclusion, Exclusion and the Formative Role of Museums," 266; Stuart Frost, "Secret Museums: Hidden Histories of Sex and Sexuality," *Museums & Social Issues* 3, no. 1 (Spring 2008): 29–40; Klaus Muller, "Invisible Visitors: Museums and the Gay and Lesbian Community," *Museum News* 80, no. 5 (October 2001), http://www.aam-us.org/pubs/mn/MN_SO01_InvisibleVisitors.cfm; John Fraser and Joe E. Heimlich, "Where Are We?," *Museums & Social Issues* 3, no. 1 (Spring 2008): 5–14; James H. Sanders III, "The Museum's Silent Sexual Performance," *Museums & Social Issues* 3, no. 1 (Spring 2008): 15–25; Joshua G. Adair, "House Museums or Walk-In Closets? The (Non) Representation of Gay Men in the Museums They Called Home," in Amy K. Levin, ed., *Gender, Sexuality, and Museums: A Routledge Reader* (New York: Routledge, 2010), 269; Robert Mills, "Theorizing the Queer Museum," *Museums & Social Issues* 3, no. 1 (April 1, 2008): 41–52; Patrik Steorn, "Curating Queer Heritage: Queer Knowledge and Museum Practice," *Curator* 55, no. 3 (July 2012): 355–65; Jennifer Tyburczy, "All Museums Are Sex Museums," *Radical History Review*, no. 113 (Spring 2012): 199–211.

10. Erin Bailey, Jill Austin, and Viviane Gosselin, "Revealing Urban Histories through LGBTQ Museum Programming" (paper presented at the American Alliance of Museums Annual Meeting, Seattle, 2014); Nick Merriman and Nima Poovaya-Smith, "Making Culturally Diverse Histories," in Gaynor Kavanagh, ed., *Making Histories in Museums* (London: Leicester University Press, 1996), 176–87.

11. Joe Heimlich and Judy Koke, "Gay and Lesbian Visitors and Cultural Institutions: Do They Come? Do They Care? A Pilot Study," *Museums & Social Issues* 3, no. 1 (April 1, 2008): 97, 102.

12. Edward Phillips, "Nazi Persecution of Homosexuals: The Curator's View," *Museums & Social Issues* 3, no. 1 (April 1, 2008): 105–14, quotations from 108 and 106.
13. Ibid., 113; Lehner, "Becoming Visible," 50–63.
14. Lehner, "Becoming Visible," 30–46, quotation from 37; Wesley Chenault, curator of *Unspoken Past: Atlanta Lesbian and Gay History, 1940–1970* (Atlanta History Center) and member of the John Q Collective, phone interview with Susan Ferentinos, May 15, 2014; Stacia Kuceyeski, "The Gay Ohio History Initiative as a Model for Collecting Institutions," *Museums & Social Issues* 3, no. 1 (April 1, 2008): 125–32.
15. Stacia Kuceyeski, director of outreach at the Ohio History Connection and liaison to the Gay Ohio History Initiative, phone interview with Susan Ferentinos, April 3, 2014.
16. Kelly Farrell, "Exposing the Soul: An Unexpected Encounter with Community-Based Interpretation," *Legacy: The Journal of the National Association of Interpretation* (February 2010): 21.
17. Ibid., 23.
18. Gregory Hinton, "Out West" (keynote address, LGBTQ Alliance Luncheon presented at the American Alliance of Museums, Seattle, May 18, 2014), 12.
19. Clark and Wexler, "Queer Collections Appear," 120; Alison Oram, "Going on an Outing: The Historic House and Queer Public History," *Rethinking History* 15, no. 2 (June 2011): 193.
20. David W. Dunlap, "Library's Gay Show Is an Eye-Opener, Even for Its Subjects," *New York Times*, September 6, 1994, sec. Arts, http://www.nytimes.com/1994/09/06/arts/library-s-gay-show-is-an-eye-opener-even-for-its-subjects.html.

PART II

HISTORICAL OVERVIEW

CHAPTER 3

Approaching LGBT History

LIKE NEARLY every historian I know, I fell in love with history through the work of a gifted teacher.[1] However, I chose to make history my career only after reading an article by Martin Duberman titled "'Writhing Bedfellows,'" in which the author explores the intricacies of trying to understand same-sex desire in the past.[2] This article is still one of my favorites, and I continue to delight in exploring the changing meanings of same-sex attraction over time. In the chapters that follow, I provide a general overview of the history of same-sex love and desire in the United States from the colonial period until the present. Before we begin, however, I would like to offer an introductory discussion about the field of LGBT history, the ways historians conceptualize sexuality, and some of the particular challenges involved in attempting to uncover the queer past.[3]

The Chapters That Follow

This part of *Interpreting LGBT History* furnishes readers with a synthesis of US history as it relates to same-sex love and desire. Three main chapters comprise the bulk of the material. The first chapter covers the period from European settlement to the late nineteenth century, roughly the period of US history before the medical concept of sexual orientation emerged. The second chapter examines the era from the late nineteenth century to the mid-1960s, from the development of medical formulations of homosexuality to the beginnings of a political movement advocating for equal treatment for gays and lesbians. (Although bisexuals and people we would now call transgender were also active in this movement, their specific concerns were not consistently addressed by this activism.) The third chapter of this part begins in the mid-1960s by considering important precursors to the Stonewall riots of 1969 and continues to the June 2013 Supreme Court decision that paved the way for federal recognition of same-sex marriages (*United States v. Windsor*). A short coda following this historical overview presents a few of the events that took place in the first year after the *Windsor* decision.

Although political activism has clearly had an influence on my periodization, these chapters take a more holistic view of LGBT history. I seek to integrate dominant views of sexual and gender variance, glimpses of intimate feelings and behavior, politics, law, science, economics, and culture. Doing so places the history of same-sex love and desire within the larger context of US history and demonstrates the ways that larger societal trends have influenced sexual choices and our ideas about them.

The Field of LGBT History

The history of variant sexuality has only garnered consistent scholarly attention for about forty years. As with other identity politics of the era, the gay liberation movement of the 1970s sparked an interest in the history of its community. Within the academy, a few brave historians risked their professional reputations to research gay and lesbian topics. (Investigations into fluid sexualities and transgender identities would come later.) More widely, in this early period, grassroots organizations formed to collect and preserve the history of queer communities that were undergoing rapid change.

The field of LGBT history owes a great debt to these mostly amateur community historians, for they saw a need to collect this history long before mainstream archives, and these early efforts form essential contributions to the historical collections of today. In a similar vein, many of the earliest books on LGBT history in the United States were written by historians (professionally trained or otherwise) who were unaffiliated with universities.

These origins shaped the discipline of LGBT history in particular ways. As a result of its gay liberation roots, many early offerings were published by alternative presses rather than university presses and were intended for a popular audience. In a similar vein, when searching for primary sources and artifacts related to queer history, researchers can potentially benefit by going beyond mainstream archival collections to seek out community historians and local LGBT history projects. Finally, writings on LGBT history from the 1970s to the 1990s bear the mark of its political origins. Studies from this era tend to focus on community formation and efforts to resist the oppression of the larger society.

It was not until the 1990s that university presses began publishing a significant body of scholarship on this topic. This decade also witnessed an extensive debate about the nature of sexuality. Influenced by the work of Michel Foucault and others, scholars argued whether sexuality is essential and inborn or socially constructed (that is, influenced by time, place, and context).[4] Eventually, the social constructionists won the point. After about 2000, it is uncommon to find a book published by an academic press that does not assume sexuality is a fluid category, dependent on time and place for its meaning. I mention this old argument, however, because although social constructionism has gained ascendency within the historical profession, many LGBT activists still maintain a belief in the immutability of sexual expression.[5] As such, museums and historic sites must interpret the queer past cautiously. On the one hand, high-quality interpretation will engage with current scholarly understandings. On the other hand, some visitors might resist a nuanced discussion of the changing understandings of same-sex desire over time, seeing it as equivocation. In the words of historian Leila Rupp, "There are complex and confusing questions that run counter to our intuitive understandings of sexuality. The important point here is that sexuality is not a fixed essence, understood and practiced the same way across history and around the globe."[6]

During the same period that historians were grappling with the question of essentialism versus social construction, they also began to move beyond a strictly liberationist approach to their subject. Rather than assuming an overarching march toward increasing acceptance and civil rights, historians began instead to look at nuances: the shifting ways various eras opened up space for homosexual expression and others restricted it; the means by which queer lives were influenced by events outside the queer community; and the different meanings same-sex activity had for different social groups during the same era. In addition, the concept of a unified LGBT "community" became destabilized, as historians explored the intersections between sexual orientation and other categories, such as race, gender, class, and political vision.[7] Finally, historians began to broaden their focus, considering the ways that the larger society used the category of "sexual deviance," along with race, class, and gender, to define boundaries of acceptable behavior and create a hierarchy by which certain groups were supported and affirmed while others, representing cultural difference, became scapegoats for societal ills.[8]

Issues in Researching LGBT History

Unearthing the history of alternative sexuality can present a unique set of challenges that are different from the task of studying other parts of the American past. Researchers may well find that documentary sources are hard to come by, and even when they are uncovered, the shifting nature of sexuality—the fact that different sexual activities are understood differently depending on the culture, subculture, and historical time period—means that interpreters must take special care to interpret evidence of same-sex desire in a way that would be recognizable to people of that era, rather than simply imposing a contemporary interpretation onto the past.

To begin with, when considering questions of sexuality, historical sources can be scarce. Given cultural taboos, sex was not discussed as publicly as many other topics a historian might investigate. Nevertheless, when considering heterosexuals we can follow the babies and birth records to learn a good bit about who was having sex with whom and how; likewise, marriage records provide a glimpse into much of the cultural infrastructure that governed sexual behavior between the sexes.[9]

While the limited range of documentary evidence is challenging within the history of sexuality generally, the problem of sources is even more pronounced for same-sex desire and behavior. Because of the specific stigma attached to same-sex sexual activity—and the fact that it was usually a criminal offense—people who engaged in this behavior were understandably reticent to leave a written record of their activities. Those who did record their actions tended to be circumspect, often relying on innuendo or code to obscure their true meaning.[10]

Even in those cases when experience and desire were captured, such records were unlikely to survive. Individuals worried about incriminating themselves, or families mindful of potential scandal after the death of a loved one, too often destroyed documents that may have revealed troves of knowledge. Indeed, a particularly frustrating aspect of LGBT

Figure 3.1.
Often, historical sources offer only a glimpse at same-sex attraction without ever being explicit.
Untitled (*Two Girls at a Window*), by Jennie Augusta Browncombe. Courtesy of the National Gallery of Art, 2008.115.684

historical research is the number of references that exist to sources being destroyed. The reasons behind the destruction are not certain, but circumstantial evidence suggests it may well have been because of homoerotic content. Historical figures suspected of having same-sex desires whose personal documents were destroyed include suffragist Alice Paul, educator M. Carey Thomas, interior designer Henry Davis Sleeper, and reformers Jane Addams, Molly Dewson, and Miriam Van Waters.[11]

Furthermore, the nuances of researching same-sex desire extend beyond simple lack of sources. When evidence of love and physical affection exists between two members of the same sex, we cannot always assume that the historical agents assigned the same meanings to that desire that we as contemporary readers would. Likewise, we cannot assume that love and affection—even physical affection—necessarily implies a sexual (that is, genital) relationship. This brings us to a second challenge of interpreting the queer past.

As discussed previously, the meanings of sexual desire, behavior, and expression vary depending on time and place. Even if we limit our view to the United States in one particular era, specific circumstances, regional variation, and class, race, and gender differences change the interpretation of what we are seeing. For instance, substantial evidence exists that same-sex behavior was generally tolerated in the nineteenth century in all-male environments such as frontier mining camps or on whaling ships, while at the same time, male-male sexual activity taking place during the same period in the anonymity of growing American cities was met with outrage and treated as a symbol of urban vice.

While such cultural variations are important to keep in mind no matter what the topic, it is even more essential to remember that the meanings attached to same-sex activity varied greatly from one era to another. As we will discuss in the next chapter, the concept of sexual orientation only became firmly established in the late nineteenth century. Before that time, medically based categories of desire such as heterosexuality and homosexuality did not exist. Thus, it becomes problematic to use these concepts to describe activity in an era before these ideas had developed.[12]

In addition, even after the concept of homosexuality was widely accepted, the term did not always mean the same as it does today. The early concept of homosexuality had as much to do with gender nonconformity (what was known at the time as "inversion") as with desire for those of the same sex. As such, there was a certain conflation of homosexuality with transgender identity, as we understand both these terms today. In addition, most of the writing on homosexuality at the turn of the twentieth century emphasized sexual behavior rather than emotional connection. Within this context, relationships based on abiding love, which may or may not have involved a sexual component, often escaped the stigma of homosexuality in the early decades of this new concept.

At this time, the label of homosexuality also did not apply equally to everyone who experienced same-sex desire. The definition of homosexuality carried class connotations, in keeping with its association with the urban underworld of vice and with the desires of more "primitive" (i.e., non-European) races. Wealthier people, unconnected from this subculture, did not necessarily understand their relationships to fall under this new category of deviance. Instead, they drew on an older nineteenth-century tradition of romantic friendship, in which declarations of love and desire among same-sex pairs were quite acceptable. Similarly, before World War II, negative slang for those who desired their own sex (such as "fairy") seems to have applied to men who permitted penetration by other men but *not* to men who did the penetrating, a distinction that remains in certain US subcultures today. Finally, at different times, same-sex relationships within sex-segregated environments—prisons, female colleges, boarding schools, and immigrant communities with disproportionate sex ratios—were relatively accepted and seen to be more of a result of circumstance than of any inborn homosexual tendencies.[13]

The changing meanings of sexual desire, coupled with the lack of documentary evidence, create implications for those who want to interpret this topic. To begin, if an organization wants to focus its interpretation on LGBT "communities," we need to be aware that the type of subcultures we would identify as communities didn't exist in any consistent way in the United States until the late nineteenth century. Without an established concept of homosexuality, people who desired their own sex didn't necessarily see this desire as a rallying point of commonality with others. Thus, the tendency to gather with others who shared this desire was not as common. Because of these historical circumstances, interpretation of "queer communities" will almost necessarily require a focus of the twentieth century or later. In addition, a consideration of subcultures requires a sensitivity to differences *among* people who shared variant sexuality or gender. There is no single LGBT community, now or in the past.

If instead, or in addition, an exhibit will examine the lives of specific historical actors, planners need to be cautious about referring to them by modern labels that the actors themselves would not have recognized (because those labels did not exist in their lifetimes) or would not have chosen for themselves, either because those labels meant something different during the era in question or because the historical actors chose not to reveal their desire publically.

Despite the need for sensitivity and an understanding of historical nuances, it remains possible to present material on sexual variance that neither circumvents the evidence nor takes interpretive leaps beyond what the evidence will support. A good example of a museum that rises to this challenge is the Jane Addams Hull-House Museum in Chicago. Addams was the founder of the Hull House Settlement in 1889, and the museum is currently housed in the last remaining buildings of the settlement. The museum interprets a wide range of topics and seeks to make connections between the history it interprets and the social justice issues of today. Among its interpretive topics is Addams's long-term relationship with Mary Rozet Smith, a resident and benefactor of Hull House. The museum interprets this relationship in Addams's bedroom, the interpretive focus of which is Addams's personal life. Exhibit panels describe the relationship between the two, noting its closeness and longevity, including pictures of the two women together, and offering the (documented) fact that the two women traveled together and would wire ahead to request a single room with a double bed for them to share. The exhibit also notes that there is very little surviving correspondence between Addams and Smith because Addams requested that all letters between them be destroyed upon her death. It also relates that female partnerships such as this were common among female reformers in the late nineteenth and early twentieth centuries. However, the museum stops there in interpreting the relationship. It sticks to verifiable information and stays clear of making assumptions (such as that of a genital component to the partnership) that cannot be substantiated. It also does not apply labels that the women did not choose for themselves.[14]

As shown by this example, interpreters need not be daunted by the challenges of accessing variant sexualities in the past. Rather, LGBT history provides a particularly exciting opportunity to discuss the realities of historical research. The truth is, we don't know everything that came before, and what we do know is often more complex than visitors assume. By presenting what evidence and context we have and allowing visitors to ponder its implications, we bring them into the historical process and encourage them to perform their own historical analysis.

Notes

1. In my case, this teacher was Simone Caron, now a professor at Wake Forest University, who introduced me to the freedom struggles of the past and helped me see their potential power for the future.
2. Martin B. Duberman, "'Writhing Bedfellows' in Antebellum South Carolina: Historical Interpretation and the Politics of Evidence," in *About Time: Exploring the Gay Past*, rev. and

expanded ed. (New York: Meridian, 1991), 3–23; reprinted in John Howard, ed., *Carryin' on in the Lesbian and Gay South* (New York: New York University Press, 1997), 15–33.

3. Because LGBT history is still a relatively new subfield, it has not experienced the same historiographical shifts as other more established areas of study. As a result, I will limit my historiographical discussion to only the broadest trends. Those interested in learning more will find a number of recent articles described in appendix 2 of this volume.

4. See, for example, Michel Foucault, *The History of Sexuality* (New York: Pantheon, 1978); Eve Kosofsky Sedgwick, *Epistemology of the Closet* (Berkeley: University of California Press, 1990); Jeffrey Weeks, *Sexuality*, 3rd ed. (New York: Routledge, 2010).

5. John D'Emilio and Estelle B. Freedman, *Intimate Matters: A History of Sexuality in America*, 3rd ed. (Chicago: University of Chicago Press, 2012), 254–56.

6. Leila J. Rupp, *A Desired Past: A Short History of Same-Sex Love in America* (Chicago: University of Chicago Press, 1999), 9–10.

7. Martha Vicinus, "The History of Lesbian History," *Feminist Studies* 38, no. 3 (Fall 2012): 577; Victoria Harris, "Sex on the Margins: New Directions in the Historiography of Sexuality and Gender," *Historical Journal* 53, no. 4 (December 2010): 1093; Larry Gross, "The Past and the Future of Gay, Lesbian, Bisexual, and Transgender Studies," *Journal of Communication* 55, no. 3 (September 2005): 515–17; D'Emilio and Freedman, *Intimate Matters*, 293; Cornelia H. Dayton and Lisa Levenstein, "The Big Tent of U.S. Women's and Gender History: A State of the Field," *Journal of American History* 99, no. 3 (December 1, 2012): 793–802.

8. Leila J. Rupp, "What's Queer Got to Do with It?," *Reviews in American History* 38, no. 2 (June 2010): 189–98; Harris, "Sex on the Margins," 1096–97.

9. However, I would argue that we tend to let marriage stand in as an indication of heterosexuality more often than we should. In an era when the consequences of variant sexual behavior were severe (and among classes where marriage served to bind families and preserve wealth), people married for many reasons beyond affection and desire.

10. On the challenges of decoding sexual sources, see John D. Wrathall, "Provenance as Text: Reading the Silences around Sexuality in Manuscript Collections," *Journal of American History* 79, no. 1 (June 1992): 165–78; Sally Newman, "The Archival Traces of Desire: Vernon Lee's Failed Sexuality and the Interpretation of Letters in Lesbian History," *Journal of the History of Sexuality* 14, no. 1/2 (January 2005): 51–75; Timothy J. Gilfoyle, "Prostitutes in the Archives: Problems and Possibilities in Documenting the History of Sexuality," *American Archivist* 57, no. 3 (Summer 1994): 514–27; Estelle B. Freedman, "'The Burning of Letters Continues': Elusive Identities and the Historical Construction of Sexuality," *Journal of Women's History* 9, no. 4 (Winter 1998): 181–200; Duberman, "Writhing Bedfellows."

11. Freedman, "'The Burning of Letters Continues.'"

12. Vicki Lynn Eaklor, *Queer America: A GLBT History of the 20th Century* (Westport, CT: Greenwood, 2008), 6–10.

13. See, for example, Freedman, "'The Burning of Letters Continues'"; George Chauncey, *Gay New York: Gender, Urban Culture, and the Making of a Gay Male World, 1890–1940* (New York: Basic, 1994); Regina G. Kunzel, *Criminal Intimacy: Prison and the Uneven History of Modern American Sexuality* (Chicago: University of Chicago Press, 2008).

14. Description based on a visit to the museum. For more on the issues of interpreting Addams's sexuality, see Victoria Bissell Brown, "Queer or Not: What Jane Addams Teaches Us about Not Knowing," in *Out in Chicago: LGBT History at the Crossroads*, ed. Jill Austin and Jennifer Brier (Chicago: Chicago History Museum, 2011), 63–75.

CHAPTER 4

"The Abominable Sin"
European Contact to the Late Nineteenth Century

LET US BEGIN our consideration of LGBT history in the United States with a bold statement: homosexuality did not exist before the late nineteenth century. This, of course, is an oversimplification, but for the modern reader, perhaps the most distinctive characteristic of early LGBT history in the North American colonies is that the concept of homosexuality as a personal characteristic was not yet firmly and consistently entrenched. Europeans and, later, Americans were well aware that men sometimes behaved sexually with other men, and, to a lesser extent, they knew that women sometimes behaved sexually with other women and that people sometimes lived their lives as members of the opposite gender. By and large, they saw this behavior as threatening to the social and natural order. Such activities were outlawed, and religious leaders condemned these acts from the pulpit. However, throughout all of this, the focus was on the *behavior*. The idea that this behavior was only committed by one particular *type of person*—and, indeed, that engaging in this behavior indicated that one *was* this type of person—would not consistently appear in popular understandings of same-sex and transgender behavior until they were put forth by the medical community in the late nineteenth century.[1] As curators Molly McGarry and Fred Wasserman have put it, "The sodomite was seen as a sinner or a criminal, but no more a distinct type of person, with a particular psychology or physiology, than was an adulterer, fornicator, thief, or liar."[2]

Of course, people of the European tradition were aware that some individuals were drawn to this particular type of behavior more than others. In 1677, for example, Nicholas Sension came before the General Court of the Connecticut Colony, charged with the crime of sodomy. Testimony from the case makes clear that Sension was something of a repeat offender; witnesses attested to his numerous sexual advances toward other men over a period of three decades. By the beginning of the eighteenth century, there were reports of small subcultures of effeminate men seeking sex with other men in the largest European cities, and by the mid-nineteenth century, such subcultures had developed in US cities as well, part of a larger underworld that sought to satisfy illicit desires. Nevertheless, it is important to understand that prior to the late nineteenth century, Americans were much more likely to understand same-sex and cross-gender behavior in terms of disorderly conduct and sin rather than psychological disposition or innate character.[3]

The Early Colonial Era

In comparison to European ideas, we know less about North American native cultures' attitudes about same-sex sexuality and gender variance at the time of European colonization. This lack of understanding is due in large part to the fact that what scanty records survive were written from the perspective of European observers. We do know that, generally speaking, native cultures accepted a much wider range of sexual expression than the colonists, and this fact suggests that Native Americans may have been more accepting of same-sex activity in particular, though evidence to support this theory is limited.[4]

Native American sexual systems caused much consternation for European colonists, who saw them as depraved and animalistic. The Spanish missionaries who colonized the American Southwest, for example, were coming from a religious worldview—Catholicism—that defined all forms of sexual activity as sinful and all behavior that did not directly lead to reproduction as unnatural. Sodomy, which they referred to as *el pecado nefando*, or "the abominable sin," was particularly loathsome because, as Tracy Brown points out, it "not only undermined the reproductive function of sex, but for a man to take the submissive position in sex also violated gender prescriptions."[5]

Violations of gender roles and same-sex sexuality were both confounding for Europeans, a fact particularly brought to light by the existence, in many native cultures, of a class of anatomical males who dressed and lived as women and who engaged in sexual acts with other men. The Europeans named these people *berdache*, after a Persian word for male sexual slave. (There is also some evidence of a similar phenomenon of anatomical females living as men. In the twenty-first century, the term "Two-Spirit" is more widely used than *berdache*.) The existence of this class of gender-crossers throughout many native cultures is clear; its significance and meaning is less so. Most historical writing before the 1990s saw the *berdache* as people who defied gender conventions and acted on same-sex desire while still holding important spiritual positions in their societies. More recently, historians have argued that the existence of the *berdache* has more to do with dominance and power relations than with personal expression. According to this interpretation, their role as sexual servicers to a community's male elite was a forced act of subjugation for males who had violated social norms or who had been captured in war.[6]

Elsewhere on the North American continent, in the English colonies of New England, the Puritans also took a stern view of sodomy. A product of the Protestant Reformation, Puritanism challenged the Catholic notion that all sexual expression was sinful. Nevertheless, Puritans confined acceptable sexuality to marriage and set up a system of moral regulation that they believed would prevent societal disorder. As such, the penalties for sexual deviance were severe, and sodomy was a capital offense throughout New England (as it was in all other English, Spanish, French, and Dutch colonies in the New World). Execution for sodomy was relatively rare, however. Only a half-dozen men are known to have been executed for this crime in colonial North America: two in New England, one in Virginia, one in Spanish Florida, and two in New Amsterdam. Nevertheless, punishments for sodomy were severe and could include banishment, whipping, and branding with a hot iron.[7]

The laws in most of New England defined sodomy as sexual activity between men, but magistrates disagreed about whether penetration was required. In the case of sexual activity among females, English colonists were more likely to understand the behavior as the result of hermaphroditism (the term used at the time; today the term "intersex" is more widely accepted). That is, one of the women was assumed to have ambiguous genitals that were not clearly male or female. Although living as a woman, the alleged hermaphrodite was assumed to have the sexual urges of a man and a clitoris that was long enough to allow sexual penetration of a vagina. Only New Haven specifically outlawed sexual activity between women, citing the biblical verse Romans 1:26, and declared it an "abomination" equal to male sodomy and thus also punishable by death. While only New Haven specifically outlawed sexual activity between females, the two known women brought before New England colonial courts for such deeds were tried for lewd behavior. In addition, Puritan religious leaders denounced female same-sex sexual activity as equally sinful to male-male sexual acts.[8]

Intriguingly, while court records and religious writings are quite vocal in their condemnation of same-sex sexual activity, historian Richard Godbeer has argued that the average populace may have been more tolerant of the idea. He points to the limited number of people actually executed for same-sex behavior and evidence suggesting that community members were sometimes aware of such activity without reporting it to the authorities. Similarly, John Murrin, although looking primarily at cases involving bestiality (which was often lumped with sodomy in colonial sources, both being seen as abominable acts, "things fearful to name"), draws parallels between accusations of sexual deviance and accusations of witchcraft, suggesting that the threat of such accusations fell disproportionately on certain demographics deemed threatening to the social order (adolescent men for sexual deviance, older unmarried women for witchcraft).[9]

Because the Puritan colonies of New England had such an established practice of regulating moral behavior and trying transgressions in the courts, we know a great deal more about this region than about the English colonies of the Mid-Atlantic and farther south. However, there is some evidence to suggest that these colonies had a more lenient attitude toward same-sex desire.[10] The Puritan colonies were established for more religious purposes and were thus more family centered than the southern English colonies, which had a more exclusively economic focus. As such, they drew settlers from a greater range of backgrounds, and their populations were more disproportionately male. Whereas New England had two women for every three men during the first generation of European settlement, the Chesapeake had only one woman for every four men. This gender imbalance led to a somewhat more permissive attitude toward nonmarital sexual activity generally, and it seems likely that it also fostered a practice of men seeking sexual gratification from other men.[11]

In addition, after 1670, slavery became more common than indentured servitude, and, like English settlers, enslaved Africans in the early years were predominantly male. The presence of Africans introduced "a diversity of sexual systems in the southern colonies."[12] Sixteenth- and seventeenth-century European sources note male-male sexual activity among a number of cultures in Africa, while some cultures also possessed fluid (that is, nonbinary) gender systems. At the same time, European perpetuators of colonial slavery deliberately aimed to break cultural bonds among Africans, so it is unclear to what extent such practices survived in the New World.[13]

The Eighteenth Century

By the early eighteenth century, the differences between the North American colonies began to lessen. While still part of the Spanish Empire and thus subject to different cultural influences, the section of Mexico that would eventually become the southwestern United States became more secular in its governance. The Pueblo Revolt of 1680 had, to some extent, mitigated the repressive surveillance of all aspects of native lives and called into question the rule of Catholic missionaries stationed in the area. With the lessening of the church's power in the region, civil authorities took over the role of policing behavior, and because this area was a frontier outpost, the Spanish did not take on this role with particular zeal.[14]

In the English colonies, the differences between New England and the more southern colonies waned as well. The population of the English colonies increased sixfold between 1700 and 1760, and such expansive population growth had numerous implications.[15] An increasingly diverse populace meant greater contention over the meanings of various behaviors, challenging the Puritans' ability to govern communities purely by the tenets of their faith. Furthermore, much of the population growth took place in the newer colony of Pennsylvania, founded by Quakers in 1681 and premised on religious tolerance. While these factors contributed to a less strident approach to sexual variance in the North, population growth lessened the gender imbalance in the Chesapeake and southern colonies, making a social system based on the marital regulation of sexuality more feasible.[16] Taken together, these demographic changes brought the attitudes of the various colonies into closer alignment.

Population growth was just one cause of the shift in moral attitudes in the eighteenth century. Even more influential were the sweeping changes in thinking about faith, science, and society that are known collectively as the Enlightenment. During this era, the rational method of inquiry was favored over blind religious faith, and the individual (unquestioningly assumed to be a white man) was given unprecedented authority in determining his own destiny. The natural world was highly prized, and cultural conventions that went against humans' "natural" inclinations became suspect. These ideas challenged the role of government in regulating individual morality and had an obvious influence on the founders of the United States, who chose the separation of church and state as a founding principle.[17]

While the beliefs of the Enlightenment went a long way toward reducing the power of the state to regulate sexual behavior and opened the door to a growing acceptance of sexual gratification generally, its effect on same-sex behavior was more equivocal. Sodomy, by and large, continued to be outlawed, although the reasoning behind its criminalization shifted. In light of the trend away from regulating individual moral choices, the arguments against sodomy transitioned from an emphasis on sin to a focus on same-sex sexuality's potential to destabilize society. Similarly, although Enlightenment thinking prized "natural" behavior, sex between members of the same sex was still seen as "unnatural," which prevented it from being included in the growing acceptance of other forms of sexual expression.[18]

Historian Clare A. Lyons argues convincingly that there were four models of male-male intimacy in play in the European world of the eighteenth century. (Intimacy among females, removed as they were from the Enlightenment role of "citizen," captured nowhere near the same amount of attention and thus is much less evident in surviving sources.) Two of the models Lyons identifies were holdovers from an earlier era and occupied different ends of the gender spectrum. The aristocratic libertine engaged in a wide range of sexual encounters—including those with males—as a demonstration of privilege and masculinity. The unmarried, effeminate "fop" possessed overtly feminine characteristics and thus symbolized social instability and sexual deviance (since his sexuality existed outside of marriage and standard masculine expression). The other two models of male intimacy that Lyons identifies—the sodomite and the heroic friend—grew specifically out of the circumstances of the eighteenth century.[19]

While the word "sodomite" was used in the sixteenth and seventeenth centuries to refer to a man who had engaged in penetrative sexual activity with another man, Lyons uses it to refer specifically to the men—usually overtly effeminate—who began to gather together in European cities in the eighteenth century. These men were explicitly seeking sex with other men (though many were also married) and congregated together in certain taverns or public spaces that became known as sites to find same-sex sexual partners and appear to have been frequented by members of various classes. While we know that news of these subcultures reached North America as part of a transatlantic print culture, there is no evidence that similar groups existed in the American colonies during this era, most likely because of the lack of cities the size of the European urban centers.[20]

Lyons's sodomites represent the first nascent subcultures of people attracted to others of their same sex, and as such, they indicate a number of new approaches to same-sex behavior. For one, these groups of men occasionally received mention in the press (which is how we know about them). Such coverage spread the word about their existence and no doubt alerted others with similar predilections that they were not alone in these desires. Lyons's model of the sodomite also represents the first popular construction of male-male sexual activity among equals; previously, this behavior was generally understood as involving a power differential (occurring between old and young, master and servant, etc.) similar to understandings of male-female sexual encounters. The existence of these groups also suggests that as early as the eighteenth century, some people recognized a connection between sexual behavior and one's larger identity. Finally, we see in these subcultures—and the subsequent discussion about them in the press—the first linkage among Europeans of same-sex sexual behavior with gender variance—a concept that would be crucial to the development of medical models in the late nineteenth century.[21]

Lyons's final model of eighteenth-century male intimacy is perhaps the most complicated: the heroic friend. Among middle-class men, Enlightenment thinking led to an increased respect for intense, affectionate male friendships. According to this new form of thought, the sympathy and sensibility fostered by such attachments would create moral citizens (assumed to be male) and men of good character. As such, intense, sometimes long-term friendships between educated men were quite common and aroused no particular suspicion. The writings these men left behind are full of explicitly romantic and sometimes erotic depictions of their feelings for each other, leaving historians to grapple with questions of what these relationships entailed. Lyons points out that the noble purposes ascribed to such friendships likely provided a respectable cover to men whose affection had moved into the realm of the sexual. Richard Godbeer, while admitting that some relationships surely had a sexual component, argues that to assume sexual attraction is to misunderstand the very purpose of the heroic friendship ideal. William Benemann, on the other hand, finds it worth pondering why contemporary historians are so insistent that these relationships were largely nonsexual, despite abundant evidence describing love and extended physical affection between men. Historians have not yet reached consensus on these issues, but regardless of any sexual component, it seems reasonable to include heroic friendships on the continuum of same-sex love and affection.[22]

The American Revolution—along with other revolutions in France and Haiti that took place in the late eighteenth century—was in many ways an embodiment of the Enlightenment ideals of self-determination and a rational citizenry. Yet the acting out of these ideals threw into question many established social norms. Heroic friendships provided a training ground for men to practice the skills of sympathy and sensitivity, which would be necessary in a new society. As such, special friendships among soldiers were common during the revolution and were not seen as anything troubling.[23] More vexing, perhaps, was the potential for revolutionary ideas of equality to upset established gender hierarchies. In the midst of the American revolt against its patriarchal monarch, it was easy for many to see a parallel potential for women to rebel against a system that declared them the inferiors of men. In a few well-publicized cases, white women rejected their assigned gender roles in favor of the freedoms promised by the philosophy of the time. One such gender rebel was Jemima Wilkinson, who in 1775 experienced a religious epiphany that led her to reject the concept of male and female (and thus her own assignation to either category) and become an evangelist preaching the concept of universal friendship to all. In two other widely publicized cases, Deborah Sampson and Ann Bailey each adopted a male identity in order to enlist and fight in the Continental army during the revolution.[24]

Despite these intriguing exceptions, however, in the years following the American Revolution a new understanding of gender emerged, which served to mitigate the threat of a gender revolution. In this new conceptualization, men and women were understood to be binary opposites. Women's sexuality was deemphasized and their passivity exaggerated in order to distinguish them from the vigor and aggressiveness of the American male. Historians disagree on the impact of these new gender divisions on attitudes about sodomy during the Revolutionary War period, but Lyons makes a compelling case for the overlooking of such behavior in order to create a cohesive class of white men, all of whom embodied similar masculine characteristics.[25]

It should come as no surprise that the founding principles of equality and freedom were applied inconsistently in the United States. Indeed, in many ways, the fledgling United States created its democratic citizenry by drawing circles of privilege around some (white, landed men) while excluding others (blacks, women, the poor). In particular, the decision to condone slavery in the Constitution unleashed centuries of repercussions for US society. Michael Bronski argues that the continuation of slavery in the new nation institutionalized two concepts

Figure 4.1. Deborah Sampson (1760–1827) disguised herself as a man during the Revolutionary War and served in the Continental Army. Courtesy of the Library of Congress, LC-USZ61-20.2

that continue to define the experiences of minorities. First, slavery allowed for a "hierarchical citizenship," where not all members of a nation are granted the same access to the rights of full citizenship. Second, it enshrined the concept that certain classes of people are sexually and morally inferior to others. Such legacies are still evident in the twenty-first century as the United States grapples with racism, poverty, and the question of LGBT civil rights.[26]

The Nineteenth Century

As the revolutionary period ended and the United States became more established as an independent country, the segmentation of American society became even more pronounced. Changes in the nation's economic structure combined with the gender transformations of the revolutionary era to create a distinctly sex-segregated society, particularly for the newly emerging middle class. At the same time, race and class differences intensified, which made it all the more easy for those in power to associate certain sexual behavior, including same-sex sexuality, with groups they perceived as inferior.[27]

The first half of the nineteenth century witnessed a profound economic shift known as the Market Revolution. With improvements in transportation and industry, production could take place on a larger scale and thus became increasingly concentrated in factories and towns. Whereas the colonial era had seen a household economy, where all members worked side by side at a mostly subsistence level, the Market Revolution moved the site of most production outside of the household. With production occurring outside the home, families began buying things they had previously produced themselves (such as furniture and textiles) or done without (such as decorative items). This in turn required money, necessitating that someone in the family work outside the home for wages.

This economic transformation had numerous consequences for American society and for sexual behavior in particular. American culture grew increasingly stratified. Slavery eliminated a sizable portion of the US population from free economic engagement, while the popular association of all African Americans with enslaved status—despite a sizable free African American population—also limited free blacks' ability to interact competitively with the market economy. Varied access to market goods created distinct economic classes, including an expanding middle class. More and more people moved to urban centers—the sites of production—and this in turn increased anonymity and exposed people to a greater variety of moral systems. The waning of the household economy also made marriage and reproduction less of a business transaction, opening the way to marriages based on affection and a reduced birthrate, since children were no longer essential to the economic survival of many families.[28]

Amid these increasing stratifications, the growing distance between male and female gender roles was particularly extreme. The movement of production outside of the home and the growing dependence on wages meant that, particularly among the middle class, men increasingly worked someplace other than where they lived, while women remained in the home, tending to the domestic arena. This gender segregation dovetailed with the gender role extremes that had begun in the postrevolutionary period to create the ideology of separate spheres, where women oversaw the private realm and men interacted with the wider world.[29]

While the idea of separate spheres no longer carries the weight among historians that it once did, the early to mid-nineteenth century was nevertheless a particularly sex-segregated era of American history. Men increasingly spent their days surrounded by other men, and women with other women. Differences between the sexes were emphasized. Within this context, it is perhaps not surprising that fierce, loving commitments with members of the same sex were quite common in the nineteenth century. Known as "romantic friendships," these attachments included pledges of undying devotion, proclamations of love, erotic language, and physical fondling. This model of friendship for both women and men first developed in the eighteenth century—as evidenced by the male ideal of heroic friendship, which shared many of the same characteristics—but its frequency among the middle class in the nineteenth century is rather striking.[30]

Furthermore, while romantic friendships were most common among middle-class whites, evidence suggests that these relationships also existed among working-class whites and African Americans. However, since written sources from these groups are so much less common, we cannot be sure whether the practice was rarer among African Americans and the working class or simply that less of this kind of source made it into archives. Given these

Figure 4.2. This 1818 cartoon demonstrates discomfort with men who strayed outside of established gender norms, in this case by showing excessive interest in their appearance. It calls to mind the eighteenth-century stereotype of the Fop. *Exquisite Dandies*, by Isaac Robert Cruikshank. Courtesy of the Library of Congress, LC-USZC2-605

circumstances, the relationship between Addie Brown, a free black domestic, and Rebecca Primus, an African American schoolteacher, is especially intriguing. Surviving correspondence between the women, spanning the years 1859–1869, reveals an abiding love for each other and also hints at a sexual component to their friendship.[31] In one letter from 1859, Brown writes:

> You are the first girl that I ever <u>love</u> so and you are the <u>last</u> one. Dear Rebeca, do not say anything against me <u>loving</u> you so, for I mean just what I say. O Rebbeca, it seem I can see you now, casting those loving eyes at me. If you was a man, what would things come to? They would after come to something very quick. What do you think the matter? Don't laugh at me. I not exactly crazy yet.[32]

Romantic friendships have fascinated historians for at least two generations. Common among both women and men (though more common for women), they often coexisted with heterosexual marriage. The explicitly erotic language used in letters between romantic friends seems clearly sexual to modern readers, and it is difficult for us to grasp that these

Figure 4.3. Intense, affectionate same-sex friendships were common in the nineteenth century, particularly among middle-class women. These relationships quite often involved physical affection and were considered quite socially acceptable.
Courtesy of the Library of Congress, LC-USZ62-124650

attachments were perfectly acceptable within mainstream society and carried no suggestion of sexual impropriety. Nevertheless, the unabashed ways in which nineteenth-century Americans proclaimed their love for members of their same sex and the sheer amount of this type of evidence that survives affirms that these relationships were exceedingly common and widely accepted during this era. Yet the question remains: How are we to understand them within the context of queer history?

In the early decades of the LGBT history subfield, historians were eager to find in the past evidence of same-sex desire that mirrored contemporary understandings of homosexuality. As such, they tended to see romantic friendships as homosexual (despite the fact that this concept developed later), assuming either that they had involved a genital dimension or failed to do so only because of Victorian repression, not for lack of desire. In more recent decades, LGBT historians have become more committed to understanding same-sex relationships of the past within the context of the era in which they existed. With the acknowledgment that sexual identity is socially constructed has come a greater comfort with avoiding easy labels. We must remember that for most of the nineteenth century there was no medical-psychological category that grouped strong emotional bonds, physical intimacy, love, and genital gratification with members of the same sex all under one label, "homosexual," and classified such behavior abnormal.

Jonathan Ned Katz has argued that nineteenth-century Americans had a significantly different moral landscape than the one that would emerge in the twentieth century. According to Katz, in the twentieth century, under the influence of Freudian psychology, the erotic world was described as a spectrum between "good" and "bad" behavior, as represented by heterosexuality on one end and homosexuality on the other. Early nineteenth-century Americans, not yet exposed to Sigmund Freud, or any other psychology for that matter, understood the moral landscape differently. For them, "good" and "bad" were represented by love and lust. Love letters between members of the same sex, nights spent lying in each other's arms, and earnest references to each other as "my own dear heart" could thus escape censure because, within the nineteenth-century worldview, this behavior occupied the world of love, the "good" end of the moral spectrum, rather than lust, which was the terrain of the lower classes and the urban underworld.[33]

While Katz's argument is particularly helpful in explaining the existence of romantic friendships, the love-lust dichotomy is but one of many frameworks for understanding sexuality in the nineteenth-century United States. Indeed, Helen Lefkowitz Horowitz has described four distinct schools of sexual thought at play in antebellum America, and when we consider the extreme regional differences of this era—increasing urbanization in the North, slavery in the South, the multicultural frontier in the West—it is likely that even more sexual systems were simultaneously operating within the United States. The nineteenth century, like our own era, represented a range of subcultures and sexual ways of being.[34]

Virtually nothing has been written about consensual same-sex sexual behavior among the enslaved, presumably because of a scarcity of historical sources. We do know, however, that slavery required a system of complete domination over the enslaved and that one weapon of that domination was sexual violence. While the sexual violence perpetuated upon enslaved women by their captors has been explored in far greater detail, Aliyyah I. Abdur-Rahman and Thomas A. Foster each have noted that sexual violence extended to all those held in slavery, regardless of gender, and included the rape of enslaved males by male captors.[35] In addition, numerous historians have noted that white assumptions about the sexual proclivities of people of color generally, and African Americans in particular, helped to construct concepts of "normal" and "deviant" sexual expression, a practice that would be applied in the twentieth century to those who desired their own sex.[36]

Among the slaveholding class of the Old South, romantic friendships were common, as they were among the educated classes of the Northeast. Anya Jabour, however, has argued that southern friendships—both among males and females—were more consistently devoid of overt sexuality than their northern counterparts. In contrast, Martin Duberman has offered evidence of at least one male-male relationship among the southern elite that he believes was more sexual than romantic. Nevertheless, most historians, when discussing romantic friendships, tend not to distinguish between the North and the South, noting similar trends for the elite of both regions.[37]

In contrast to genteel society in the East, the frontier West represented an opportunity for rebirth and self-determinism. In the American imagination, the frontier offered a means to flee the confines of "civilization," and for many Americans in the nineteenth century, "civilization" meant a society stratified by class and race distinctions, where women were the arbiters of propriety. The region did experience a range of cultural conflicts, as Mexicans, Native

Americans, Chinese immigrants, and Anglo-American and African American settlers came into extended contact with each other. Nevertheless, societal divisions and the demands of morality were more relaxed in the frontier West. Marriage between people of different races was more common than in the East, and the rigors of life in a sparsely populated region prone to warfare between settlers and indigenous populations meant that one couldn't be too picky about one's associates, based on class or religious pretensions.[38]

This moral flexibility was accompanied by another distinctive feature of the frontier: sex-segregated communities. As already discussed, the nineteenth century in general was a highly sex-segregated era, but in the East this primarily meant that men and women—particularly middle-class men and women—spent most of their day among members of their own sex. On the frontier—for those living in mining camps, Chinese labor camps, military outposts, ranches, and even to some extent Mormon settlements—sex segregation was even more extreme. Settler and immigrant men could quite literally go weeks or longer without sustained contact with women, although this was less true for Native American and Mexican populations that had resided in the region longer. Brothels represented a type of all-female frontier community, where—although the women were in frequent contact with men—survival depended on other women.[39]

The scarcity of women (particularly white women) in many areas of the frontier fostered an all-male settler culture that accepted cross-dressing and female impersonation. It is also possible that such communities were influenced by the Two-Spirit tradition, which continued among many native cultures during the nineteenth century. At social activities, settler men danced with other men, and often a portion of the men would dress like women in order to more clearly act out female gender roles during such occasions. Later in the course of American settlement of the West, shows featuring female impersonators became a standard form of entertainment, with gender-crossing performers living as accepted members of their communities.[40]

In addition to the presence of male-to-female cross-dressing in frontier settlements, there is substantial evidence to suggest that intense male-male bonds were also rather common and generally accepted. "Cowboy" poems and songs praised the devotion and comfort of male partnerships, such as in this excerpt from the 1915 Badger Clark poem, "The Lost Pardner":

> We loved each other in the way men do
> And never spoke about it, Al and me,
> But we both knowed, and knowin' it so true
> Was more than any woman's kiss could be.[41]

Susan Lee Johnson, in discussing male partnerships in the West, recounts the relationship of Jason Chamberlain and John Chafee, who lived together for more than fifty years in nineteenth-century California. Chamberlain eventually ran a way station for travelers to the Yosemite Valley, and a surviving guest book indicates that visitors recognized the men as partners, referring to "the wedded batchelors [sic]" and the two men's "Golden Wedding" of a half-century together. Chafee and Chamberlain died within a few months of each other as well; ten weeks after Chafee's death in 1903, Chamberlain committed suicide.[42]

Part of the explanation for these frontier partnerships among men lies in the romantic friendship model prevalent in the United States at this time. No doubt, many of these relationships were more romantic than sexual and followed the conventions of the era by emphasizing emotion and loyalty over sexual gratification. However, evidence suggests that a greater number *were* sexual (or, at least, less care was taken to hide their sexual component) than in the East. Numerous firsthand accounts of the frontier period refer to casual encounters between men that appear to be sexual in nature.[43] Popular culture, too—from songs to stories to cowboy limericks—seem to delight in a double entendre suggestive of bawdy practices between men, as in this excerpt from an 1836 tale of a fight with a stagecoach driver:

> I jumped right down upon the driver and he tore my trowsers [sic] right off me ... luckily there was a poker in the fire which I thrust down his throat, and by that means mastered him.

Or this limerick:

> Young cowboys had a great fear,
> That old studs once filled with beer,
> Completely addle'
> They'd throw on a saddle,
> And ride them on the rear.

Traditionally, such evidence was explained in terms of pure circumstance—in the absence of women, heterosexual men chose male sexual partners. However, it also seems feasible that the sex-segregated lifestyles of the frontier may have been particularly appealing to men seeking to avoid the pressures of traditional courtship and marriage and who were aware of the comparative acceptance of same-sex sexuality within these groups.

Historian Peter Boag offers a similar explanation for the prevalence of cross-dressing in the West, which he describes as "ubiquitous." Indeed, there are a surprising number of cases that have survived in the historical record, particularly of anatomical females who assumed male identities and lived for varying periods of time as men, quite often partnering or legally marrying women along the way. Examples of anatomical males who took on female identities full time or made their livings as female impersonators are also prevalent. Boag argues that this component of the frontier has been largely forgotten in popular memory, and the cases that are remembered have been explained in ways that foster our prevailing national myths about the frontier. Anatomical females dressing as men are explained in terms of expediency: because of the frontier's wild nature, a male identity was required for protection, access to adventure, or employment. In popular imagination, anatomical males dressed as women are invariably nonwhite (usually Mexican or Native American), contributing to our dominant national narrative of the West as a place of recklessness that required the stabilizing influence of white gender norms. Instead, Boag puts forward the idea that many cross-dressers (a term he admits is problematic) possessed a gender opposite of their biological sex and chose to live in the West precisely because of its less rigid social structures.[44]

Like the frontier, the battlefields of the American Civil War also provided a site where traditional societal norms were strained and where men lived in close proximity with each other under stressful conditions, far from the company of many women. Given these circumstances, it seems likely that same-sex sexual activity occurred between soldiers. However, such behavior was apparently extremely well hidden or, more likely, not of major concern to the US military. No evidence exists of soldiers being disciplined for sodomy during the Civil War, and only three pairs of navy sailors were court-martialed for sodomy during this period. More common were anatomical females serving in battle under male identities. Loreta Janeta Velazquez, a Cuban American, fought for the Confederacy under the name of Lt. Harry T. Buford and seems to have moved between categories of gender and race more easily than most Confederates. Velazquez returned to living as a female after the war. In contrast, Pvt. Albert Cashier, who fought for the Union with the Ninety-Fifth Illinois, retained his male identity. Cashier spent his childhood as Jennie Hodgers but assumed the name Albert Cashier some time before enlisting in the army in 1862. He lived the rest of his life as Cashier, until his death in 1915.[45]

In the aftermath of the Civil War, Americans struggled to find a national identity that would reconcile the country's deep divisions, though for most, particularly after the 1870s, this concern was limited to reconciliation among native-born whites. Art provided one path through which the new American identity was explored, and the male body became a subject of particular interest to artists working in a variety of media. This is not surprising when we consider the devastation the war wreaked. Nearly 2 percent of the population, 620,000 men, died between 1861 and 1865, and this tragedy severely affected the national ethos. Many of those who survived with their lives were physically maimed or psychologically scarred. Within this context of national loss, the virile male body came to symbolize a healthy democracy. A certain homoeroticism emerged, made all the more remarkable by the fact that many prominent artists of this era—including Thomas Eakins, F. Holland Day, John Singer Sargent, Harriet Hosmer, Edmonia Lewis, and Anne Whitney—had intense romantic attachments with members of their own sex.[46]

Of course, no discussion of homoeroticism in nineteenth-century American art would be complete without reference to the author Walt Whitman, who has been a long-standing object of fascination for those seeking to uncover the queer past. Whitman intrigues because his poetry sets forth such a compelling vision of the American character while also being unabashedly adoring of men and the bonds they share. His personal life was also overtly male oriented, though he never explicitly acknowledged engaging in sexual activity with other males. Whitman spent his adult life in a series of relationships with men, usually younger and from the working class, and he spent the Civil War years engaged in a variety of flirtations with soldiers. He also engaged in a long-running correspondence with the British art critic John Addington Symonds and British political organizer Edward Carpenter, both of whom were early advocates for legal leniency for those who engaged in same-sex behavior. As the letters with Carpenter and Symonds attest, many people who desired others of the same sex saw in Whitman a kindred spirit; his poetry spoke of the potential of the nation, and for some, the imagery he chose spoke of a different potential, where those who loved their own sex were essential members of the democratic whole.[47]

Whitman represents yet another facet of late nineteenth-century American life: the city. His poetry often employs industrial images, and Whitman himself spent long periods of his

Figure 4.4. Author Walt Whitman with his friend Peter Doyle, 1865. Courtesy of the Library of Congress, LC-DIG-ppmsca-07387

life within an urban milieu, where he could pursue his relationships with working-class men in relative privacy. In this, he was not alone. As mentioned earlier, the Market Revolution concentrated sites of production, which in turn expanded the number of people who lived in cities in order to be close to economic opportunities. In the last two decades of the nineteenth century, the urban population of the United States grew by fifteen million people.[48]

Urbanization reduced the amount of community surveillance that was possible and enabled people to find others who shared their sexual interests. The anonymity available in cities, coupled with a firm line between public and private among the middle class, enabled the development of an urban underworld in which Americans could relate to each other in a host of ways that were considered offensive to mainstream sensibilities. Prostitution, gambling, and drinking flourished in these underworlds, as did male sexual liaisons with other men. These urban enclaves created an environment where it was significantly easier for people—middle-class men among them—to indulge their vices away from the censorious eye of their familes and community. For men inclined to have sex with other men, the underworld made it far simpler to find a willing partner.[49]

Such behaviors were considered immoral, to be sure, and urban "vice" in all its forms caused considerable anxiety among social commentators and reformers. As such, the late nineteenth century also saw a surge in efforts to maintain a system of traditional morality based on Protestant ethics. Movements to regulate prostitution and outlaw alcohol were active during this era, and one citizen-activist—Anthony Comstock—succeeded in getting Congress to revise federal postal law to prohibit the mailing of any material deemed even vaguely salacious. The 1873 Comstock Law, as it was called, was strictly enforced until the late 1950s, greatly limiting the ability of gays, lesbians, and gender crossers to access information about themselves in the form of magazines, books, or organizational newsletters.[50]

The Young Men's Christian Association (YMCA), of which Anthony Comstock was a member, was but the most prominent of a number of late nineteenth-century reform organizations that sought to direct the sympathies of young people away from urban vices. The YMCA's mission was to provide an upstanding Christian environment in which young men separated from their families could live and/or spend their leisure time. Ironically, the YMCA's emphasis on male companionship created an environment where same-sex attachments could grow, and its dormitories, showers, and locker rooms afforded relative privacy in which men could physically express these attachments. Despite its goal of creating a community that adhered to Protestant values, the YMCA developed a reputation as a meeting ground for men interested in men that would last for nearly a century.[51]

By the last quarter of the nineteenth century, the United States was undergoing rapid change brought on by urbanization, immigration, shifting gender roles, economic transformations, and new ideas about the self and human behavior. From this shifting terrain came a new approach to same-sex love and desire, one grounded in the medical and psychological knowledge of the day. At the turn of the twentieth century, scientists would introduce the idea that one's sexual object choice was fixed and unchanging and provided a glimpse into a person's mental health. Desire for the opposite sex was deemed normal; desire for the same sex—now labeled homosexuality—became an indicator of flawed character. This transition to a heterosexual/homosexual binary and its subsequent impact on American culture is the subject of the next chapter.

Notes

1. John D'Emilio and Estelle B. Freedman, *Intimate Matters: A History of Sexuality in America*, 3rd ed. (Chicago: University of Chicago Press, 2012), 30–31; Leila J. Rupp, *A Desired Past: A Short History of Same-Sex Love in America* (Chicago: University of Chicago Press, 1999), 27–35; Thomas A. Foster, introduction to *Long before Stonewall: Histories of Same-Sex Sexuality in Early America* (New York: New York University Press, 2007), 8–9; Richard Godbeer, "'The Cry of Sodom': Discourse, Intercourse, and Desire in Colonial New England," *William and Mary Quarterly* 52, no. 2 (April 1, 1995): 259–86.
2. Molly McGarry and Fred Wasserman, *Becoming Visible: An Illustrated History of Lesbian and Gay Life in Twentieth-Century America* (New York: Penguin Studio, 1998), 39.
3. Nicholas C. Edsall, *Toward Stonewall: Homosexuality and Society in the Modern Western World* (Charlottesville: University of Virginia Press, 2003), 3–16; Foster, introduction, 8–9; Godbeer, "'The Cry of Sodom.'"

4. Rupp, *Desired Past*, 15–19; Ramón A. Gutiérrez, *When Jesus Came, the Corn Mothers Went Away: Marriage, Sexuality, and Power in New Mexico, 1500–1846* (Stanford, CA: Stanford University Press, 1991), 72.
5. Tracy Brown, "'Abominable Sin' in Colonial New Mexico: Spanish and Pueblo Perceptions of Same-Sex Sexuality," in *Long before Stonewall: Histories of Same-Sex Sexuality in Early America*, ed. Thomas A. Foster (New York: New York University Press, 2007), 55–57.
6. Rupp, *Desired Past*, 15–19; Gutiérrez, *When Jesus Came, the Corn Mothers Went Away*, 32–35; Richard C. Trexler, *Sex and Conquest: Gendered Violence, Political Order, and the European Conquest of the Americas* (Cambridge: Polity, 1995); Ramón A. Gutiérrez, "Warfare, Homosexuality, and Gender Status among American Indian Men in the Southwest," in *Long before Stonewall: Histories of Same-Sex Sexuality in Early America*, ed. Thomas A. Foster (New York: New York University Press, 2007), 19–31; Gunlög Fur, "Weibe-Town and the Delawares-as-Women: Gender Crossing and Same-Sex Relations in Eighteenth-Century Northeastern Indian Culture," in *Long before Stonewall: Histories of Same-Sex Sexuality in Early America*, ed. Thomas A. Foster (New York: New York University Press, 2007), 32–50; Marc Stein, ed., *Encyclopedia of Lesbian, Gay, Bisexual, and Transgender History in America* (New York: Scribner/Thomson-Gale, 2004), 3:213–16.
7. D'Emilio and Freedman, *Intimate Matters*, 23–24, 30; Michael Bronski, *A Queer History of the United States* (Boston: Beacon, 2011), 7–8; Godbeer, "'The Cry of Sodom,'" 263, 272; Foster, introduction, 5–6; John M. Murrin, "'Things Fearful to Name': Bestiality in Colonial America," *Pennsylvania History* 65 (January 1, 1998): 8–43; Roger Thompson, *Sex in Middlesex: Popular Mores in a Massachusetts County, 1649–1699* (Amherst: University of Massachusetts Press, 1986), 72–75.
8. Elizabeth Reis, "Hermaphrodites and 'Same-Sex' Sex in Early America," in *Long before Stonewall: Histories of Same-Sex Sexuality in Early America*, ed. Thomas A. Foster (New York: New York University Press, 2007), 144–63; Clare A. Lyons, "Mapping an Atlantic Sexual Culture: Homoeroticism in Eighteenth-Century Philadelphia," *William and Mary Quarterly* 60, no. 1 (January 1, 2003): 127; Jonathan Katz, *Gay American History: Lesbians and Gay Men in the U.S.A.: A Documentary History*, rev. ed. (New York: Meridian, 1992), 23; Godbeer, "'The Cry of Sodom,'" 267–68.
9. Godbeer, "'The Cry of Sodom,'" 262–72; Murrin, "'Things Fearful to Name,'" 28–33.
10. Foster, introduction, 5; Lyons, "Mapping an Atlantic Sexual Culture," 138.
11. D'Emilio and Freedman, *Intimate Matters*, 9–11.
12. Ibid., 13.
13. Rupp, *Desired Past*, 24–27.
14. Brown, "'Abominable Sin' in Colonial New Mexico"; Gutiérrez, *When Jesus Came, the Corn Mothers Went Away*, 130–40.
15. Bronski, *A Queer History of the United States*, 19.
16. D'Emilio and Freedman, *Intimate Matters*, 13–14, 38; Bronski, *A Queer History of the United States*, 19; Clare A. Lyons, *Sex among the Rabble: An Intimate History of Gender & Power in the Age of Revolution, Philadelphia, 1730–1830* (Chapel Hill: Omohundro Institute of Early American History and Culture, Williamsburg, Virginia / University of North Carolina Press, 2006), 1–10.
17. D'Emilio and Freedman, *Intimate Matters*, 39–42; Foster, introduction, 5–6; Lyons, *Sex among the Rabble*, 9; Bronski, *A Queer History of the United States*, 26–28; Jay Hatheway, *The Gilded Age Construction of Modern American Homophobia* (New York: Palgrave Macmillan, 2003), 15–20.

18. Edsall, *Toward Stonewall*, 33–46; Bronski, *A Queer History of the United States*, 26–27; Mark E. Kann, *Taming Passion for the Public Good: Policing Sex in the Early Republic* (New York: New York University Press, 2013), 1–22.
19. Lyons, "Mapping an Atlantic Sexual Culture," 123–27; Thomas A. Foster, *Sex and the Eighteenth-Century Man: Massachusetts and the History of Sexuality in America* (Boston: Beacon, 2006), 101–27.
20. Lyons, "Mapping an Atlantic Sexual Culture," esp. 123–27; Godbeer, "'The Cry of Sodom'"; Richard Godbeer, *The Overflowing of Friendship: Love between Men and the Creation of the American Republic* (Baltimore: Johns Hopkins University Press, 2009), 6–7; Foster, *Sex and the Eighteenth-Century Man*, 155–77; History Project, *Improper Bostonians: Lesbian and Gay History from the Puritans to Playland* (Boston: Beacon, 1998), 28–29; William Benemann, *Male-Male Intimacy in Early America: Beyond Romantic Friendships* (New York: Harrington Park, 2006), 29–56.
21. Lyons, "Mapping an Atlantic Sexual Culture," esp. 123–27; Godbeer, "'The Cry of Sodom'"; Edsall, *Toward Stonewall*, 17–32; Benemann, *Male-Male Intimacy in Early America*, 29–56; Godbeer, *The Overflowing of Friendship*, 6–7; Foster, *Sex and the Eighteenth-Century Man*, 155–77.
22. Lyons, "Mapping an Atlantic Sexual Culture," esp. 123–27; Godbeer, *The Overflowing of Friendship*; Benemann, *Male-Male Intimacy in Early America*. See also History Project, *Improper Bostonians*, 33–37; Bronski, *A Queer History of the United States*, 32–35.
23. Godbeer, *The Overflowing of Friendship*, 119–54; Benemann, *Male-Male Intimacy in Early America*, 71–120.
24. Bronski, *A Queer History of the United States*, 35–39; History Project, *Improper Bostonians*, 30–31; Alfred F. Young, *Masquerade: The Life and Times of Deborah Sampson, Continental Soldier* (New York: Knopf, 2004).
25. Lyons, *Sex among the Rabble*; Lyons, "Mapping an Atlantic Sexual Culture"; Bronski, *A Queer History of the United States*, 35–39; Kann, *Taming Passion for the Public Good*, 103–7.
26. Bronski, *A Queer History of the United States*, 22–23, quote from 22; Godbeer, *The Overflowing of Friendship*, 145; Lyons, *Sex among the Rabble*.
27. Rupp, *Desired Past*, 41–42; D'Emilio and Freedman, *Intimate Matters*, 37–38; Kann, *Taming Passion for the Public Good*, 103–27.
28. D'Emilio and Freedman, *Intimate Matters*, 73–78; Rupp, *Desired Past*, 40; Walter Licht, *Industrializing America: The Nineteenth Century* (Baltimore: Johns Hopkins University Press, 1995), 63–68; John D'Emilio, "Capitalism and Gay Identity," in *Powers of Desire: The Politics of Sexuality*, ed. Ann Barr Snitow, Christine Stansell, and Sharon Thompson (New York: Monthly Review Press, 1983), 100–113.
29. Rupp, *Desired Past*, 40–41.
30. Ibid., 43–53; Leila Rupp, "Romantic Friendships," in *Modern American Queer History*, ed. Allida Mae Black (Philadelphia: Temple University Press, 2001), 13–23; Carroll Smith-Rosenberg, "The Female World of Love and Ritual: Relations between Women in Nineteenth-Century America," *Signs: Journal of Women in Culture & Society* 1, no. 1 (1975): 1–29; Anthony Rotundo, "Romantic Friendship: Male Intimacy and Middle-Class Youth in the Northern United States, 1800–1900," *Journal of Social History* 23 (Fall 1989): 1–26; D'Emilio and Freedman, *Intimate Matters*, 125–29; Edsall, *Toward Stonewall*, 72.
31. Karen V. Hansen, "'No *Kisses* Is Like Youres': An Erotic Friendship between Two African-American Women during the Mid-Nineteenth Century," *Gender & History* 7, no. 2 (August 1, 1995): 153–82.
32. Ibid., 162.

33. Jonathan Katz, *Love Stories: Sex between Men before Homosexuality* (Chicago: University of Chicago Press, 2001), 332–36. See also Rupp, "Romantic Friendships," 8–12.
34. Helen Lefkowitz Horowitz, *Rereading Sex: Battles over Sexual Knowledge and Suppression in Nineteenth-Century America* (New York: Knopf, 2002); Helen Lefkowitz Horowitz, *Attitudes toward Sex in Antebellum America: A Brief History with Documents* (New York: Palgrave Macmillan, 2006), 1–31.
35. Aliyyah I. Abdur-Rahman, "'The Strangest Freaks of Despotism': Queer Sexuality in Antebellum African American Slave Narratives," *African American Review* 40, no. 2 (Summer 2006): 223–37; Thomas A. Foster, "The Sexual Abuse of Black Men under American Slavery," *Journal of the History of Sexuality* 30, no. 3 (September 2011): 452–54.
36. Abdur-Rahman, "'The Strangest Freaks of Despotism'"; Bronski, *A Queer History of the United States*, 22–23; Siobhan B. Somerville, *Queering the Color Line: Race and the Invention of Homosexuality in American Culture*, Series Q (Durham, NC: Duke University Press, 2000); Julian B. Carter, *The Heart of Whiteness: Normal Sexuality and Race in America, 1880–1940* (Durham, NC: Duke University Press, 2007); Stein, *Encyclopedia of Lesbian, Gay, Bisexual, and Transgender History in America*, 3:123–24.
37. Anya Jabour, *Scarlett's Sisters: Young Women in the Old South* (Chapel Hill: University of North Carolina Press, 2007), 70–76; Anya Jabour, "Male Friendship and Masculinity in the Early National South: William Wirt and His Friends," *Journal of the Early Republic* 20, no. 1 (April 1, 2000): 83–111; Martin B. Duberman, "'Writhing Bedfellows' in Antebellum South Carolina: Historical Interpretation and the Politics of Evidence," in *About Time: Exploring the Gay Past*, rev. and expanded ed. (New York: Meridian, 1991), 3–23.
38. Susan Lee Johnson, *Roaring Camp: The Social World of the California Gold Rush* (New York: Norton, 2000), esp. 141–44; Bronski, *A Queer History of the United States*, 41–46; D'Emilio and Freedman, *Intimate Matters*, 86–93.
39. Johnson, *Roaring Camp*, 100–30; Bronski, *A Queer History of the United States*, 42–46; Rupp, *Desired Past*, 53–60; Stein, *Encyclopedia of Lesbian, Gay, Bisexual, and Transgender History in America*, 1:88.
40. Rupp, *Desired Past*, 53–67; Johnson, *Roaring Camp*, 172–74; Peter Boag, *Re-Dressing America's Frontier Past* (Berkeley: University of California Press, 2011), 64–66, 70–71.
41. Badger Clark, *Sun and Saddle Leather* (Boston: Gorham, 1919), 67–69, quoted in Katz, *Gay American History*, 511. See also Bronski, *A Queer History of the United States*, 41–46; Rupp, *Desired Past*, 55.
42. Johnson, *Roaring Camp*, 335–37.
43. Ibid., 170–76.
44. Boag, *Re-Dressing America's Frontier Past*. See also Jennifer Brier and Anne Parsons, "Gender Crossroads: Representations of Gender Transgressions in Chicago's Press, 1850–1920," in *Out in Chicago: LGBT History at the Crossroads*, ed. Jill Austin and Jennifer Brier (Chicago: Chicago History Museum, 2011), 23–40.
45. Bronski, *A Queer History of the United States*, 63–70; Thomas P. Lowry, *The Story the Soldiers Wouldn't Tell: Sex in the Civil War* (Mechanicsburg, PA: Stackpole, 1994), 109–22; Robin C. Sager, "The Multiple Metaphoric Civil Wars of Loreta Janeta Velazquez's 'The Woman in Battle,'" *Southern Quarterly* 48, no. 1 (Fall 2010): 27–45.
46. Bronski, *A Queer History of the United States*, 63–68, 74–77; Hatheway, *The Gilded Age Construction of Modern American Homophobia*, 53–55; Drew Gilpin Faust, *This Republic of Suffering: Death and the American Civil War* (New York: Knopf, 2008), xi.

47. Katz, *Love Stories*, 150–63; Bronski, *A Queer History of the United States*, 77–81; Rupp, *Desired Past*, 68–71; D'Emilio and Freedman, *Intimate Matters*, 127–29; David S. Reynolds, *Walt Whitman* (New York: Oxford University Press, 2005), 118–122.
48. "City Life in the Late 19th Century," online lesson plan, *Library of Congress Teacher Resources*, accessed June 8, 2014, http://www.loc.gov/teachers/classroommaterials/presentationsandactivities/presentations/timeline/riseind/city/.
49. Rupp, *Desired Past*, 67–70, 77–79; D'Emilio and Freedman, *Intimate Matters*, 122–23, 130–33, 180–83; Hatheway, *The Gilded Age Construction of Modern American Homophobia*, 55–60.
50. D'Emilio and Freedman, *Intimate Matters*, 155–61, 284; Bronski, *A Queer History of the United States*, 83–87; Horowitz, *Rereading Sex*, 358–407.
51. Paula Lupkin, *Manhood Factories: YMCA Architecture and the Making of Modern Urban Culture* (Minneapolis: University of Minnesota Press, 2010), 1–35; John D. Gustav-Wrathall, *Take the Young Stranger by the Hand: Same Sex-Relations and the YMCA* (Chicago: University of Chicago Press, 1998).

CHAPTER 5

Creating Communities
Late Nineteenth Century to the Mid-1960s

THE END OF the nineteenth century in the United States was marked by conflict and change. Immigrants flooded the cities. Discrepancies grew between rich and poor, sparking a labor movement that sought fair working conditions and compensation for all. African Americans experienced a period of heightened oppression and terrorism. Jim Crow laws throughout the South created rigid segregation, and mob violence against African Americans became quite common. At the same time, women—particularly middle-class women and white women of all classes—experienced unprecedented opportunities to engage with the public world of work, leisure, education, and reform. Within this culture of conflict and change, the field of sexology emerged and introduced the world to new ideas about same-sex desire and behavior. The late nineteenth-century concepts of homosexuality and heterosexuality structured understanding of sexual desire for more than a century and continue, to some extent, to influence LGBT lives today. Yet such medical writings on same-sex desire were also very much a product of the world that created them. I thus begin with a larger description of the turn-of-the-twentieth-century United States to describe the context in which scientists began to theorize about sexual "deviance."

1880–1920

The period between roughly 1880 and 1920 was marked in the United States by extreme racism as well as class and gender strife. Many Americans—particularly the white, wealthy, and educated, whose power seemed the most threatened—understood this cultural flux as a crisis of morality and responded with efforts at social control, many of which related to sexuality.[1] In the words of John D'Emilio and Estelle Freedman:

Sexuality became a vehicle for exercising control over the lower classes, especially immigrants in the urbanized North and blacks in the rural South. The range of political responses that took shape—a social hygiene movement to halt the spread of venereal disease, campaigns against white slavery and prostitution, and the wave of lynching that accompanied segregation in the South—suggest the depth of concern over sexual issues at the turn of the century.[2]

In addition to these phenomena, an interest in studying, classifying, and labeling various elements of society emerged. In the midst of this cultural milieu, people who desired their own sex came to be defined as homosexuals.

Many of the changes taking place in the United States at the turn of the twentieth century come into focus when we consider the issue of urbanization. Between 1880 and 1920, the percentage of the US population living in urban centers doubled, from 26 percent in 1880 to 50 percent in 1920.[3] The economy was diversifying, creating the need for a new class of workers to manage people and knowledge. This newly expanding professional class in turn required legions of clerical workers to support its work, and a significant proportion of these new jobs were located in urban centers. Young people, often unaccompanied by other family members, flocked to the city in hopes of economic opportunity. This motivation was reinforced for many African Americans by a desire to escape the oppression, racial violence, and extreme poverty of the Jim Crow South. Known as the Great Migration, this massive African American mobility constituted a major demographic shift. Finally, immigrants contributed to the growth of cities at the turn of the twentieth century. Twelve million immigrants arrived in the United States between 1870 and 1900, and by 1920, 75 percent of the foreign-born population of the country lived in urban areas.[4]

Many of the people moving to the city were young, unmarried, and arriving without family members to govern their conduct. While this was true of both men and women, it was more common for men, and whole subcultures of bachelors existed in most large American cities by the early twentieth century. In addition, the population of certain ethnic groups—such as Italian and Chinese—were disproportionately male at this time, because these groups tended to immigrate temporarily to earn money, leaving their families behind in their countries of origin.[5] At various points during the 1880–1920 period, bachelors accounted for 40 percent or more of the male populations over the age of fifteen in New York City, Chicago, and Boston.[6]

The preponderance of single men created all-male subcultures, which in turn provided an opportunity for same-sex experimentation. Certain entertainment establishments, restaurants, and neighborhoods became known as places where those who desired their own sex could meet each other (although this was more true for men, who had greater access to public nightlife, than for women), and as people with same-sex desires were increasingly able to find each other, communities began to develop. At the same time (and not necessarily in opposition), opportunities for anonymous same-sex encounters became far more common, and the practice of "cruising" emerged.[7]

One example of the spread of queer gathering places was Columbia Hall, operating by the 1890s in the Bowery district of New York City. Colloquially known as Paresis Hall (a turn-of-the-century term for mental illness), this establishment provided a meeting ground for men seeking sex with other men, the companionship of those with similar desires, and/or the freedom to interact socially while assuming a female persona. Evidence suggests that a fraternal organization for such men, called the Cercle [*sic*] Hermaphroditis, operated out of the hall. According to George Chauncey, the group rented a room in the building where club members could store belongings and change into feminine attire once safely off the public street, since cross-dressing was illegal at the turn of the century.[8]

Also by the 1890s, masquerade balls catering specifically to those who wanted to explore cross-dressing and same-sex sociability were coming into existence. These dances, known as "drag balls," allowed men and women to dress in the clothing of the opposite sex, disguise their identity, and dance with whomever they liked. Police often condoned these events as carnival-like nights that disrupted normal social hierarchies. While drag balls gained a higher profile in the 1920s and 1930s and continued into the 1960s, their existence as early as the 1890s indicates early social networks sophisticated enough to create long-running social traditions.[9]

In addition to the development of early queer communities, by the end of the nineteenth century opportunities for anonymous same-sex encounters were also increasing in number. Cruising was primarily a male phenomenon and involved the informal designation of certain sites, such as parks or docks, as places for men to meet other men and engage in anonymous sexual activity, often in secluded but still public areas (such as public bathroom stalls or wooded areas of public parks). D'Emilio and Freedman point out that places that became cruising sites for gay men "tended to be sites of either moral ambiguity in American society or of transient relationships." Such sites included waterfronts, bohemian neighborhoods, and YMCA boardinghouses catering to travelers.[10]

Three raids in not particularly large urban centers offer a glimpse at the extent of gay male cruising in the early twentieth century. In 1912, Benjamin Trout, a young man being questioned by the police in Portland, Oregon, revealed an extensive homosexual cruising community operating in the city. The revelations, which the press reported widely, shocked residents of the city in part because they involved white, middle-class men at a time when popular portrayals of same-sex desire associated it with people of color and the poor.[11]

In 1914, police in Long Beach, California, arrested fifty men and charged them with social vagrancy. Their offenses included engaging in oral sex with other men in a public restroom. This case is interesting not only because of the extent of the arrests but also because of the charges. Most sodomy laws at this time covered only anal penetration, and because the men had engaged in oral sex only, the authorities had to use a creative approach when determining what law they had broken, hence the charges of social vagrancy. Five years later, in 1919 and 1920, the Newport Naval Training Station in Newport, Rhode Island, launched a major investigation of male cruising within its ranks, which resulted in charges brought against numerous sailors, an Episcopal clergy member, and an administrator at the local YMCA.[12]

Although they did not reach the same numbers as men, many unmarried women also migrated alone to the city, often to find jobs in the expanding clerical fields. Social commentators worried a great deal about these young women and the sexual predators who awaited them upon their unchaperoned arrival. To ensure the safety and virtue of these "women adrift," various organizations formed to provide them with all-female lodging and "safe"

Figure 5.1. This 1893 photograph of the Black Crook all-female theater company provides a glimpse into the homosocial female world of the late nineteenth and early twentieth centuries.
Courtesy of the Library of Congress, LC-USZ62-6270407387

outlets for socializing. Ironically, while these environments did provide a safe, nonsexualized haven for some, they also created a means for women who desired the company of other women to meet like-minded companions without arousing suspicion.[13]

The expansion of jobs for women and subsequent ability for them to earn an independent living was just one of the dramatic changes affecting women's lives in the late nineteenth and early twentieth centuries. Female higher education also grew during this era for middle-class women both white and black. In the two decades following the Civil War, Vassar (1865), Smith (1872), Wellesley (1875), Atlanta Baptist Female Academy (1881, now the historically black Spelman College), and Bryn Mawr (1886) all opened their doors to educate all-female student bodies. Mt. Holyoke College had opened even earlier, in 1837. By 1880, over a third of the higher education student population was female, and these numbers only increased as the nineteenth century came to a close.[14]

Female colleges provided another primarily single-sex environment where same-sex attachments could flourish. As part of one of the first surveys of "normal" female sexuality (that is, of women who were not considered sexually deviant), the section dealing with unmarried women found that "[t]wenty-eight percent of the women's college graduates and twenty percent of those from coeducational schools had experienced intense ties with other women that included a physical component recognized as sexual. Almost equal numbers had enjoyed intense emotional attachments that involved kissing and hugging."[15] In addition to creating an environment conducive to same-sex attachments, college also exposed young women to alternatives beyond the domestic roles of wife and mother, and many college-educated women chose to heed other calls. As an example, between 1889 and 1908, 53 percent of women who graduated from prestigious Bryn Mawr College remained unwed. Perhaps even more telling, 75 percent of American women granted PhD degrees between 1877 and 1924 remained unmarried.[16]

Many of the newly educated women of this era sought meaningful work in the public sphere. A large number stayed in academia, educating the next generations of female learners; some pursued arts and letters; some devoted themselves to the fight for women's suffrage; and many chose to address the needs of the downtrodden in the nation's cities. The Progressive Era, as the period between 1880 and 1920 is known, saw the rise of the settlement house movement, improvements in public health and safety, the creation of the juvenile justice system, expansion of charitable organizations serving children and the poor, and the birth of the social sciences. Women, including many who had chosen to forgo traditional marriage, played a crucial role in all of these developments.

While many female Progressive Era reformers chose not to marry, this is not to say that they remained uncoupled. During this period, unmarried women often coupled together as long-term companions, sharing their lives, their homes, their finances, and quite often their beds. The phenomenon was so common, in fact, that such arrangements were known by the colloquial term "Boston marriage," a reference to the 1886 novel *The Bostonians*, by Henry James. Some of the most influential women of this era lived in such relationships. Jane Addams, founder of the American settlement house movement; Emily Blackwell, one of the first female medical doctors in the United States and a pioneer in providing medical training to other women; M. Carey Thomas, president of Bryn Mawr College; Sara Josephine Baker, an early advocate for childhood public health; and author Willa Cather are but a few examples.[17]

Surviving documents make it clear that the women involved understood these relationships to be serious, emotional unions. They refer to their partners as "My Ever Dear," "devoted companion," "lover," "dearest," and often describe lifelong devotion, as when reformer Jane Addams wrote to Mary Rozet Smith, her partner of more than thirty years, "I miss you dreadfully and am yours 'til death." Whether or not these relationships involved a sexual component is less clear. At the end of the nineteenth century, most women of the middle and upper classes would have understood female sexuality as existing primarily within the confines of heterosexual marriage. It is quite possible that many women also associated acceptable female sexual expression with the limiting role of traditional motherhood. As such, it seems a safe assumption that at least some of these relationships remained nonsexual, although it seems equally likely that others did occupy a sexual terrain. Take, for example, Rose Cleveland, sister of President Grover Cleveland, who exhorted her companion Evangeline Simpson to "carry my body to the summit of joy, the end of search, the goal of love!" and who declared, "Yes, I dare it now—I will no longer fear to claim you—you are mine by everything in earth and heaven—by every sign in soul and spirit and body."[18]

Lillian Faderman asserts that economic circumstances are important to consider when looking at the ways women made their lives together. In many ways, Boston marriages were an extension of the romantic friendships of earlier years. However, until the final decades of the nineteenth century, most women could not feasibly live a middle-class lifestyle independently from men because their options for employment were so limited. Once they had the option to earn their own living in middle-class professions, many women chose to forgo

Figure 5.2. At the turn of the twentieth century, educated women who chose to have careers often chose to forego heterosexual marriage; many partnered with other professional women instead. Shown here (left to right) are reformers Julia Lathrop, Jane Addams, and Mary Eliza McDowell on a 1913 suffrage trip to Capitol Hill. None of them ever married.
Courtesy of the Library of Congress, LC-USZ62-50050

heterosexual marriage in favor of partnerships that better suited their aspirations to have careers and, presumably, their desires as well.[19]

The situation was different for women of the laboring classes, who would still have found it difficult to live comfortably on only the wages of two women. Faderman suggests that female working-class couples wishing to cohabitate would have greatly improved their chances of economic comfort if one of them assumed a male identity and earned male wages. We do know that many females did just that, but it is difficult to ascertain whether their public presentation was an expression of their gender identities, of economic expediency, or of some combination of the two.[20]

The "Invention" of Homosexuality, 1880–1920

As mentioned earlier, the growth, excitement, and diversity of the late nineteenth-century city caused many middle-class observers to feel that their way of life, based as it was on a "civilized morality," was in decline. Indeed, the ethnic/racial and class prejudices of Progressive Era reforms have been well documented, and we can see much anxiety over changing morals represented in reformers' efforts to control the sexual expression of other groups, through "anti-vice" campaigns.[21] Science provided another arena in which educated white Americans sought to defend their moral system in the midst of a changing world.

Nineteenth-century scientific practice favored classification and labeling of the natural world, including a growing interest in discerning and detailing differences between various types of humans. As they sought to make sense of the world they saw around them, scientists searched for biological differences between people of different cultures and classes, positing that people from non-Western cultures and from the "lower orders" of their own societies were further down on the human evolutionary scale—more "primitive"—and would bear physical marks of that primitivism on their bodies. At the same time, academically trained medical doctors labored to professionalize the field of medicine, to bring it more in line with scientific knowledge, and to establish its authority in matters of human behavior and morality. Finally, social science emerged during this era and sought to apply scientific principles to the study of human society and culture.[22]

The late nineteenth-century blending of science and medicine with social issues reached some troubling conclusions. A majority of the white elite, fearing the rapid changes in the United States and Europe, believed that careful study would reveal new ways to return "order" to their world. Within all these disciplinary realms—natural science, social science, medicine—arose an interest in bettering society through the conscious control of human breeding, although not all practitioners agreed with this direction. "Social Darwinism" applied the principles of evolutionary biology, as outlined by Charles Darwin, to argue that the human condition could improve if reproduction were encouraged among people possessing desirable traits (which for the theory's proponents meant middle-class whites of northern European descent) and controlled among those who possessed undesirable traits (who were assumed to be people of color, the poor, and particularly, people with physical, intellectual, or mental disabilities). These ideas became more sophisticated in the early twentieth century, when eugenics-inspired laws passed in many states, allowing for the forcible sterilization of those whom the state deemed "unfit" to reproduce.[23]

The concepts of homosexuality and heterosexuality arose out of this intellectual environment. Previously, as we have seen, sexual expression was understood more as a set of behaviors rather than as a reflection of one's core identity, and the regulation of sexual behavior was more the domain of religion and the law rather than science and medicine. That changed in the late nineteenth century, when theorists first posited the concept of the homosexual—an individual whose physical attraction to others of the same sex was an essential part of who they were as a person.[24]

The first observers to formulate these ideas were based in Europe, primarily the area that is now Germany and England. Karl Heinrich Ulrichs, a German, was the first. In 1864, he articulated a theory of same-sex attraction that identified that desire as an inborn characteristic, although he was not formally trained in either science or medicine. Ulrichs, and many who came after him, saw same-sex desire as intimately tied to gender expression. That is, individuals desired members of their same sex because they did not possess the full range of characteristics normal to their sex but instead possessed elements of both sexes. In other words, their gender was *inverted* (think masculine women and effeminate men), and, possessing the opposite gender's sex drive, inverts desired the object of that sex drive.[25]

Ulrichs took a sympathetic view of homosexuality and was himself a homosexual, as were some other early writers on the subject, including Karl Maria Kertbeny, Edward Carpenter, John Addington Symonds, and Magnus Hirschfeld.[26] Ulrichs saw same-sex desire as an inborn sexual variation that was not particularly abhorrent or threatening to society. As such, he urged compassion in the legal and medical treatment of homosexuals. Later theorists, particularly Richard von Krafft-Ebing (also German), built on Ulrichs's ideas but understood homosexuality as a defect that represented a lower stage of human development than did heterosexuality. Krafft-Ebing's *Psychopathia Sexualis* (1886) grouped homosexuality as one of four broad categories of degeneracy, along with fetishism, sadism, and masochism.[27]

Europeans would continue to be leaders in the conceptualization and research of sexual variance for the next fifty years. In 1897, the British researcher Havelock Ellis published *Sexual Inversion*, cowritten by John Addington Symonds, which was the first full-length English-language book on the topic. Magnus Hirschfeld, a German, was both a researcher and an advocate for fair treatment of homosexuals under the law. In 1919, he founded the Institute of Sexual Science in Berlin and organized the first international conference of sex researchers in 1921. He also pioneered the study of people with variant gender identities, first publishing a book on the subject, *The Transvestites*, in 1910 and arranging the first surgical modifications (or "sex changes" as they were then called) in the 1920s. Tragically, on May 6, 1933, Nazis broke into Hirschfeld's institute and burned its extensive library and data holdings, destroying a treasure trove of sexual research. Hirschfeld himself was out of the country at the time, where he remained until his death in France two years later.[28]

Famed psychoanalyst Sigmund Freud, working in Vienna, was among the first to argue for a "psychogenic" approach to homosexuality in the early twentieth century. Unlike his predecessors and many of his contemporaries who saw homosexuality as an inborn trait, Freud argued that it was a perversion of the normal sex drive that occurred in early childhood. He saw homosexuality as a stage of sexual development that all people experienced, where some people's development became arrested. He also introduced the concept of "latent homosexuality," where a person's homosexual desires, not acted upon, could manifest other psychological problems.[29]

In the United States, the first writings about homosexuality appeared around 1890. Early research came out of Chicago, then the second-largest city in the United States and also the center of the newly emerging field of social science research. In 1889, Dr. G. Frank Lydston conceptualized same-sex desire as a congenital defect common among "primitive types," which could be ameliorated by surgical interventions such as the cauterization of nerves and clitoridectomies. Dr. James G. Kiernan, another Chicago-based researcher, wrote about homosexuality as a form of pathology. He argued against compassionate treatment, which he felt only exacerbated the problem. Kiernan was also responsible for the first known published use of the terms "homosexual" and "heterosexual" in the United States.[30]

Research into homosexuality in the United States proceeded on a slightly different trajectory than research in Europe. To begin with, both Vern L. Bullough and Jennifer Terry have noted that American research advanced more slowly because of an American reticence to publicly discuss sexual matters. Many felt that sexuality was not a topic for polite discussion, even within the confines of professional conferences. The situation was further stymied by the 1873 Comstock Law, which prevented sexually explicit material being sent through the mail, a circumstance that led many journal editors and book publishers to avoid printing sexual content of any kind.[31]

US researchers were also more likely to recommend harsh treatment of homosexuals and to link same-sex desire to urban environments, racial minorities, and the lower classes. Siobhan Somerville has explored the ways that the construction of homosexuality in opposition to "normal" sexuality paralleled the ways that the sexuality of African Americans was juxtaposed with the sexuality of native-born white Americans (unquestioningly assumed to represent the "normal"). Both Somerville and Heather Lee Miller, among others, have chronicled the disturbing ways that scientists observed and described in minutest detail the bodies—particularly the sexual organs—of women deemed deviant (African Americans, lesbians, prostitutes) in the name of scientific study. Historians generally now understand these early studies of homosexuality to be part of a larger desire on the part of middle-class, educated whites to enforce their understanding of sexual morality on the larger population by using science to define what was acceptable and what was deviant.[32]

At the same time, these early sexologists were not simply crafting moralistic treatises; they were responding to the world they saw around them. Evidence indicates that urban subcultures of men who desired other men developed around the same time, or slightly before, the medical construction of homosexuality. The presence of these subcultures in cities may account for the fact that early sexologists identified homosexuality as a particularly urban malady. Similarly, early medical literature on homosexuality employed the case study, a detailed biography of a patient diagnosed with the particular condition under study. As such, it provides some of the most detailed sources we have on homosexual lives before 1920. Jennifer Brier and Ann Parsons have argued that urban newspapers were the first to employ the rhetorical device of the case study, which they used when reporting on people who had been discovered to be living under the guise of the opposite sex. In adopting it for their own professional ends, sexologists unwittingly left evidence of the ways they were influenced by—as well as shaping—the culture in which they lived.[33]

Just as the reality of queer experience at the turn of the twentieth century influenced sexologists, so too did developments in the field of sexology affect queer people's lives. Most obviously, the scientific discussion of homosexuality put a name to same-sex desire and brought it into public awareness. Sexologic writing on the subject provided a means by which people could learn they were not alone in their attraction to the same sex or their identification with the gender of the opposite sex. Michael Bronksi makes the point that the medical construction of the homosexual—which relied heavily on the concept of gender inversion—actually provided queer people with a language through which they could identify themselves to others who shared their predilections, by incorporating subtle cues of gender transgression, such as uncommon red neckties for men or short hair for women.[34] At the same time, the new prevailing concept of homosexuality as a characteristic present from birth no doubt changed people's experience of their sexual truth. Whereas previously they could understand their sexual experience with members of their own sex as a temporary misstep, people now were given to believe that they were, at core, abnormal.

Even though many of the characteristics of the late nineteenth-century construction of homosexuality continue to inform mainstream understandings in the twenty-first century, much of the queer landscape of a hundred years ago would be surprising to a modern,

Figure 5.3. Homosexuals often used subtle clues to find each other. For men these clues included jaunty dress (red ties in particular), an effusive manner, and poses that emphasized the hips. *Second Avenue Lunch/Posed Portraits, New York,* by Walker Evans, c. 1933. Gelatin silver print. Courtesy of the J. Paul Getty Museum.

uninformed reader. Contemporary understanding of same-sex desire as innate and essential to a person's sense of self has its origins in this time period. Likewise, the understanding of homosexuality as closely linked to nonnormative gender expression continues to this day, though many of the specifics have changed over time. Finally, neither the turn of the twentieth century nor the turn of the twenty-first offers a particularly sophisticated understanding of bisexuality. Bisexuals confound the binary world of homosexual and heterosexual as much now as they did then, and so they are quite often simply ignored.

Nevertheless, two important features of the early twentieth-century understanding of homosexuality have *not* survived and so warrant specific mention. First, not everyone who engaged in sexual acts with members of the same sex was originally considered homosexual. George Chauncey has demonstrated that, particularly among working-class and immigrant communities during this era, men who took an active role in sexual encounters (that is, men who did the penetrating) were not understood to be doing anything terribly different from what they did sexually with women, and thus they escaped the label of deviance. Only men who allowed themselves to be penetrated (anally or orally) by other men earned the title of homosexual.[35]

Additionally, the label seems to have had a class component. In other words, the behavior of working-class individuals was much more likely to be categorized as homosexual. The reasons for this were threefold. First, many of the early sexologists obtained their data from studying inmates of prisons and mental asylums, populations more likely to come from the working class, who lacked the resources to resist incarceration. Thus, the behavior and outlook identified as belonging to homosexuals actually belonged to working-class homosexuals (and a specific subpopulation to boot). Second, as Chauncey has demonstrated, working-class gay culture was much more publicly visible in the turn-of-the-century city than was middle-class gay culture, in part because the working class socialized more in the public arena generally and partly because middle-class gays were more likely to be mindful of their reputations and hence more discreet. Finally, as we have seen, the construction of homosexuality was part of a larger endeavor to shore up the "civilized morality" of the middle class, and as such the observers of sexuality more frequently saw deviance in those different from themselves. As an example of this last point, Boston marriages—those long-term partnerships of middle-class professional women—somehow mostly escaped the taint of lesbianism for at least a generation after ideas of homosexuality had emerged. Not until the 1920s did these relationships draw regular suspicion from outsiders, and even then, societal pressure was not severe enough to separate the women involved or bring criminal repercussions. Many of these partnerships continued until one of the women's death, lasting well into mid-century.[36]

By the 1920s, however, the risk of being labeled a lesbian was limiting women's behavior regardless of class. As discussed earlier, this era brought great change in women's status. Employment opportunities were increasing, allowing for greater economic independence from men. Large numbers of women were attending college, and some went on to earn graduate degrees as well. Women were taking a growing part in civic life through reform work, the women's club movement, and political activism. Suffrage, in particular, expanded core understandings of the abilities and proper role of women in society. In fact, many observers began to suspect that women were vying to take over roles traditionally reserved for men. Political opponents proclaimed such active women gender deviant, thus marking them with an overt symptom of homosexuality. Hence, lesbianism became a means to taint women's efforts toward equality with men in the early twentieth century, just as it did fifty years later during the women's movement of the 1960s and 1970s.[37]

The 1920s and 1930s

Yet despite the moralizers' best efforts, changes in gender roles only gained momentum. With the 1920s came the United States' first sexual revolution, where sexual understandings and practices rapidly transformed and culminated in a new moral order. Beth Bailey poetically sums up these changes as experienced by middle-class heterosexual youth with the title of her book, *From Front Porch to Back Seat*. This phrase captures the dramatic changes of the 1920s as heterosexual youth moved outside of the realm of family and chaperones and began exercising much more autonomy in choosing their companions and romantic activities. In truth, working-class youth had enthusiastically embraced these new freedoms for more than a decade; the changes were deemed revolutionary in the 1920s only because the middle class and popular culture joined in the cultural shift.[38]

Nevertheless, a new feeling of permissiveness permeated American society in the 1920s, as leisure activities and fashion changed to allow for more freedom, new musical rhythms and dances encouraged more bodily expression, and moving pictures exposed the population to repeated tales of romance and lust. Within the world of adult sexuality, female sexual satisfaction became an important aspect of healthy marriages, and the number of people sexually experimenting before marriage jumped significantly. Approximately half of the women who came of age in the 1920s had engaged in sexual intercourse before marriage, and a 1924 study of Muncie, Indiana, found that nearly half of high school boys and a third of the girls had engaged in "petting."[39] Among the more adventurous, this milieu of sexual experimentation led to a relative acceptance of same-sex sexual experience among women in bohemian circles, although Faderman points out that—at least among bohemian men—such attraction was consistently understood as less serious than attraction to the opposite sex.[40]

Chauncey has also chronicled the flamboyance of this period. In large cities, drag balls proliferated. Local newspapers covered these events, and heterosexual spectators often attended. In fact, the phrase "to come out," meaning to accept one's homosexuality and inform others of this identity, originated from these extravaganzas. According to Chauncey, the term originally parodied debutantes' coming-out balls and referred to men coming out into gay society.[41]

The prohibition of alcohol sales during the 1920s pushed urban nightlife to more marginal parts of American cities, quite often to predominantly African American neighborhoods. Adventurous whites went "slumming" in these sections of town, titillating themselves by engaging in a world not normally visible to them. As described by one observer of an establishment in New York City's Harlem, "Every night we find the place crowded with both races, the black and the white, both types of lovers, the homo and heterosexual."[42] In addition to the diversity of the clientele, the entertainment also pushed the boundaries of dominant culture by including jazz music and shows with racy sexual content (both gay and straight).[43]

Homosexuality was also visible in the larger popular culture of the 1920s, particularly in the music and literature of the Harlem Renaissance. Numerous African American blues singers, including Bessie Smith, Ma Rainey, and Gladys Bentley, engaged in romantic relationships with other females (Smith and Rainey had relationships with both men and women) and sang songs that were tantalizing in their references to same-sex desire.[44] Rainey's "Sissy Blues" (1926), for example, included these lyrics:

> I dreamed last night I was far from harm
> Woke up and found my man in a sissy's arms
> "Hello, Central, it's 'bout to run me wild
> Can I get that number, or will I have to wait awhile?"
>
> Some are young, some are old
> My man says sissy's got good jelly roll . . .

> My man got a sissy, his name is Miss Kate
> He shook that thing like jelly on a plate . . .
>
> Now all the people ask me why I'm all alone
> A sissy shook that thing and took my man from me.[45]

Likewise, a number of Harlem Renaissance writers, including Wallace Thurman, Claude McKay, Countee Cullen, and possibly Langston Hughes, had relationships with men, and the writing of this genre often included references to homosexual life. McKay's 1928 *Home to Harlem* included a scene where "the dark dandies were loving up their pansies"; Thurman's *The Blacker the Berry* (1929) and *The Infants of the Spring* (1932) also referenced this world.[46]

Overall, homosexuality was surprisingly visible between the end of World War I and the middle of the Great Depression. Doctors still believed same-sex desire to be a sign of mental illness, and laws still outlawed sodomy and cross-dressing, but simultaneously, certain parts of the United States tolerated such activity, a fact that was largely forgotten amid the social entrenchment of the Cold War. Ironically, this newfound visibility was not unequivocally liberating. As awareness of homosexuality spread into the mainstream, choices previously assumed to be innocent now carried a taint of suspicion. The long-term female partnerships of middle-class women are but one example; where they had previously appeared to be a practical extension of romantic friendship, allowing unmarried women to pool their financial resources, these relationships were now seen as potentially subversive and diseased. Avowed bachelors now met with similar suspicions. As a result, the interwar period saw the start of the elaborate double lives that marked homosexual experience throughout much of the twentieth century, where some homosexuals chose to hide their sexual orientation behind a constructed front of acceptable sexuality.[47]

While lesbian subcultures were not yet as visible as gay male ones, evidence suggests a growing sense of community among homosexual women at this time. Nascent subcultures of lesbians developed in places as diverse as Harlem, San Francisco, Salt Lake City, Buffalo, and Cherry Grove on New York's Fire Island. The lesbian bar as a cultural phenomenon also spread in the 1920s and 1930s, primarily catering to working-class women.[48]

The relative visibility of queer subcultures continued into the 1930s, but as the full impact of the Great Depression revealed itself, tolerance of difference waned. In the midst of tough economic times, many individuals chose to conceal their same-sex preferences in order to hold onto difficult-to-acquire jobs. The economic uncertainty affected people of color and women even more strongly, as they were often seen as stealing jobs from white men. For the members of these groups who also loved their own sex, the call to hide their sexuality carried economic expediency.[49]

In addition, the popularization of Freudian psychology shifted the general understanding of homosexuality from a predilection people were born with to a product of retarded emotional development. Popular parenting advice in the 1930s held that same-sex attraction was a normal developmental phase for children in early adolescence, but the objects of their affection should switch to the opposite sex by about age sixteen or seventeen. Experts urged parents to be vigilant against same-sex attraction that lingered as their children grew older, and within this construction, adults with homosexual desires were cast as children perpetually stuck in an immature developmental phase.[50]

As the Great Depression wore on, a backlash against homosexual visibility developed in the form of public panic over sexual psychopaths. We see here the first conflation of male homosexuality with pedophilia (the sexual desire for children) and child sexual abuse. In various locations such as Washington, DC, and Philadelphia, the discovery of a series of sexual crimes against children led to a public outcry against homosexuality, calls to stamp out gay male cruising areas, and the passage of "sexual psychopath laws," which explicitly outlawed a series of activities associated with gay men far beyond committing actual acts of sodomy.[51]

World War II and the Cold War

The history of LGBT Americans in the middle of the twentieth century is an interesting balance between societal oppression and the creation of communities that would coalesce in the 1960s and 1970s as a cohesive political minority. World War II is but one example. Wartime mobilization afforded gays and lesbians unprecedented opportunities. The population became newly mobile, as young men were drafted into the military and much of the rest of the population gravitated to centers of wartime industry in the hopes of finding well-paying employment. These circumstances drew many residents of rural areas to US cities and offered a certain level of anonymity and freedom, allowing them to experiment with their sense of identity. Skewed gender ratios within the military and on the home front fostered the establishment of strong same-sex attachments, while war industry jobs and the newly established female branches of the military facilitated women's ability to live outside of heterosexual marriage, leaving them free to build deep relationships with other women.[52]

Yet even while the war created many opportunities for gay men and lesbians, it also carried risks. Same-sex sexual acts had long been grounds for dismissal from the US military; however, during World War II, for the first time in its history the US government decreed homosexuals unfit to serve (regardless of their actual sexual behavior) and named homosexuality grounds for a dishonorable discharge. Induction interviews that probed one's sexual interests reinforced the idea in the popular imagination that same-sex desire was a disease. And for those men and women dismissed from service because of their alleged homosexuality, scandal and employment discrimination awaited them back home. These soldiers were also denied veterans' benefits because of their dishonorable discharges, excluding them from the postwar opportunities afforded by the GI Bill.[53]

After World War II, the threat of atomic (and later nuclear) annihilation loomed large as the United States engaged in the Cold War with the Soviet Union. Historians such as Elaine Tyler May have detailed the ways in which these global anxieties created a national "containment culture." This era, roughly 1945–1965, demanded conformity, considered difference dangerous, and portrayed marriage and children as the fulfillment of patriotic duty.[54]

Within this cultural climate, homosexuality went from being simply deviant to downright subversive. Federal policies supported this understanding, declaring homosexuals security risks because of their susceptibility to blackmail. Under pressure from Congress, individuals suspected of "sexual perversion" were dismissed from federal employment in large

Figure 5.4. World War II created a more sex-segregated society, allowing those who were attracted to their own sex to develop relationships with others like them without drawing suspicion to themselves.

Courtesy of the Library of Congress, LC-USW3- 035302-D

numbers in the late 1940s. The purge intensified after 1950, was an aspect of McCarthyism, and became enshrined in federal policy in 1953. Signed by President Dwight Eisenhower within months of taking office, Executive Order 10450 explicitly disqualified homosexuals from employment by prohibiting "any behavior which suggests the individual is not reliable or trustworthy." Such behavior included "[a]ny criminal, infamous, dishonest, immoral, or notoriously disgraceful conduct, habitual use of intoxicants to excess, drug addiction, or sexual perversion." Although the federal government's harassment of leftists is far better known, between 1947 and 1953 twice as many civil servants lost their jobs because of alleged homosexuality than because of communist sympathies, and by the end of the 1950s as many as five thousand federal public servants had lost their jobs because of their sexual orientation. The numbers dismissed from the US military were even greater.[55]

These purges set the tone for an overall suspicion of sexual variance during the Cold War. The federal government also required companies receiving federal contracts to follow its policies concerning security risks. State governments, particularly in the South, formed their own committees to investigate security threats. While these committees most often used their mission to harass those advocating racial equality, homosexuals also experienced the wrath of such investigations. In addition, the federal government did not limit its investigation only to its employees but expanded its surveillance of private citizens, including suspected homosexuals.[56]

Socially, too, queer lives were marked by the danger of discovery, although numerous historians have made the point that this did not mean they lived lives of isolation. Rather, most (but not all) queers in the Cold War era lived double lives, establishing a front of heterosexuality and gender conformity in order to maintain social acceptability and stay employed. However, many also engaged to varying degrees with underground communities of others who shared their same-sex attraction. Although this surely was a difficult life, evidence suggests that these demands for secrecy also helped create a growing sense among homosexuals that their problems stemmed from societal discrimination rather than their own perversity.[57]

For a small percentage—mostly those already living close to society's margins—the public embrace of a homosexual or transgender identity, despite the societal rejection and physical dangers, offered entry into a world beyond others' expectations. Interracial relationships appear to have been more common among same-sex couples (though it is also possible that theorists simply mentioned them more often when discussing homosexuality, once again conflating alternative sexuality with "racial disorder"). Anatomical males who chose to live full-time as women were largely barred from standard paid employment opportunities, and many survived by working as female impersonators or sex workers. In addition, working-class lesbians in the 1950s often took on a "butch" presentation, adopting masculine markers (pants, short hair, physical labor, a personal style gruffer than the traditional expectations of femininity) without fully rejecting their identity as female. While it is probable that some 1950s butches would resonate with the idea that they were in fact transgender (an idea that became more common in later decades), for others butch was an insistence that being a woman entailed a larger range of gender expression than was then widely accepted.[58]

While the medical and psychiatric professions still generally assumed a link between same-sex desire and gender variance, a few members began to differentiate the two. Harry Benjamin, Karl Bowman, and Alfred Kinsey conducted early US research into gender variance. Benjamin, in particular, served as an advocate for medical intervention to assist people wishing to modify their bodies to match their gender identities. Born and medically trained in Germany and professionally acquainted with Magnus Hirschfeld, Benjamin was an anomaly in the mid-twentieth-century United States, when most doctors adhered to the idea that the removal of healthy tissue constituted "mayhem" and violated medical ethics. Because of this widespread medical opinion in the United States, many people seeking to alter their bodies to better match their gender identity traveled to Europe to receive such treatment.[59]

As with the World War II era, the Cold War provided new opportunities for LGBT Americans as well as challenges. Historians of sexuality interpret the twentieth century as a slow transition toward sexual liberalism, where personal desire and sexual satisfaction are highly valued and sexual morality becomes more a matter of individual decision making. Even within the containment culture of the late 1940s, 1950s, and early 1960s, there were significant challenges to the sexual status quo. Three were particularly relevant to LGBT lives: the publication of the Kinsey Report, the celebrity of Christine Jorgensen, and the increasing representation of same-sex desire in popular culture.

In the late 1930s, Alfred Kinsey, a biology professor at Indiana University, began an extensive survey of American sexual experiences. His findings, published in two volumes

(1948 and 1953) and known collectively as the Kinsey Report, revealed that American sexual preferences and behavior were far more varied than conventional morality had led everyone to believe. Although the surprises covered a full range of sexual topics—from masturbation to oral sex to the prevalence of premarital intercourse—some of Kinsey's most noteworthy findings pertained to same-sex desire and experience. According to Kinsey's data, far more white Americans (he only included data on whites) had homosexual experience than previously imagined; 37 percent of males and 13 percent of females reported same-sex experiences that had led to orgasm. Furthermore, from his data, Kinsey determined that 10 percent of the male population and 2–6 percent of the female population were more or less exclusively homosexual. These findings affected US culture in two ways. First, the controversy caused by the Kinsey Report brought the subject of so-called sexual deviance into the public spotlight for a time, demanding that the mainstream grapple with the very real possibility that "perverts" lived in their midst. Second, these books provided yet another means for queer people—particularly those living in smaller towns and rural areas—to know that there were others like them; they were not alone.[60]

While the nation was still digesting the information in the Kinsey Report, a second event captured the national spotlight. Christine Jorgensen achieved celebrity after receiving gender reassignment surgery (known at the time as a "sex change") performed in Denmark. Born with a male body, Jorgensen served the United States as a male soldier in World War II before traveling to Europe in the early 1950s to undergo treatment and eventual surgery to make her body better conform to her identity as a woman. The press first reported the story in 1952, under the sensational headline "Ex-G.I. Becomes Blonde Beauty," and Jorgensen became an object of fascination and notoriety upon her return to the United States in 1953. Although she was not the first person to undergo gender reassignment, Jorgensen became the subject of public fascination. Her status as a war veteran, her willingness to be in the public spotlight, and her traditionally feminine beauty challenged popular American understanding of the sexually variant as shamefaced and mentally diseased, inherently different from "true" Americans.[61]

A final element countered the general trend of Cold War containment culture: an ever-growing supply of homosexual characters inhabited literature and film. This was the heyday of pulp fiction, cheaply manufactured and mass-produced novels sold at a price that was affordable to nearly everyone. While pulp novels covered a range of genres, including westerns and detective novels, many also dealt with sexually explicit topics, including homosexuality. With titles such as *Warped*, *Sin Girls*, and *The Odd Ones*, these novels intended to be salacious and almost always ended badly for the homosexual characters. However, they also brought same-sex sexuality and subcultures into broader awareness and provided a means for newly identified queers to learn about people like themselves. At the same time, Hollywood films also began including more overt references to those who desired their own sex. Same-sex desire and gender play had been present in feature films from the beginning of the medium, but the Hays Code, which outlined standards of propriety for the film industry, drove most of these characters from the movies beginning in 1934. By the 1950s, references were again appearing in American film, though the portrayals were always circumspect and, like pulp novels, ended tragically. *Tea and Sympathy*, *Rebel without a Cause*, *Suddenly Last Summer*, and *The Children's Hour* are some of the more well-known examples of this trend.[62]

The Homophile Movement

While the queer and straight worlds alike pondered the implications of these new representations of alternative sexuality, some gays and lesbians also slowly began to recognize the need to organize politically against society's mistreatment of them. Although popular wisdom holds that the Stonewall riots of 1969 sparked the LGBT civil rights movement, in reality, efforts to mobilize politically had been underway for nearly twenty years prior. Known collectively as the homophile movement (to distinguish it from the post-Stonewall gay liberation movement), these early enterprises represent the first consistent inroads into promoting fair treatment for homosexuals and indicate that increasingly gays and lesbians were coming to understand themselves as a cohesive minority deserving legal protection against discrimination.

To be sure, some attempts to organize preceded even the homophile movement. A man named Henry Gerber organized the first homosexual rights organization in the United States—the short-lived Society for Human Rights (SHR)—in Chicago in 1924, though it lasted only a few months before a police raid ended the group. In 1945, in New York City, the Veterans Benevolent Association formed as a social club for gay veterans, while in 1947, Edith Eyde began writing and circulating a mimeographed lesbian newsletter under the pseudonym of Lisa Ben (an anagram for "lesbian"). Entitled *Vice Versa*, this one-woman effort out of Los Angeles is usually credited as the first homosexual periodical in the United States, although SHR did put out a publication, *Friendship and Freedom*, during its brief existence in the 1920s. Also in late-1940s Los Angeles, an African American man, Merton L. Bird, formed the Knights of the Clock, an interracial group aimed at increasing understanding about homosexuality.[63]

Despite these earlier efforts, the Mattachine Society, established in Los Angeles in 1951, was the first homosexual rights organization to achieve a national following and make substantive strides in challenging the widespread assumption that homosexuals deserved the discrimination they received. Although Harry Hay is generally credited as the founder of Mattachine, C. Todd White has meticulously detailed the early history of the organization and argues that it was a substantial group effort between Harry Hay, Rudi Gernreich, Bob Hull, Chuck Rowland, Dale Jennings, and (joining the group slightly later) Konrad Stevens and James Gruber. Hay had been active in Communist Party politics since the 1930s, and many of the other founders had left-wing backgrounds as well. This ideological outlook allowed the group's organizers to conceptualize homosexuality in a new way, arguing that gays and lesbians were an oppressed minority who, like the workers in Marx's writings, needed to come together, shake off their false consciousness, and fight injustice. This approach was groundbreaking at the time and informed the group's efforts to "unify," "educate," and "lead" homosexuals. And in another nod toward communism, the group originally structured itself as a series of cell meetings, which enabled members to engage actively in the group while still maintaining some anonymity.[64]

Although the Mattachine Society began as a series of discussion groups around southern California, within a year the group received national attention for its role in supporting one of its founders, Dale Jennings, in a run-in with the police. In February 1952, Jennings was arrested for allegedly engaging in sexual activity with an undercover police officer. At the urging of the other Mattachine founders, Jennings chose to contest the case in court, a rare move in this era when arrest on such charges could ruin a person's reputation and trigger widespread ostracism. The Mattachine Society, operating as the Citizens' Committee to Outlaw Entrapment, publicized the trial and used it as an opportunity to speak out against police harassment of gay men. At the trial, Jennings admitted he was a homosexual (another bold move) but denied the specific allegations. When the trial resulted in a hung jury, the case was thrown out, and Mattachine declared its first legal victory. After this, enrollment in the organization greatly increased, and cells were founded throughout California and eventually spread throughout the nation.[65]

Also in 1952, some members of the Mattachine Society in Los Angeles organized a separate group to begin publishing a magazine devoted to gay and lesbian issues. *ONE*, as the magazine was called, published its first issue in January 1953 and soon had a national circulation in the thousands. It provided a communication network among homosexuals, many of whom led extremely isolated and secretive lives. In the words of scholar Craig Loftin, "In an acutely repressive moment, when gay people were being entrapped by police, rooted out of jobs, and demonized as political subversives, *ONE* challenged its readers to believe that homosexuals had a fundamental right to exist in American society."[66]

Within a few months of its first publication, *ONE* ran into difficulty with the US Postal Service, which (operating under the 1873 Comstock Law) confiscated the August/September 1953 issue as obscene (interestingly, that issue sported the cover story "Homosexual Marriage?"). Although postal authorities eventually released that issue, they intervened again with the October 1954 issue, which featured a cover story on government censorship. ONE, Inc., the magazine's parent company, sued the government in a case that went all the way to the US Supreme Court. In 1958, the court ruled in *ONE v. Olesen* that homosexual content did not in and of itself constitute obscenity, effectively opening the door for much wider distribution of LGBT-related publications and literature.[67]

Although white males dominated the leadership of both the Mattachine Society and ONE, Inc., white women and a few African Americans were involved in both organizations from their early days. In particular, Irma Wolf, publishing under the pseudonym Ann Carll Reid, served as chief editor of *ONE* from 1954 to 1957 and regularly contributed to the magazine. Her long-time partner, Joan Corbin, publishing under the pseudonym Eve Elloree, served as the magazine's main illustrator. Nevertheless, women in these two organizations were often frustrated by what they felt was a predominantly male focus. In 1955, a lesbian organization emerged that would become an advocate for women's issues within the homophile movement.[68]

The Daughters of Bilitis (pronounced be-LEE-tus and abbreviated DOB) began in 1955 in San Francisco as a middle-class social club for lesbians wishing to avoid the bar scene. Rose Bamberger, a Filipina American, had the initial idea for the group and enlisted the aid of her partner and three other lesbian couples. Phyllis Lyon and Del Martin were one of the couples, and they are more famously associated with the group's founding. Historians credit Lyon and Martin with switching the group's focus from socializing to organizing and educating. In 1956, the group began publishing *The Ladder*, a magazine focused specifically on lesbian lives. Through this publication and the other DOB groups that formed around the country, the organization created a forum to advocate for the specific concerns of women who loved other women. Many of the most well-known female activists of the pre-Stonewall gay and lesbian movement—Lyon, Martin, Kay Tobin (Lahusen), and Barbara Gitting—held leadership positions within DOB at one time or another, as did a number of lesbians of color, including Cleo Bonner, Ernestine Eckstein, and Ada Bello. In addition, as the feminist movement gained momentum in the 1960s, DOB provided a critical voice advocating for sexual minorities.[69]

Gender-variant people also began to organize and build communities in the middle of the twentieth century. Beginning in the late 1940s, Louise Lawrence, a male-bodied individual living full time as a woman, became an advocate for research related to people like herself. She served as a crucial link between sexologists and research subjects. In 1952, Virginia Prince (at that time a male-to-female transvestite who would choose to live full-time as a woman in 1968), along with a small group of associates in Long Beach, California, produced the first US periodical aimed at a gender-variant audience. Although it only ran for two issues, *Transvestia: Journal for the American Society for Equality in Dress* (actually a mimeographed newsletter) made a point of differentiating gender variance from homosexuality.[70]

Moving into the 1960s, grassroots political activism in the United States became more visible to the wider population, most memorably through the movement against the Vietnam War, the African American civil rights movement, and the women's movement. Organized public protest became more common, and identity politics—the idea that a group of people could organize around a common experience of oppression based on their identity—became increasingly sophisticated.[71]

On the homophile front, increasing numbers of homosexuals became aware of groups like the Mattachine Society, ONE, Inc., and DOB, and many joined their cause. At the same time other organizations were springing up throughout the country. Marc Stein estimates that by the spring of 1969 (right before the Stonewall riots), there were as many as fifty

Figure 5.5. Frank Kameny was a civil servant who was fired from the federal government in 1957 because of his homosexuality. He became a key figure in the East Coast homophile movement and coined the phrase, "Gay is Good." He is shown here in 2009 at the opening of the Velvet Foundation in Washington, DC. Behind him are protest signs from the homophile era.
Courtesy of DCVirago

homophile groups in the United States.[72] In addition, after a decade of organizing and community building among themselves, homophile organizations began in the 1960s to protest for fairer treatment from the larger society, which they did through direct political action, legislative politics, and the nation's court system. These efforts, along with other factors to be discussed in the next chapter, provided a critical precursor to the 1969 Stonewall riots, which are popularly recognized as the start of the modern LGBT movement.

Much of the political activity took place in San Francisco. In 1961, José Sarria, a well-known Latino drag performer, ran for the San Francisco Board of Supervisors, becoming the first openly gay political candidate in the United States. Although he did not win election, Sarria garnered nearly six thousand votes, suggesting that LGBT populations had the potential to form a voting bloc. In 1966, also in San Francisco, the country's first gay community center was founded by the Society for Individual Rights (SIR), an organization that became the largest homophile organization in the country by 1967.[73]

In 1964, a group of clergy members and homophile activists in San Francisco joined forces to form the Council on Religion and the Homosexual (CRH). As one of their first events, they held a New Year's Eve ball as a fund-raiser. The San Francisco Police Department arrived at the event and harassed attendees by parking paddy wagons in front of the venue, filming attendees as they entered the ball, and ultimately shutting down the event. While this treatment of homosexuals by police was standard for the day, the heterosexual clergy members were shocked at the disrespectful treatment. As a result, CRH became an active and vocal force for change in San Francisco.[74]

The homophile movement made strides on other fronts as well. In 1961, Illinois became the first state to repeal its sodomy laws, followed by Connecticut in 1969. The Washington, DC, affiliate of Mattachine, led by Frank Kameny and representing an increasingly militant branch of the movement, staged a number of actions throughout the 1960s. These included a 1963 campaign to repeal District of Columbia sodomy laws, a 1965 protest against the firing of homosexuals from the federal government, and a 1965 resolution (later adopted by other groups) declaring that "homosexuality is not a sickness, disturbance, or other pathology in any sense, but is merely a preference, orientation, or propensity, on par with, and not different in kind from, heterosexuality." Beginning on July 4, 1965, an annual Independence Day protest in front of Philadelphia's Liberty Bell advocated for fair protection of homosexuals under the law. Called the annual reminders, these protests continued through Independence Day 1969. The final reminder occurred a week after the Stonewall riots, and the following year these events were absorbed into Christopher Street Liberation Day, held to mark the first anniversary of Stonewall and eventually evolving into an annual gay pride celebration.[75]

The period between the late nineteenth century and the mid-1960s represents a crucial period in LGBT history marked by widespread adoption of the idea that same-sex desire and gender nonconformity represented a mental health condition that set people apart from the "norm." Emerging in tandem with this medical model of homosexuality were subcultures of people who met these definitions and sought out each other for companionship, intimacy, and support. These subcultures grew more sophisticated as the twentieth century wore on and more and more people learned about their existence through references in popular culture, the national media, and scientific studies such as the Kinsey Report. Eventually, some homosexuals began to understand their experiences within a political context of oppression and began advocating for change. These early political efforts, encapsulated in the homophile movement, laid the groundwork for the Stonewall riots and their aftermath.

Notes

1. Vern L. Bullough, *Science in the Bedroom: A History of Sex Research* (New York: Basic, 1994), 96; John D'Emilio and Estelle B. Freedman, *Intimate Matters: A History of Sexuality in America*, 3rd ed. (Chicago: University of Chicago Press, 2012), 171–201; Jay Hatheway, *The Gilded Age Construction of Modern American Homophobia* (New York: Palgrave Macmillan, 2003), 61–62; Julie Abraham, *Metropolitan Lovers: The Homosexuality of Cities* (Minneapolis: University of Minnesota Press, 2008), 91–94.
2. D'Emilio and Freedman, *Intimate Matters*, 203.
3. David I. Macleod, *The Age of the Child: Children in America, 1890–1920* (New York: Twayne, 1998), 2–3; Hatheway, *The Gilded Age Construction of Modern American Homophobia*, 34. These figures reflect US Census Bureau numbers, which at the time defined urban areas as any area containing more than 2,500 people. Macleod makes the point that if we use a more restrictive cap of 25,000 people, only 36 percent of the American population lived in cities by 1920.
4. Hatheway, *The Gilded Age Construction of Modern American Homophobia*, 34–38; Michael Bronski, *A Queer History of the United States* (Boston: Beacon, 2011), 106–8; Joanne J. Meyerowitz, *Women Adrift: Independent Wage Earners in Chicago, 1880–1930* (Chicago: University of Chicago Press, 1988), 1–20; George Chauncey, *Gay New York: Gender, Urban Culture, and the Making of a Gay Male World, 1890–1940* (New York: Basic, 1994), 11, 245; US Census Bureau, "Historical Statistics of the United States," *Millennial Online Edition*, 2006, http://hsus.cambridge.org.ezproxy.lib.indiana.edu/HSUSWeb/index.do, table Ad707-710.
5. Meyerowitz, *Women Adrift*, 1–20; Chauncey, *Gay New York*, 74–86; Sucheta Mazumdar, "Beyond Bound Feet: Relocating Asian American Women," *OAH Magazine of History* 10, no. 4 (Summer 1996): 23–27; Howard P. Chudacoff, *The Age of the Bachelor: Creating an American Subculture* (Princeton, NJ: Princeton University Press, 1999), 45–55.
6. Chudacoff, *The Age of the Bachelor*, 52; Chauncey, *Gay New York*, 76.
7. Bronski, *A Queer History of the United States*, 106–8; D'Emilio and Freedman, *Intimate Matters*, 227–28; Molly McGarry and Fred Wasserman, *Becoming Visible: An Illustrated History of Lesbian and Gay Life in Twentieth-Century America* (New York: Penguin Studio, 1998), 66–67; Leila J. Rupp, *A Desired Past: A Short History of Same-Sex Love in America* (Chicago: University of Chicago Press, 1999), 104–23; Chauncey, *Gay New York*, 33–45; Hatheway, *The Gilded Age Construction of Modern American Homophobia*, 55–60; Nan Alamilla Boyd, *Wide-Open Town: A History of Queer San Francisco to 1965* (Berkeley: University of California Press, 2003), 25–29.
8. Chauncey, *Gay New York*, 42–44; Hatheway, *The Gilded Age Construction of Modern American Homophobia*, 55–56; Terence S. Kissack, *Free Comrades: Anarchism and Homosexuality in the United States, 1895–1917* (Oakland: AK Press, 2008), 2–3; Susan Stryker, *Transgender History* (Berkeley: Seal, 2008), 41.
9. Chauncey, *Gay New York*, 291–99.
10. D'Emilio and Freedman, *Intimate Matters*, 228; Bronski, *A Queer History of the United States*, 106–8; Rupp, *Desired Past*, 104–23; McGarry and Wasserman, *Becoming Visible*, 62–66; Chauncey, *Gay New York*, 180–84; Hatheway, *The Gilded Age Construction of Modern American*

Homophobia, 55–60; John D. Gustav-Wrathall, *Take the Young Stranger by the Hand: Same-Sex Relations and the YMCA* (Chicago: University of Chicago Press, 1998), 158–79; Marc Stein, ed., *Encyclopedia of Lesbian, Gay, Bisexual, and Transgender History in America* (New York: Scribner / Thomson-Gale, 2004), 1:270–73.

11. Peter Boag, *Same-Sex Affairs: Constructing and Controlling Homosexuality in the Pacific Northwest* (Berkeley: University of California Press, 2003), 1–3, 135–47.
12. Rupp, *Desired Past*, 94–100; Margot Canaday, *The Straight State: Sexuality and Citizenship in Twentieth-Century America* (Princeton, NJ: Princeton University Press, 2009), 72–75.
13. Meyerowitz, *Women Adrift*, 79–91.
14. Lillian Faderman, *Odd Girls and Twilight Lovers: A History of Lesbian Life in Twentieth-Century America* (New York: Columbia University Press, 1991), 13; "About Spelman College," *Spelman College*, 2012, http://www.spelman.edu/about-us.
15. Katharine Bement Davis, *Factors in the Sex Life of Twenty-Two Hundred Women* (New York: Harper & Brothers, 1929); referenced in D'Emilio and Freedman, *Intimate Matters*, 193. This study examined women who had attended college in the last decades of the nineteenth century and first decades of the twentieth century.
16. D'Emilio and Freedman, *Intimate Matters*, 189; Katy Coyle and Nadiene Van Dyke, "Sex, Smashing, and Storyville in Turn-of-the-Century New Orleans: Reexamining the Continuum of Lesbian Sexuality," in *Carryin' On in the Lesbian and Gay South*, ed. John Howard (New York: New York University Press, 1997), 54–72; McGarry and Wasserman, *Becoming Visible*, 52.
17. D'Emilio and Freedman, *Intimate Matters*, 189–94; Abraham, *Metropolitan Lovers*, 111–23; Bronski, *A Queer History of the United States*, 72–74, 145–48; Faderman, *Odd Girls and Twilight Lovers*, 11–36; Lillian Faderman, *Surpassing the Love of Men: Romantic Friendship and Love between Women from the Renaissance to the Present* (London: Women's Press, 1985), 201–3; Patricia Bradley, *Making American Culture: A Social History, 1900–1920* (New York: Palgrave Macmillan, 2009), 109–10; "Sara Josephine Baker: Public Health Pioneer," *OutHistory.org*, accessed March 18, 2014, http://outhistory.org/exhibits/show/sara-josephine-baker/background.
18. Faderman, *Odd Girls and Twilight Lovers*, 31–36; quotations from 26, 30, 31, 34, 26, 33, and 32–33.
19. Ibid., 11–13.
20. Ibid.
21. D'Emilio and Freedman, *Intimate Matters*, 221; Hatheway, *The Gilded Age Construction of Modern American Homophobia*, 61–62; Bullough, *Science in the Bedroom*, 96.
22. Jennifer Terry, *An American Obsession: Science, Medicine, and Homosexuality in Modern Society* (Chicago: University of Chicago Press, 1999), 27–29; Hatheway, *The Gilded Age Construction of Modern American Homophobia*, 63–69; Bullough, *Science in the Bedroom*, 50–52.
23. D'Emilio and Freedman, *Intimate Matters*, 150–51; Abraham, *Metropolitan Lovers*, 133–38; Bullough, *Science in the Bedroom*, 49–52; Terry, *An American Obsession*, 100–3.
24. The medical history of homosexuality is a complicated topic, worth detailed investigation. For those who wish to learn more, see Bullough, *Science in the Bedroom*; Terry, *An American Obsession*; Jonathan Katz, *The Invention of Heterosexuality* (New York: Dutton, 1995).
25. Terry, *An American Obsession*, 40–73; Katz, *The Invention of Heterosexuality*, 51–55; Bullough, *Science in the Bedroom*, 35–40.
26. Bullough, *Science in the Bedroom*, 34–35; Terry, *An American Obsession*, 43–44, 53–55, 70–71; Jonathan Katz, *Love Stories: Sex between Men before Homosexuality* (Chicago: University of Chicago Press, 2001), 269–71. Note that, of this group, only Hirschfeld was scientifically or

medically trained; also, although not himself a homosexual, Havelock Ellis was married to a woman, Edith Lees, whom he identified as a lesbian. See Terry, 65–66.

27. Bullough, *Science in the Bedroom*, 40–43; Terry, *An American Obsession*, 45–50.
28. Bullough, *Science in the Bedroom*, 61–86; Terry, *An American Obsession*, 50–55; Joanne J. Meyerowitz, *How Sex Changed: A History of Transsexuality in the United States* (Cambridge, MA: Harvard University Press, 2002), 18–21; Stryker, *Transgender History*, 39–43.
29. Bullough, *Science in the Bedroom*, 86–91; Terry, *An American Obsession*, 55–60.
30. Terry, *An American Obsession*, 80–83; Bullough, *Science in the Bedroom*, 45; Katz, *Love Stories*, 19–21; Abraham, *Metropolitan Lovers*, 133–38.
31. Bullough, *Science in the Bedroom*, 92–96; Terry, *An American Obsession*, 74–79.
32. Katz, *Love Stories*; Katz, *The Invention of Heterosexuality*; Siobhan B. Somerville, *Queering the Color Line: Race and the Invention of Homosexuality in American Culture*, Series Q (Durham, NC: Duke University Press, 2000); Heather Lee Miller, "Sexologists Examine Lesbians and Prostitutes in the United States, 1840–1940," *NWSA Journal* 12, no. 3 (Fall 2000): 67–91; Lisa Duggan, *Sapphic Slashers: Sex, Violence, and American Modernity* (Durham, NC: Duke University Press, 2000); Bronski, *A Queer History of the United States*, 127–28; Bullough, *Science in the Bedroom*, 50–52; Hatheway, *The Gilded Age Construction of Modern American Homophobia*, 38–43.
33. Jennifer Brier and Anne Parsons, "Gender Crossroads: Representations of Gender Transgressions in Chicago's Press, 1850–1920," in *Out in Chicago: LGBT History at the Crossroads*, ed. Jill Austin and Jennifer Brier (Chicago: Chicago History Museum, 2011), 23–40; D'Emilio and Freedman, *Intimate Matters*, 226; Hatheway, *The Gilded Age Construction of Modern American Homophobia*, 55–56.
34. Bronski, *A Queer History of the United States*, 123; Chauncey, *Gay New York*, 52.
35. Chauncey, *Gay New York*; Rupp, *Desired Past*, 96–100.
36. Rupp, *Desired Past*, 86–96; D'Emilio and Freedman, *Intimate Matters*, 193–94; Chauncey, *Gay New York*; Estelle B. Freedman, "'The Burning of Letters Continues': Elusive Identities and the Historical Construction of Sexuality," *Journal of Women's History* 9, no. 4 (Winter 1998): 181–200.
37. Christina Simmons, "Modern Sexuality and the Myth of Victorian Repression," in *Passion and Power: Sexuality in History*, ed. Kathy Peiss and Christina Simmons (Philadelphia: Temple University Press, 1989), 157–77; Miller, "Sexologists Examine Lesbians and Prostitutes in the United States, 1840–1940"; Laura L. Behling, *The Masculine Woman in America, 1890–1935* (Urbana: University of Illinois Press, 2001).
38. Beth L. Bailey, *From Front Porch to Back Seat: Courtship in Twentieth-Century America* (Baltimore: Johns Hopkins University Press, 1988); Kevin White, *The First Sexual Revolution: Male Heterosexuality in Modern America* (New York: New York University Press, 1992); D'Emilio and Freedman, *Intimate Matters*, 256–61.
39. D'Emilio and Freedman, *Intimate Matters*, 256.
40. Faderman, *Odd Girls and Twilight Lovers*, 81–89.
41. Chauncey, *Gay New York*, 7–8, 257–63.
42. Kevin J. Mumford, *Interzones: Black/White Sex Districts in Chicago and New York in the Early Twentieth Century* (New York: Columbia University Press, 1997), 81.
43. Chauncey, *Gay New York*, 244–57; Rupp, *Desired Past*, 107–10; Faderman, *Odd Girls and Twilight Lovers*, 67–79; Mumford, *Interzones*, 73–92.
44. Rupp, *Desired Past*, 107–9; Faderman, *Odd Girls and Twilight Lovers*, 74–75; McGarry and Wasserman, *Becoming Visible*, 68–71; Stein, *Encyclopedia of Lesbian, Gay, Bisexual, and Transgender History in America*, 2:9–12.

45. Gertrude "Ma" Rainey, vocal performance of "Sissy Blues," recorded June 1926, Paramount 12384-B, 78 rpm.
46. Chauncey, *Gay New York*, 263–66; Rupp, *Desired Past*, 106–8; Faderman, *Odd Girls and Twilight Lovers*, 67–71; Mumford, *Interzones*, 89–91; Stein, *Encyclopedia of Lesbian, Gay, Bisexual, and Transgender History in America*, 2:68–69.
47. Chauncey, *Gay New York*; Faderman, *Odd Girls and Twilight Lovers*, 88–92; David K. Johnson, "The Boys of Fairy Town: Gay Male Culture on Chicago's Near North Side in the 1930s," in *Creating a Place for Ourselves: Lesbian, Gay, and Bisexual Community Histories*, ed. Brett Beemyn (New York: Routledge, 1997), 97–118.
48. McGarry and Wasserman, *Becoming Visible*, 66–70; Faderman, *Surpassing the Love of Men*, 72–81; Rupp, *Desired Past*, 101–29; Esther Newton, "The 'Fun Gay Ladies': Lesbians in Cherry Grove, 1936–1960," in *Creating a Place for Ourselves: Lesbian, Gay, and Bisexual Community Histories*, ed. Brett Beemyn (New York: Routledge, 1997), 145–64; Esther Newton, *Cherry Grove, Fire Island: Sixty Years in America's First Gay and Lesbian Town* (Boston: Beacon, 1993), 207–20; Boyd, *Wide-Open Town*, 68–101; Elizabeth Lapovsky Kennedy and Madeline D. Davis, *Boots of Leather, Slippers of Gold: The History of a Lesbian Community* (New York: Routledge, 1993), 29–67.
49. Faderman, *Odd Girls and Twilight Lovers*, 93–102; David K. Johnson, *The Lavender Scare: The Cold War Persecution of Gays and Lesbians in the Federal Government* (Chicago: University of Chicago Press, 2004), 46–51.
50. Susan Ferentinos, "An Unpredictable Age: Sex, Consumption, and the Emergence of the American Teenager, 1900–1950" (PhD diss., Indiana University, 2005), 141–42.
51. Chauncey, *Gay New York*, 331–54; Johnson, *The Lavender Scare*, 55–59; Estelle B. Freedman, "'Uncontrolled Desires': The Response to the Sexual Psychopath, 1920–1960," in *Passion and Power: Sexuality in History*, ed. Kathy Peiss and Christina Simmons (Philadelphia: Temple University Press, 1989), 199–225.
52. McGarry and Wasserman, *Becoming Visible*, 75–77; Faderman, *Odd Girls and Twilight Lovers*, 118–30; D'Emilio and Freedman, *Intimate Matters*, 288–90; Leisa D. Meyer, *Creating GI Jane: Sexuality and Power in the Women's Army Corps during World War II* (New York: Columbia University Press, 1996), 148–78; Allan Bérubé, *Coming out under Fire: The History of Gay Men and Women in World War Two* (New York: Free Press, 1990).
53. D'Emilio and Freedman, *Intimate Matters*, 288–90; Bérubé, *Coming out under Fire*, 8–33; Margot Canaday, "Building a Straight State: Sexuality and Social Citizenship under the 1944 G.I. Bill," *Journal of American History* 90, no. 3 (December 2003): 935–57.
54. Elaine Tyler May, *Homeward Bound: American Families in the Cold War Era*, rev. and updated ed. (New York: Basic, 1999).
55. Faderman, *Odd Girls and Twilight Lovers*, 139–45; John D'Emilio, *Sexual Politics, Sexual Communities: The Making of a Homosexual Minority in the United States, 1940–1970*, 2nd ed. (Chicago: University of Chicago Press, 1998), 40–46; statistics from Craig M. Loftin, *Masked Voices: Gay Men and Lesbians in Cold War America* (Albany: SUNY Press, 2012), 6; Johnson, *The Lavender Scare*, 166, quotation from ibid.
56. D'Emilio, *Sexual Politics, Sexual Communities*, 46–49; Loftin, *Masked Voices*; Johnson, *The Lavender Scare*; Stacy Lorraine Braukman, *Communists and Perverts under the Palms: The Johns Committee in Florida, 1956–1965* (Gainesville: University Press of Florida, 2012).
57. Loftin, *Masked Voices*; D'Emilio, *Sexual Politics, Sexual Communities*; Faderman, *Odd Girls and Twilight Lovers*, 157–87; Kennedy and Davis, *Boots of Leather, Slippers of Gold*, 113–90; John

Howard, *Men Like That: A Southern Queer History* (Chicago: University of Chicago Press, 1999).
58. Faderman, *Odd Girls and Twilight Lovers*, 157–87; Kennedy and Davis, *Boots of Leather, Slippers of Gold*, 67–112.
59. Meyerowitz, *How Sex Changed*, 45–48, 120–21; Stryker, *Transgender History*, 44–46; Stein, *Encyclopedia of Lesbian, Gay, Bisexual, and Transgender History in America*, 1:133–34.
60. D'Emilio and Freedman, *Intimate Matters*, 285–87; Rupp, *Desired Past*, 143–44; Kinsey Institute, "Data from Alfred Kinsey's Studies," *Kinsey Institute for Research in Sex, Gender, and Reproduction*, accessed April 3, 2014, http://www.kinseyinstitute.org/research/ak-data.html.
61. Stryker, *Transgender History*, 47–50; Meyerowitz, *How Sex Changed*.
62. Bronski, *A Queer History of the United States*, 183–201; Vito Russo, *The Celluloid Closet: Homosexuality in the Movies*, rev. ed. (New York: Harper & Row, 1987); Faderman, *Odd Girls and Twilight Lovers*, 146–48.
63. St. Sukie de la Croix, *Chicago Whispers: A History of LGBT Chicago before Stonewall* (Madison: University of Wisconsin Press, 2012), 70–87; Michelle McClellan et al., "Henry Gerber House: Draft" (National Historic Landmark nomination, University of Michigan Public History Initiative, National Park Service, 2014), section 8; Bronski, *A Queer History of the United States*, 176; D'Emilio, *Sexual Politics, Sexual Communities*, 32; C. Todd White, *Pre-Gay L.A.: A Social History of the Movement for Homosexual Rights* (Urbana: University of Illinois Press, 2009), 1–2, 30. Sources disagree on some details of the Knights of the Clock. Bronski calls it Knights of the Clocks, and White claims it was formed in 1950.
64. White, *Pre-Gay L.A.*, 11–27; D'Emilio, *Sexual Politics, Sexual Communities*, 59–74; Marc Stein, *Rethinking the Gay and Lesbian Movement* (New York: Routledge, 2012), 45–52.
65. White, *Pre-Gay L.A.*, 23–27; D'Emilio, *Sexual Politics, Sexual Communities*, 70–71; Stein, *Rethinking the Gay and Lesbian Movement*, 49–50.
66. White, *Pre-Gay L.A.*, 28–40; Stein, *Rethinking the Gay and Lesbian Movement*, 50; Loftin, *Masked Voices*, 17–41, quotation from 18.
67. Joyce Murdoch and Deb Price, *Courting Justice: Gay Men and Lesbians v. the Supreme Court* (New York: Basic, 2001), 27–50.
68. Loftin, *Masked Voices*, 23; Stein, *Rethinking the Gay and Lesbian Movement*, 50, 55–57.
69. Stein, *Rethinking the Gay and Lesbian Movement*, 55–57, 68; Marcia M. Gallo, "Different Daughters," *OAH Magazine of History* 20, no. 2 (March 1, 2006): 27–30; Marcia M. Gallo, *Different Daughters: A History of the Daughters of Bilitis and the Rise of the Lesbian Rights Movement* (New York: Carroll & Graf, 2006).
70. Meyerowitz, *How Sex Changed*, 179–82; Stryker, *Transgender History*, 44–47.
71. Bronski, *A Queer History of the United States*, 205–8.
72. Stein, *Rethinking the Gay and Lesbian Movement*, 67.
73. David Carter, *Stonewall: The Riots That Sparked the Gay Revolution* (New York: St. Martin's, 2004), 104–5; McGarry and Wasserman, *Becoming Visible*, 82–83; D'Emilio, *Sexual Politics, Sexual Communities*, 187–88, 201–5.
74. Josh Sides, *Erotic City: Sexual Revolutions and the Making of Modern San Francisco* (New York: Oxford University Press, 2009), 85–86; Carter, *Stonewall*, 105; D'Emilio, *Sexual Politics, Sexual Communities*, 103–5.
75. Stein, *Rethinking the Gay and Lesbian Movement*, 65, 70; McGarry and Wasserman, *Becoming Visible*, 151–52; D'Emilio, *Sexual Politics, Sexual Communities*, 150–57.

CHAPTER 6

We're Here, We're Queer, Get Used to It

Mid-1960s to *United States v. Windsor* (2013)

I F YOU ASK the average museum visitor in the United States to name one event in LGBT history, chances are they will say the Stonewall riots of 1969. This event—when a police raid on a gay bar in New York City sparked five days of spontaneous protests—is popularly accepted as the start of the LGBT fight for civil rights, and as a result, it has taken on an almost hagiographic status in the story of LGBT history. The Stonewall Inn, the bar where the riots began, was the first site in the United States to be listed on the National Register of Historic Places specifically because of its association with LGBT history, and for more than a decade, 1999–2011, it was the *only* site that held that honor.[1] To be sure, the Stonewall riots were a very significant event in LGBT history. We know from the previous chapter, however, that LGBT political activism had existed within the homophile movement for nearly two decades before the riots. In reality, Stonewall was part of a much longer trajectory in which LGBT people became increasingly organized, and eventually radicalized, in their efforts to improve the circumstances of their lives. In the words of Michael Bronski, "Stonewall was less a turning point than a final stimulus in a series of public altercations."[2] Let us, then, briefly turn our attention to the context of the 1960s so that we can better understand Stonewall's catalysts before moving forward to examine the event itself and its legacy.

The Context of the 1960s

The decade of the 1960s was a period of extreme cultural transformation, influenced by changing demographics, sexual experimentation, grassroots political activism, and racial tensions. At a basic demographic level, the 1960s saw the first members of the baby boom enter adulthood, and this, to some extent, skewed American culture toward youth. Seventy million Americans became teenagers during this decade. Between 1964 and 1970, twenty million reached the age of eighteen. What's more, an increasing proportion of Americans were attending college, which provided a youth-segregated environment in which to develop new visions of the future. While not all young people took part, a sizable counterculture developed during this era.[3]

As is perhaps inevitable when millions of young people come of age simultaneously, traditional morality began to erode in the 1960s and continued to do so into the 1970s. The changes in attitudes and behavior were significant enough that this time is known as the sexual revolution (although historians recognize that a comparably seismic shift took place in the 1920s and thus often refer to the 1960s as the *second* sexual revolution). In addition to the development of the counterculture, the freer attitude toward sexual expression was influenced by the release of the birth control pill; court decisions that made birth control more widely accessible; and the fact that during the 1960s and 1970s, the medical risks of having sex were relatively low. Cures had been found for syphilis and gonorrhea (although not for herpes), and AIDS was not yet known. The ethic of sexual experimentation in this era encouraged many people—particularly within the youth culture—to open themselves to a wider range of sexual expression and contributed to a more laissez-faire approach to personal choices in some countercultural circles.[4]

The 1960s were also a time of grassroots political activism, most memorably through the movement against the Vietnam War, the African American civil rights movement, and the women's movement. These efforts, combined with the work of the homophile movement, set the stage for the post-Stonewall LGBT movement in a number of ways. To begin with, many people who would later join gay liberation (as the movement was called in the 1970s) were active in these earlier movements, learning the skills of political action and analyzing the dynamics of oppression. Second, in the words of Michael Bronski, "The progressive politics of the late 1960s were predicated on the principle that a person had complete autonomy and control over her or his own body." This premise was crucial to the development of the gay liberation philosophy.[5]

Street-level mass protest was a common form of demonstration among the leftist movements of the 1960s, and by the end of the decade "taking to the streets" increasingly carried the potential for violence. The protests surrounding the 1968 Democratic National Convention in Chicago are probably the most memorable example from organized leftist politics, but we can also understand the urban riots of the late 1960s as part of the same trend. American cities underwent a great deal of flux in the 1950s and 1960s as middle-class whites moved to the suburbs and government-sponsored urban renewal projects destroyed many poor neighborhoods, most often inhabited by African Americans. The tensions created by these circumstances frequently exploded into violence. Between 1964 and 1969, nearly seventy-five race-related riots took place in US cities, including Los Angeles (the Watts riot of 1965), Detroit (1967), and Newark (1967).[6]

From this briefest of overviews, we can see many potential catalysts for the Stonewall riots of 1969. Young queers, influenced by the changing cultural expectations and increasingly radical politics they saw around them, staged their own spontaneous protest against police in June 1969. And like many other attempts by oppressed groups to express their frustration against the status quo during those years, the protest at the Stonewall Inn was unorganized and frightening enough to be described as a "riot" by outside observers.

Increasing Calls to End Homosexual Oppression

In addition to all the factors just described, the 1960s saw a growing mobilization among gays and lesbians themselves and an increasing recognition of the need to advocate for fairer treatment within society. This idea was developing in queer subcultures long before Stonewall. The previous chapter described the birth of the homophile movement in the early 1950s and its efforts to effect change by working within electoral politics and the court system on through the 1960s. But like so many other movements of the mid-twentieth century, the effort to obtain wider acceptance of homosexuality underwent a sea change in the late 1960s that can be understood as a shift from a liberal to a radical orientation. As with the women's movement and the African American civil rights movement, efforts by gays and lesbians to achieve reform within the arena of mainstream politics continued well into the 1970s, but by the late 1960s more radical arms of these movements were calling for a complete overhaul of a society that they saw as rooted in hierarchy and dominance. Thus, we pick up the story of homophile activism here, with an exploration of a few of its more radical elements, which foreshadowed the events of Stonewall and its aftermath. However, it is important to remember that all of these developments—more mainstream homophile efforts, the increasingly radical efforts described below, the sexual revolution, larger forays into identity politics, and urban unrest—were happening simultaneously.

By the late 1960s, under the influence of the New Left's critique of mainstream society, the Black Power movement, and radical feminism, some homosexuals began to call for a revolution. At a national movement conference in 1968, homophile activists adopted the slogan "Gay Is Good," a clear homage to the phrase "Black Is Beautiful," coined by the Black Power movement.[7] And in early 1969, Carl Wittman, a well-known figure in the New Left then living in San Francisco, penned an essay called "Refugees from Amerika: A Gay Manifesto," in which he stated:

> In the past year there has been an awakening of gay liberation ideas and energy.... Where once there was frustration, alienation, and cynicism, there are new characteristics among us. We are full of love for each other and are showing it; we are full of anger at what has been done to us.[8]

The "Gay Manifesto" would eventually become a classic of the post-Stonewall gay liberation movement.

The sexual revolution also had an impact on the movement; some LGBT people saw themselves as vanguards in the overthrow of traditional morality. Seizing the momentum of changing attitudes about sexuality, they embraced a vision of expanded options for sexual expression of all kinds. For instance, the Janus Society, a group out of Philadelphia, drew connections between homosexual discrimination and laws governing other aspects of sexuality such as abortion, birth control, adultery, prostitution, and obscenity. In 1964, the

Janus Society's publication *Drum* became the widest-circulating homosexual periodical in the United States, in large part because of its more sexualized content aimed at a gay male audience. Marc Stein also makes the point that the gay sex industry—pornography and the nation's extensive network of bathhouses catering to gay men and providing a place for anonymous sexual encounters—provided significant funding for political efforts of the larger gay and lesbian movement.[9]

Clearly, there were signs of diverging philosophies within LGBT activism before Stonewall. Some had grown tired of the accommodationist politics of the older homophile organizations and were advocating for a more radical approach to change. The Committee for Homosexual Freedom (CHF), which began in San Francisco in April 1969 (a few months before the Stonewall riots), represented this newer vision, so much so that Josh Sides has identified it as the first gay liberation organization in the United States.[10] The CHF clearly envisioned a revolution and was critical of other homophile organizations, stating:

> Homosexual organizations on the West Coast are doing very little to spark the Homosexual revolution of '69. Timid leaders with enormous ego-trips, middle class bigotry and racism, and too many middle-aged up-tight conservatives are hurting almost every major homosexual organization on the West Coast and probably throughout the nation.[11]

Throughout the major cities of the United States, then, LGBT activists were losing patience with the status quo.

In addition to the LGBT activism, societal critique, and publications that came out of the late 1960s, the growing presence of queer street youth in the nation's cities was also a significant factor leading up to the Stonewall riots. Of the homeless or marginally housed youth that congregated near urban sex districts such as the Tenderloin in San Francisco or Greenwich Village and Times Square in New York City, many were gender variant and/or attracted to the same sex. Their very nonconformity often contributed to their predicament; they had become runaways after being rejected by their families of origin or because they could not live their true identities within mainstream culture. Often unable to obtain traditional employment because of their lack of address or unconventional gender presentation, many made their living hustling (that is, performing sex acts for hire). They also formed tight bonds among themselves and challenged the wider society to pay attention to their plight.[12]

In San Francisco, thanks in part to the advocacy of transgender residents of the Tenderloin, a number of social service organizations reaching out to street youth in the 1960s recognized that a significant part of their constituency was gender and/or sexually variant. The Council on Religion and Homosexuality, spurred on by one of its founders, Reverend Tim McIlvenna and his Glide Urban Center, worked from 1964 onward to raise awareness of gender and sexual identity issues among street youth. The San Francisco Public Health Department established a "Center for Special Problems" in the 1960s to specifically address the needs of transgender San Franciscans, offering hormone prescriptions, counseling, and assistance with obtaining identification documents that matched patients' lived gender. Even the San Francisco Police Department assigned an officer to liaise with the city's gays, lesbians, and transgenders, and much of that work also focused on the street culture of the Tenderloin. The presence of any kind of LGBT advocate within a police department during this era is particularly noteworthy, as police throughout the country were far better known for harassing LGBT people and raiding the bars and taverns where queer people congregated.[13]

The summer of 1966 proved a crucial turning point. In San Francisco, Vanguard, a self-proclaimed "organization of, by, and for the kids on the streets," organized to provide mutual support for street youth and advocate for fairer treatment. Vanguard is believed to be the nation's first queer youth organization. Members would meet in a local Tenderloin hangout, Gene Compton's Cafeteria, whose owners grew increasingly frustrated with the presence of these socially marginal customers who would spend very little money. Under increasing harassment, Vanguard joined with the Glide Urban Center and other homosexual organizations to picket the business. In August 1966, tensions reached a breaking point. Police arrived at Compton's to disperse the young people, and in the course of their efforts, violence broke out. The youth physically attacked the officers, resisted arrest, and broke windows and dishes.[14]

Although the Compton's riot did not spark the wave of radical activism that followed the Stonewall riots three years later, the event does point to the fact that economically marginalized, gender-variant urban queers played a significant role in the changes LGBT activism underwent in the 1960s. Street youth and transgender people were also among the instigators in the Stonewall riots; they were some of the first to resist arrest that night and participated in sustaining the protests for multiple days.

The Stonewall Riots and Their Aftermath

In the early morning of June 28, 1969, New York City police officers raided the Stonewall Inn, a gay bar located on Christopher Street in the Greenwich Village neighborhood of New York City. Police raids on gay bars were quite common during this era, and it is likely the officers expected nothing out of the ordinary. Yet, for whatever reason, the response of the bar patrons that night was far from common. Several patrons—mostly young working-class men and trans women—resisted arrest and physically assaulted the police officers. The commotion attracted additional people from the surrounding neighborhood (this being a section of the city known to be relatively safe for alternative expressions of sexuality and gender), who joined in the altercation. The ruckus grew in magnitude until the city's riot control unit was called to the scene and managed to disperse the crowd. The "riots"—more accurately a series of unorganized street protests against police harassment—continued intermittently for another five nights. In its aftermath, numerous groups formed to advocate for better treatment of homosexuals, and this is why Stonewall has been credited in popular memory with starting the modern LGBT movement.[15] As David Carter has argued, the riots were a moment of redefinition, when gays, lesbians, bisexuals, and transgender people fought back against a larger society that defined them as lesser human beings.[16]

Seizing on the energy and momentum of Stonewall and the various events that preceded it, LGBT communities began a new era of political organizing in mid-1969. Whereas the pre-Stonewall homophile movement largely focused on the efforts of homosexuals to maintain their privacy and live their lives free of harassment, activism after Stonewall adopted a more visible and collective flavor. Naming their movement "gay liberation," these activists challenged traditional sexual morality and proclaimed pride in their sexual orientation.

Figure 6.1. Gays and lesbians are a button-loving people. Here, a display of gay liberation buttons are exhibited at the opening of the Velvet Foundation in Washington, DC.
Courtesy of DCVirago

Inspired by feminism's assessment that "the personal is political," gay liberation saw the emancipatory power of individuals speaking the truth about their sexual desires. The concept of coming out of the closet (that is, admitting same-sex desire to oneself and others) developed during this period and was understood as a political act, essential for convincing the wider public of queers' influence and numbers. Captured in the slogan "Out of the Closets, and Into the Streets!" gay liberation argued that only by being out, loud, and proud could substantive change take place.[17]

Within a month of Stonewall, activists from various movements held a mass meeting in New York City, and from this meeting, a new organization—the Gay Liberation Front (GLF)—was created. Rejecting the accommodationist approach of the homophile movement, the GLF instead emphasized the interconnectedness of all forms of oppression and provided an umbrella for a variety of radical impulses among a younger generation of queers who were ready for immediate change. In the words of Michael Bronski, "Within a year, GLF had organized Sunday night meetings, nineteen 'cells' or action groups, twelve consciousness-raising groups, an ongoing radical study group, an all-men's meeting, a women's caucus, three communal living groups, and a series of successful community dances, in addition to publishing the newspaper *Come Out!*"[18] GLF's flame burned bright but also quickly died out. The organization was defunct by 1972, but by then many other groups throughout the country had formed with similar desires for change. These included the Gay Activists Alliance (GAA), Street Transvestite Action Revolution (STAR), and, starting in 1973, the National Gay Task Force (later the National Gay and Lesbian Task Force).[19]

The five years following Stonewall were a riot of initiatives and efforts. Political accomplishments included the first Christopher Street Liberation Day Parade, held in New York City in June 1970 (with similar events in Los Angeles, San Francisco, and Chicago) to mark the one-year anniversary of Stonewall. A mass gathering of people identifying themselves as queer, in broad daylight in a public space, was virtually unheard of in 1970 and served as a powerful message to the wider society that LGBT people were ready for respect. The event has continued annually and spread throughout the world; the gay pride parades that are held each June are the direct descendants of this 1970 event.[20]

The 1970s LGBT movement accomplished many other goals as well. In 1971, Frank Kameny launched the first run for Congress by an open homosexual, vying to become the nonvoting representative from the District of Columbia.[21] Also, throughout this period, activists from both the gay liberation and homophile camps fought a sustained effort to remove homosexuality from the *Diagnostic and Statistical Manual of Mental Disorders* (*DSM*). They finally succeeded in 1973. The *DSM* remains the definitive source used to diagnose mental illness in the United States, and the removal of homosexuality as a classified mental illness represented a huge achievement toward allowing homosexuals to live normal lives, free from discrimination. It also protected them from incarceration in mental hospitals, where in previous eras they had been forced to undergo severe treatment such as aversion therapy and lobotomies.[22]

However, Susan Stryker points out that the movement's success in removing homosexuality from the list of mental illnesses contributed to a growing wedge between transgender and LGB political collaboration that occurred in the 1970s. While the change in the *DSM* granted homosexuals and bisexuals a certain freedom from psychiatric authority, gender identity disorder (GID) remained in the *DSM* until 2012, when it was replaced with "gender dysphoria." GID was controversial among transgender people. Unlike the later category of gender dysphoria, GID labeled all gender variance as "disordered," a construction to which many objected. At the same time, others accepted the label because doctors and insurance companies often required a diagnosis of GID before approving medical treatment to alter someone's body to fit their lived gender. Throughout the late twentieth and early twenty-first centuries, transgender people battled continually for fair and respectful treatment by the medical and psychiatric professions, a goal that few nontransgendered gays, lesbians, and bisexuals lent energy to after 1973.[23]

Serious challenges remained in the gay and lesbian movement as well, a fact that was brought home in March 1970. During a police raid of the Snake Pit, a gay bar in New York City, officers rounded up over 160 customers and took them to the Sixth Precinct police station. Among those taken was Alfredo Diego Vinales, a young Argentinian who was in the United States on an expired visa. Fearing that being arrested in a gay bar would lead to his deportation, Vinales sought to escape by jumping out of a second-story window. Tragically, he landed on the iron-spiked fence surrounding the station and was impaled by six fourteen-inch spikes. Vinales, though speared, survived the fall, and an excruciating effort to remove him from the spikes followed, while others rounded up in the raid watched helplessly from the station's windows. This gruesome incident, stemming directly from continued police harassment of LGBT communities, served to renew the efforts of gay liberationists and recruit additional activists to their cause. The following day, over five hundred demonstrators assembled in Christopher Street Park (site of the Stonewall riots) to protest police harassment, making it, at that point, the largest LGBT protest ever held.[24]

Lesbians were present at the Stonewall riots and active in the early gay liberation organizations, although not in the same numbers as gay men. In part, this was because they were fighting for their rights on a different front, within second-wave feminism, where the question of homosexuality was threatening to divide the women's movement.

From the beginning, the 1960s women's movement was appealing to lesbians and bisexuals as well as heterosexual women. While not all parts of the feminist agenda were directly relevant to lesbians' lives (reproductive freedom and the ability of married women to obtain credit in their own name, for instance), its critique of rigid gender roles and call for economic and social equality between men and women certainly did appeal. Nevertheless, within a few years, it became increasingly clear that many of the leading feminist organizations were ambivalent at best regarding the presence of lesbians within their ranks.

Frustrated by the failure of feminist organizations to include lesbian issues in their platforms, and perhaps inspired by the galvanizing effect Stonewall had had in mobilizing a previously soft-spoken minority, beginning in 1970 lesbians took a more radical stance within the women's movement. At the Second Congress to Unite Women, in May 1970, a guerrilla action group calling itself the Lavender Menace (which included activists Karla Jay and Rita Mae Brown and would later rename itself Radicalesbians) confronted fellow members of the National Organization for Women (NOW), distributing a pamphlet titled "The Woman-Identified Woman" and demanding that NOW work harder to address the needs of lesbians. Although NOW did eventually pass a resolution affirming the importance of addressing the issue of lesbian rights, many lesbians had already begun to drift away from mainstream feminist organizations.[25]

Equally frustrated by what they saw as the male dominance of the gay liberation movement and the lesbian baiting of the mainstream women's movement, many lesbians proposed alternative political critiques. Lesbians of color tended to join with other women of color and argued for the intersectionality of oppressions based on race and gender. Audre Lorde and Barbara Smith, among others, spoke out about their disillusionment with the larger women's movement. In Boston, the Combahee River Collective formed in 1974 and became the most prominent African American lesbian feminist organization of the 1970s.[26]

Other lesbians within the women's movement (particularly white, college-educated lesbians) adopted their own philosophy and political agenda, known collectively as radical lesbian feminism. Represented by groups such as the Radicalesbians and producing such feminist classics as Anne Koedt's "The Myth of the Vaginal Orgasm," lesbian feminists shifted their focus away from trying to reform male attitudes and instead advocated for women leading "woman-identified" lives, relying on other women for their social support, economic livelihood, lovers, and family. Many removed themselves from the dominant culture, moving "back to the land" and forming women's collectives to meet their basic needs.[27]

1973–1981

While it is admittedly oversimplistic, we can understand LGBT history as following two significant paths of development in the 1970s. One was the development of stronger, more public subcultures; the other was a fight for legal protections and representation. In the early 1970s, these paths overlapped in many ways, but by the mid-1970s they were two distinct impulses within LGBT communities, although admittedly, many individuals chose to straddle both roads.[28]

A distinct lesbian feminist subculture was represented by the creation of a female-centered alternative economy, feminist presses, and the development of a "women's music" industry. Among gay men, a subculture of dancing, recreational drug use, and anonymous sex, revolving around the disco music scene, sprang up in urban centers throughout the country. While these aspects had all existed within gay communities before Stonewall, in the 1970s the subculture became much more visible, as gays (influenced perhaps by the political rhetoric of the time) aggressively claimed their public space. Men proudly engaged in anonymous sexual encounters in traditional gay male cruising areas (such as parks and public restrooms), back rooms of gay bars, and public bathhouses. In addition, a distinctive gay male ideal emerged from the bar scene of the 1970s, marked by overt masculinity, youth, muscled bodies, mustaches, and style references to working-class male culture such as work boots and jeans.[29]

Although the lesbian-feminist and urban gay subcultures in many ways were wildly divergent during the 1970s, they shared two characteristics worth noting. First, influenced in part by the sexual revolution and in part by the disproportionate youth of the population engaging in these subcultures (this was the baby boom, after all), both lesbian feminists and participants in the urban gay club culture, generally speaking, rejected marriage and monogamy as a model for their lives. The lesbian feminists saw these traditions as rooted in patriarchal efforts to own and control women's bodies as well as keep track of male lineage. Gay men saw such traditions as interfering with the sexual freedom that was a hallmark of their lives.[30] Second, as Susan Stryker points out, neither the hypermasculinity of gay disco culture nor the lesbian feminist disdain for rigid gender roles created a particularly welcoming environment for transgender identities.[31]

On the political front, the initial spark of gay liberation cooled to a slow burn within about five years. While the movement struggled in the mid-1970s to find its core issues, many queers continued to explore ways they could be better protected and represented within the larger culture and society. Some pursued LGBT civil rights via attempts to elect openly gay candidates to public office. As mentioned previously, the first congressional campaign by an openly queer candidate was Frank Kameny in 1971. It would be nearly thirty years before a nonincumbent candidate who publically identified as LGBT actually won a congressional election. That honor went to Tammy Baldwin of Wisconsin, who was elected to the US House of Representatives in 1999. (Before that, already elected members of Congress had come out and subsequently won reelection: Gerry Studds, D-MA, came out in 1983, and Barney Frank, D-MA, came out in 1987.) In 2012, Baldwin achieved another significant milestone, becoming the first (and so far only) openly LGBT person to gain a seat in the US Senate. This is not to say that LGBT people did not serve in public office before this; rather, they did not publically identify as such and thus ran a professional risk by allying too closely with the issue of LGBT rights.[32]

An unsung leader of the effort to increase queer representation in politics was the city of Ann Arbor, Michigan. In 1973, two city council members in this small city, Nancy Wechsler and Jerry DeGrieck, became the first public officials in the United States to publicly acknowledge their same-sex desire. The following year, 1974, Kathy Kozachenko was elected to the Ann Arbor city council, making her the first out LGBT person in the United States to win a political race. Elsewhere, the first out LGBT person to win a state-level office was Elaine Noble, elected to the Massachusetts State Assembly, also in 1974.[33]

Another 1970s LGBT political effort sought legal protection against discrimination. In 1973 and 1974, Seattle, Washington, DC, Minneapolis-St. Paul, and the small town of Alfred, New York, all passed local nondiscrimination ordinances that included sexual orientation. Thirty more cities had followed suit by 1978. These efforts reached the national level when Bella Azbug (D-NY) introduced to Congress the Equality Act of 1974, outlawing discrimination based on sexual orientation, sex, or marital status. Although the bill did not pass, it launched a series of similar antidiscrimination bills introduced to Congress throughout the 1970s and 1980s.[34]

Amid these various gains, by the late 1970s, a mounting conservative backlash had begun to emerge. Harvey Milk, an openly gay man representing an increasingly gay neighborhood (the Castro), was elected to the San Francisco Board of Supervisors in 1977. He served in city politics during a contentious moment in San Francisco's history, as residents grappled with San Francisco's sexual permissiveness and growing visibility as the home of a significant number of gay men, transgender people, lesbians, and bisexuals. The same year as Milk's campaign, California state senator John Briggs introduced Proposition 6, outlawing homosexuals from teaching in public schools. Although the Briggs Initiative, as Proposition 6 was widely known, was soundly defeated at the ballot box in 1978, the rhetoric of the campaign represented a new era of US politics where conservatives fought to prevent what they saw as the erosion of traditional morality as represented by pro-LGBT protections.[35]

In the aftermath of the Briggs Initiative, political tensions reached a tragic climax. In San Francisco on November 27, 1978, former city supervisor Dan White, who had represented the defenders of an older moral order while in office, shot and killed Mayor George Moscone and Supervisor Harvey Milk. The assassinations of Milk and Moscone caused national outrage and illustrated for many heterosexuals the depth of disgust and threat of violence that queers lived with at the time. LGBT people throughout the country understood Milk's death as a huge blow to the political gains of the previous decade. This disappointment erupted into anger in May 1979, when a jury found Milk's killer guilty only of manslaughter, sentencing him to less than eight years in prison. The ostensible reason for this minimal sentence lay in White's claim that he had committed the murders after consuming too much sugar. The "Twinkie defense," as it became known, caused so much outrage that a spontaneous street protest, known as the White Night riots, erupted on the streets of the Castro after the verdict was announced.[36]

The same climate that produced the Briggs Initiative on the West Coast produced an even more visible campaign on the East Coast. In 1977, Dade County, Florida (the county in which Miami is located), passed an ordinance protecting gays and lesbians from

Figure 6.2. Grave site of Leonard Matlovich who protested his discharge from the US military for homosexuality in 1975.
Courtesy of A.J. Lopp

discrimination, and this ordinance, although similar to other ordinances around the country, sparked a high-profile backlash. Anita Bryant, a singer and spokesperson for Florida orange juice, joined the campaign to repeal the law and draw attention to the fact that gays and lesbians were slowly gaining civil rights protections, something Bryant opposed. She created an antigay organization and, in an astute political move, named it "Save Our Children," equating homosexuality to child molestation. She also enlisted the help of evangelical television personalities, who spread the antihomosexual message throughout the conservative Christian community in the United States and launched a nationwide political effort to oppose civil rights for homosexuals.[37]

The success of the campaign in Florida invigorated the religious right. In the wake of the Florida effort, gay rights ordinances were defeated in St. Paul, Minnesota, Wichita, Kansas, and Eugene, Oregon. Troubled by the growing sexual liberalism of American society, as symbolized by the feminist and gay liberation movements, conservatives began in the late 1970s and 1980s to publicly defend a more traditional, Christian-based morality.[38] The subsequent battles heralded an era of polarization. In the words of historians John D'Emilio and Estelle Freedman:

> [W]hatever consensus existed in the mid-twentieth century about sexuality had dissolved by the 1980s. The debates about sex, rather than remaining the province of feminists and gay liberationists, were polarizing the nation's politics. The contentious quality of the debates stemmed not only from the demands of radicals, but also from the response of conservatives distressed by the reorientation of sexual values that had occurred since the 1960s.[39]

AIDS and the 1980s

By 1980, the LGBT community had experienced serious setbacks in the assassination of Harvey Milk and the repeal of the Dade County gay rights ordinance. Likewise, Ronald Reagan's election as president, due in large part to the support of the increasingly antigay religious right, did not bode well for the LGBT movement. Also by 1980, the movement had lost its focus; many of the activists of the immediate post-Stonewall years had drifted away from political activism, captivated by the urban club scene or the isolation of lesbian separatism or simply taking on more middle-aged, self-interested concerns. However, an even greater blow was about to hit the queer community, one that would create incredible loss but ultimately contribute to many of the political gains of the past twenty-five years.

In the late 1970s and early 1980s, doctors in US cities began to see a mysterious medical phenomenon. Young, previously healthy men were seeking treatment for a host of ailments not common to their demographic—an unusual pneumonia, a rare cancer. What's more, these men were dying, felled by illnesses that would not normally kill a healthy young person. Further investigation revealed another commonality among these earliest cases: these patients tended to be sexually active with other men. The first published reports of the symptoms appeared in summer 1981, when a newsletter of the Centers for Disease Control and Prevention (CDC) mentioned five cases of a rare pneumonia in Los Angeles, and a few weeks later, the *New York Times* ran an article about forty-one cases of a rare cancer among gay men. Eventually, the spectrum of symptoms came to be described as acquired immunodeficiency syndrome: AIDS.[40]

The toll of AIDS on the gay community in the early years is nearly unfathomable. Before effective prevention was developed, the disease spread exponentially. At the end of 1981, there were 251 reported cases; by spring of 1983, there were 1,400. By the summer of 1985, 15,000 people had been diagnosed, and two years later, that number had increased to 40,000.[41] Even more alarming, those diagnosed in the early years of the epidemic, before the discovery of any effective treatment, suffered an extremely high mortality rate. By 1990, 31,129 people had died from AIDS in the United States.[42]

With regard to AIDS, the early 1980s were years of panic, confusion, and misunderstanding. Although gay men acquired the disease at disproportionate rates, by the end of 1981, it was clear that they were not the only ones at risk. Hemophiliacs, intravenous drug users, prostitutes, and Haitians (because of that country's historic ties to regions of Africa that were greatly affected by the disease) were also particularly susceptible to developing AIDS, but because of the early connection made in the press between the disease and gay men, it was considered a "gay disease" in the public imagination for many years. High-profile religious leaders, such as Jerry Falwell and Pat Buchanan, also perpetuated this association, claiming that AIDS was a punishment from God for sinful behavior.[43]

The mainstream media and the federal government were slow to respond to the epidemic, resulting in its rapid spread in the first, critical years after its identification. Response within LGBT communities was swifter. Within months of the identification of the disease, in early 1982, activists in New York City formed the Gay Men's Health Crisis (GMHC) to educate the gay community about AIDS and to provide care to those who were dying, many of whom had been rejected by families of origin and were in financially precarious positions, having lost their jobs (and their health insurance) when their conditions were discovered. Another early AIDS service organization was the San Francisco AIDS Foundation, a leader in publicizing safer ways for men to sexually interact with each other (as opposed to simply calling for abstinence). Similar organizations formed around the United States as local LGBT communities rushed to fill the gap in services and information dissemination. By 1985, the Third World AIDS Advisory Task Force (TWAATF) organized, also in San Francisco, to ensure that communities of color—both gay and straight—were being considered and included in AIDS service organizations.[44]

Yet while LGBT communities mobilized to care for the sick, there was less consensus among gay and transgender communities on addressing the spread of the epidemic. In a context where little was known about the disease, where many outsiders were declaring AIDS to be the wages of sin, and where many gays saw the open expression of their sexuality as a hard-won reward of gay liberation, communities heatedly debated the proper ways to maintain queer cultures that celebrated sexuality while also preventing the spread of AIDS. The issues were further complicated by the history of ill treatment from the medical profession, which had spent most of the century immediately prior to this period declaring homosexuality and gender variance a disease. The incarceration of sexually and/or gender-variant individuals in mental institutions was a very real memory of many LGBT people in the 1980s and contributed to a broad distrust of medical authority. Likewise, memories of Nazi Germany were only forty years old. Within this context, public health recommendations that included abstinence, monogamy, registration of people with AIDS, and the closing of sites where men gathered to have sex with other men—not to mention some political efforts to quarantine those with the disease—seemed suspiciously motivated by agendas other than disease prevention.[45]

These issues were nowhere better illustrated than in the debate around closing bathhouses. These establishments, a visible symbol of gay male sexual culture, became a flashpoint in the public health discussion about curbing the spread of the disease. In San Francisco, one of the cities hit hardest by AIDS, Mayor Dianne Feinstein called for closure of the bathhouses on the grounds that they were sites of anonymous male sexual encounters and thus were vectors in the spread of AIDS. The director of the San Francisco Department of Public Health (SFDPH), Mervyn Silverman, was not convinced this was the best course of action, however. Arguing that behaviors, not businesses, spread the disease, he saw the potential to use the bathhouses as a means of educating an at-risk population. By April 1984, 80 percent of San Franciscans polled by the *San Francisco Examiner* favored either closing the bathhouses or prohibiting sexual activity in them. On the other side of the debate, the local gay press vocally opposed any restrictions, and a significant portion of the gay community agreed, seeing the closures as a violation of civil liberties and an attack on small-business owners. In 1984, the SFDPH did close the bathhouses, and New York City and Los Angeles followed suit the following year. In the words of Josh Sides, "A more complete erasure of the urban landmarks of gay male liberation could not have been imagined."[46]

In light of how rapidly AIDS spread in the early years, the federal government's slow response was egregious. During the early 1980s, as the disease spread exponentially and gay men, intravenous drug users, sex workers, and hemophiliacs were dying in great numbers, the president of the United States, Ronald Reagan, remained silent on the topic. He did not publicly use the word "AIDS" until 1985 and did not deliver a substantive speech on the topic until 1987, *six years* after the disease had been identified. Similarly, adequate funding for research and education was not forthcoming in the federal budget. When compared to National Institutes of Health (NIH) expenditures for other newly identified diseases in the early 1980s, the agency's spending on AIDS was nearly negligible. In 1982, the NIH spent $36,100 per death from toxic shock syndrome, $34,841 per death from Legionnaire's disease, and $8,991 per death from AIDS.[47]

A turning point for the Reagan administration and the nation as a whole came in 1985, when movie actor Rock Hudson succumbed to AIDS. Hudson, a symbol of American heterosexual masculinity (although privately homosexual), brought the disease home to many Americans who had previously seen it as something that happened only to the marginal. President Reagan, a former Hollywood actor himself, mourned his longtime friend and finally began to speak on the topic.[48]

This historical record of governmental inaction has led many historians to view the government response to AIDS as an example of the rise of the religious right's influence on US politics. John D'Emilio and Estelle Freeman, for instance, consider the US military's implementation of mandatory testing for HIV (the virus that causes AIDS, discovered in 1983) and the congressional decree that all immigrants be tested for the virus and conclude that these policies "transformed the disease into a new weapon to preserve inequality." More recently, however, Jennifer Brier has argued that the federal government's response was more complicated than previously understood, with different constituencies within the administration advocating for different responses.[49]

In the midst of battling government indifference to the AIDS crisis, the LGBT community received another serious political blow. In 1986, the US Supreme Court issued a ruling in *Bowers v. Hardwick* upholding the legality of sodomy laws, including those that applied only to same-sex activity while permitting the same behavior between heterosexuals. In the majority opinion, Justice Byron White claimed the argument that sodomy was protected under the right to privacy "is, at best, facetious." Within the context of public inaction on the AIDS crisis and the rise of the religious right, the *Hardwick* decision seemed to many LGBT people to be a final indignity. In fact, historian Marc Stein has identified *Hardwick* as a key component in the radicalization of AIDS activism in the late 1980s.[50]

In the wake of continued government inaction and court prejudices, AIDS activism became increasingly visible and aggressive in the late 1980s. The crisis fostered political partnerships between gay men and lesbians, and significant numbers of lesbian and bisexual women joined the fight to stem the AIDS crisis even while continuing to support a separate all-women's culture.

Figure 6.3. The NAMES Project allows people to memorialize loved ones who have died of AIDS by creating a quilt square. Here, portions of the AIDS memorial quilt are displayed on the National Mall, date unknown.
Courtesy of The Library of Congress, LC-HS503-2457

Rising out of this more radical era, the AIDS Coalition to Unleash Power (ACT UP) became one of the most vocal and successful AIDS activist groups. Begun in 1987 in New York City, the organization soon developed affiliates throughout the nation's cities and universities. Known for its flamboyant protest style, ACT UP disrupted the seats of power—government agencies, high-profile meetings, drug companies, legislators' offices—and demanded that AIDS be given the attention it deserved. They staged regular "die-ins," in which inert bodies would lie across the ground to draw attention to the numbers of people dying due to government inaction. They disrupted numerous meetings and conferences on the disease, demanding that people with AIDS (PWAs) literally have a seat at the table of public health and research decision making. And they were instrumental in the US Food and Drug Administration's decision to expedite testing of treatments for terminal illness.[51]

ACT UP offered a broad view of the AIDS epidemic, linking it to other issues of inequality such as poverty, racism, and sexism. Members of the group fought for and achieved a broader definition of the disease from the CDC, one that better encompassed the common symptoms in women, children, and people of color. In addition to fighting for the release of effective treatments for AIDS, ACT UP members protested the treatments' exorbitant prices, which effectively made the drugs inaccessible to large numbers of PWAs. The group's "feisty politics" and sweeping analysis inspired later activists as well. Two other popular and flamboyant LGBT protest groups of the 1990s—Queer Nation and the Lesbian Avengers—displayed a style clearly inspired by ACT UP. Queer Nation's slogan, "We're Here, We're Queer, Get Used to It," summed up many LGBT people's aggravation at being among the religious right's key scapegoats.[52]

In addition to the frontline of AIDS, another battle raged in LGBT communities in the 1980s as lesbians sought to create a meaningful sexual culture defined by feminism. Known as the "lesbian sex wars," these debates pitted a sharp critique of sexism's damaging effect on modes of sexual expression against an embrace of the full range of lesbian sexual desire. On the one side were feminists (many of whom were lesbians) fighting against the sex and pornography industries while striving to raise awareness of sexual violence and obtain legal protections for its victims. These activists argued that such societal ills were the result of a sexist culture that emphasized male dominance and female submission. Many in this camp extended their critique further, criticizing consensual sexual practices they saw as replicating the larger power dynamics of a sexist society. The list of suspicious activities included sado-masochism (S/M), lesbian erotica and pornography, butch-femme role playing, and adherence to heterosexual standards of feminine beauty, such as wearing makeup and high heels.[53]

On the other side of the sex wars, queer women advocated for a wide range of consensual sexual expression. These activists often had connections with the S/M community; they saw the erotic potential of lesbian pornography and became founders of the feminist porn industry; and many resurrected a butch-femme aesthetic in lesbian coupling, which had largely gone underground with the rise of the feminist movement. They also tended to be more accepting of bisexuality and transgender identity, although Susan Stryker suggests that in this debate, trans was misunderstood as an erotic practice rather than an expression of gender identity.[54]

In light of the dramatic changes that the gay male sex culture was undergoing in the 1980s, these women saw their own embrace of what they called a "sex-positive" culture as an affirmation of all that made LGBT communities "queer." Josh Sides posits that the sex-positive lesbians in San Francisco—arguably the epicenter of sex radicalism in the 1980s and 1990s—engendered a resurgence of the 1960s sexual revolution, continuing its legacy to the very turn of the twenty-first century.[55]

The Turn of the Twenty-First Century

Perhaps more than any decade of US history, the 1990s were a roller-coaster ride with regard to LGBT civil rights and acceptance. LGBT people were increasingly visible to the wider society due to a combination of individual decisions to come out to family, friends, neighbors, and coworkers and an increasing representation in national media. In some ways, this increased visibility bred greater tolerance for a range of sexual and gender expressions. In other ways, such open diversity was seen as a threat and continued a backlash that had begun with the Briggs Initiative and "Save Our Children" campaigns of the late 1970s. LGBT

Figure 6.4. The anniversary of the Stonewall riots is celebrated every year in June with LGBT Pride events throughout the world. LGBT Pride Parade, San Francisco, 2012.
Courtesy of Library of Congress, LC-DIG-highsm-21340

activists achieved some major gains during the 1990s while also experiencing significant political losses.

Despite ongoing illness and increasingly strident antigay rhetoric from the religious right, a groundswell of LGBT individuals chose to live more openly, alerting the people in their lives that LGBT issues had a real and immediate impact to them. The change was striking. In 1985, more than half of Americans believed they did not know anyone who was gay or lesbian. Fifteen years later, that number had shrunk to 20 percent. The percentage of Americans who reported having a gay or lesbian family member rose from 9 percent in 1992 to 23 percent in 2000. This national coming-out party had the effect of increasing the number of straight allies to the LGBT struggle. Membership in Parents and Friends of Lesbians and Gays (PFLAG) swelled during the 1990s, and the group led the way for a host of gay-straight alliances that would eventually spring up in communities, high schools, and universities throughout the country.[56]

Within popular culture, there was a flowering of representations of gays, lesbians, bisexuals, and transgender people. In 1993, the feature film *Philadelphia* told the heart-wrenching story of a man dying from AIDS. While certainly not the first film to deal with the disease, *Philadelphia* starred A-list actors, including Tom Hanks and Denzel Washington, and earned Hanks his first Academy Award, for Best Actor. Other popular films of the decade portraying LGBT lives included *The Crying Game* (1992), *The Wedding Banquet* (1993), *Go Fish* (1994), *The Bird Cage* (1996), *In & Out* (1997), and *Boys Don't Cry* (1999). On television, increasing numbers of shows featured LGBT characters. Television's first same-sex wedding took place in 1994 on *Northern Exposure*, and *Spin City* featured an African American gay male character. Ellen DeGeneres created a media sensation when she and the title character of her hit sitcom *Ellen* came out the same month (April 1997), and a year later, in 1998, *Will & Grace* premiered and chronicled the friendship between a gay man and his best friend, a straight woman. Star musicians also began coming out publicly, including the singers k.d. lang in 1992 and Melissa Etheridge in 1993.[57]

By the mid-1990s, the landscape of AIDS had begun to change. Awareness within middle-class gay communities about prevention of HIV transmission eventually began to slow the spread of the disease among this part of the population, and the release in 1996 of the so-called AIDS cocktail, the first consistently effective treatment, meant that AIDS no longer had to be a terminal disease for those who could afford access to the drugs. These factors furthered a trend begun in the 1980s, where the epidemiology of AIDS intersected with global and national economic realities. The epidemic became a pandemic, ravaging the Global South and the poorest sectors of industrialized nations, and eventually the focus of AIDS activism shifted to fair and equitable access to medical treatment for all. As survival rates among queer men increased, other issues captured the attention of the mainstream LGBT movement, despite the fact that poor queers of color continued to struggle with high infection and mortality rates.[58]

The wider society became more conscious of the threat of violence marking the lives of LGBT people, although sadly, this awareness came at the price of young lives. Congress passed significant hate crimes legislation in 1990, 1994, and 1996 (when it renewed the 1990 act). Sexual orientation and gender expression were included in each of these laws, despite a right-wing effort to have sexual orientation removed from the 1996 renewal. These laws did not prevent crimes motivated by hate, however. In 1993, Brandon Teena, a transgender man in rural Nebraska, was raped and murdered when two men close to him discovered his transgender status, and public awareness of this crime spread in 1999 with the release of the feature film *Boys Don't Cry*, based on Teena's life and death. In 1998, the nation was shocked by the torture and murder of Matthew Shepard, an openly gay man in Wyoming. These two deaths are noteworthy because of the national attention they received, but we should also note that many other hate-motivated murders of LGBT people—particularly transgender people of color—still regularly occur but do not receive media attention.[59]

As with hate crimes, the campaign to allow gays and lesbians to serve in the US military is an example of the ambivalent progress LGBT communities experienced in the 1990s. Public awareness of the plights of homosexuals discharged from service increased due to a number of public cases, most notably those of Leonard Matlovich and Margarethe Cammermeyer. After twelve years of military service, Matlovich was deemed unfit for service and discharged from the US Air Force after coming out to his superiors in 1975. His case received national attention when he appeared on the cover of *Time* in September of that year, becoming the first openly gay man ever to do so. (Matlovich is also remembered for the poignant epitaph that appears on his tombstone: "When I was in the military, they gave me a medal for killing two men, and a discharge for loving one"—figure 6.2.) Fifteen years later, in 1992, the discharge of Cammermeyer, another Vietnam veteran decorated for her service as an army nurse, also captured national headlines. Colonel Cammermeyer was the highest-ranking person yet dismissed solely on the grounds of homosexuality, and her commanding officer cried while decommissioning her, alerting the world to a lack of consensus about the military ban. Unlike Matlovich, Cammermeyer was eventually reinstated upon appeal.[60]

By 1992, the year of Cammermeyer's discharge, public support of the military ban appeared to be weakening. Seventy-seven members of Congress joined with Patricia Schroeder in sponsoring a bill that would prohibit discrimination in the military based on sexual orientation, signaling substantial support, although it eventually died in committee. Bill Clinton won the presidential election on a platform that included an end to the ban. However, the actual demise of this policy proved far more complicated than originally expected. Although Clinton had the power to end the ban by executive order, he faced vocal opposition not only from political conservatives but from key members of his own party. Ultimately, caught between vocal advocates on both sides of the debate, Clinton agreed to a compromise he would later refer to as "this dumb-ass 'don't ask, don't tell' thing," which stated that gays and lesbians could serve in the military as long as they concealed their sexual identity. Although ostensibly an improvement over the previous policy, "Don't Ask, Don't Tell" (DADT) was enacted into law in 1993, which made it significantly more difficult to repeal than the previous ban, which had never been legislated. It also did little to actually protect gay and lesbian military personnel, *seventeen thousand* of whom were discharged for homosexuality during the seventeen years DADT was the law of the land. Congress eventually repealed the law in December 2010, after years of work by LGBT activists and the concerted efforts of lobbyists, the Barack Obama administration, and veterans of the Iraq and Afghanistan wars.[61]

At the state level, the religious right continued its efforts to legislate the view that homosexuality was an affront to American values. The 1992 elections brought the residents of both Oregon and Colorado the opportunity to vote on constitutional amendments outlawing any protection of LGBT civil rights by state, municipality, or school district. Oregon's Measure 9 called for the government (including public schools) to teach that homosexuality was "wrong, unnatural, and perverse."[62] Although that measure was defeated, in Oregon alone, twenty-seven local antigay ordinances were introduced in the next two years, and all but one became law.[63] In Colorado, voters in the 1992 election passed an amendment to the state constitution that prohibited LGBT protections, a resounding defeat for LGBT activists and LGBT Coloradans. The amendment stood for four years before the US Supreme Court ruled it unconstitutional in the landmark 1996 decision *Romer v. Evans*. In the majority opinion, Justice Anthony Kennedy declared, "If the constitutional conception of 'equal protection of the laws' means anything, it must at the very least mean that a bare . . . desire to harm a politically unpopular group cannot constitute a legitimate government interest."[64]

Same-sex marriage emerged as a third civil rights battleground in the 1990s. We have evidence of individual same-sex couples making vows to each other and describing their relationships as similar to marriage from various eras, and from the 1920s onward same-sex couples in Harlem sometimes held public ceremonies presided over by preachers. The Metropolitan Community Church, a Christian church begun in 1968 specifically for LGBT parishioners, performed approximately eighty-five thousand marriages or holy unions between its founding and 2003, when the first same-sex marriages became legal in the United States.[65]

However, the first organized efforts to have same-sex relationships *legally* recognized did not occur until 1970, when couples in Minnesota and Kentucky filed lawsuits after being denied marriage licenses. These suits argued that no law required that marriage be between a man and a woman. While the courts agreed that neither state law specifically defined marriage as heterosexual, they nevertheless ruled that this was marriage's intent. The courts' acknowledgment of the lack of clarity in the law prompted the first efforts to legally define marriage as a heterosexual institution. Maryland, Texas, and Colorado passed such laws in 1973, and twelve more states had followed by 1978.[66]

Despite these efforts by some gays and lesbians (and their opponents), legal recognition of same-sex relationships wasn't a priority for most gays and lesbians in the 1970s. AIDS changed that. In the face of an epidemic and the untimely deaths of so many young men, gays and lesbians began to see first-hand the vulnerability of their families without legal recognition. Men with AIDS, fired from their jobs for having a stigmatized disease or being presumed gay (actions legal in most states in the 1980s) or simply too sick to work any longer, lost their health insurance at a time when they desperately needed access to quality care. While this situation pointed to larger problems in the nation's social safety net—a situation many LGBT activists were well aware of—the fact remained that being able to access their partners' benefits would have helped many of those suffering. In a similar vein, the lack of hospital visitation rights, medical decision making, custody of the dead, or inheritance of the deceased's assets made a tragic situation infinitely more disempowering for gay couples facing AIDS. Even in cases where the deceased had a will naming his partner as heir, inheritance tax (waived for legal spouses) meant many of the assets did not reach the surviving partner.[67]

Lesbians, too, were becoming newly aware of the need to protect their families. The intersection of changing cultural norms and technology in the 1980s meant that lesbian couples could more easily than in past eras make the choice to have children together. Children had always been a part of many LGBT people's lives; as divorced parents joined this community, they often brought the children they were raising with them. But the 1980s saw increasing numbers of children born or adopted into established same-sex (primarily lesbian) families, and such developments required greater legal protections so that children would be safeguarded.[68]

The case of Sharon Kowalski also brought the vulnerability of same-sex relationships into sharp focus. Kowalski was severely disabled in a car accident in 1983, and her family of origin—who learned of her lesbianism only after the accident—refused to allow her partner, Karen Thompson, a voice in decision making about her care. A guardianship battle ensued. After Kowalski's father won full guardianship in 1985, he cut off all contact between his daughter and Thompson. The ruling was appealed, but not until 1991 did Thompson finally win the right to care for her partner. The case was a wake-up call for many in the LGBT community.[69]

LGBT activists began advocating for coverage of "domestic partners" in employment benefits, and a number of court cases were filed actively seeking the legal ability to marry someone of the same sex. In 1992, Lotus (a maker of software) became the first publicly traded company to extend domestic partner benefits to its employees, and a number of other companies and universities followed. In 1993, the Hawaii Supreme Court ruled that the state's ban on same-sex marriage might violate the state constitution's equal rights amendment (since women were prohibited from doing something—marry a woman—that men were allowed to do). The issue was sent back to trial court to determine whether there was a "compelling state interest" in maintaining the ban.[70]

Although this ruling did not result in the legalization of same-sex marriage in Hawaii, it raised enough concern for conservatives that a wave of legislation spread throughout the country explicitly barring recognition of same-sex relationships. According to D'Emilio and Freedman, "Between 1995 and 1998, a majority of state legislatures approved statutes to remove any ambiguity that marriage was only the union of a man and a woman."[71] In 1996, by an overwhelming majority, the US Congress passed—and President Clinton signed—the Defense of Marriage Act (DOMA), which defined marriage as between a man and a woman for the purposes of federal law and declared that states were not required to recognize same-sex marriages performed in any other state. By 2008, nearly thirty states had constitutional amendments banning same-sex marriage, and nearly forty had laws to the same effect.[72]

Yet, at the same time, small sections of the country were reevaluating the age-old equation of marriage with heterosexuality. In 2000, Vermont became the first state to offer legal recognition of same-sex relationships, though it fell short of legalizing same-sex marriage. Instead, it allowed gay and lesbian couples to enter into "civil unions," which provided the benefits afforded to marriages, without the name. In 2003, Massachusetts became the first state to provide equal recognition for heterosexual and homosexual unions when the Massachusetts Supreme Judicial Court ruled that the state's same-sex marriage ban was illegal and required the state to begin issuing marriage licenses to same-sex couples within six months. The deadline, May 17, 2004, also happened to be the fiftieth anniversary of *Brown v. Board of Education*.[73]

On February 12, 2004, just a few months after the Massachusetts ruling, before it took effect, Mayor Gavin Newsom announced that San Francisco would begin granting marriage licenses to same-sex couples. (Long-time lesbian activists Phyllis Lyon and Del Martin, who helped found the Daughters of Bilitis in 1952, received the honor of being the first couple married under the mayor's new directive. They had been partners for over fifty years.) In the words of the *Advocate*, "Within hours the news had spread citywide: Get to City Hall. The media flocked. So did the couples. In the rain, into the night, there they were: couples waiting in line for their turn to marry." A month later, the California Supreme Court ordered Newsom to stop the marriages while it deliberated on their legality, but in the twenty-nine days same-sex marriage was permitted in San Francisco, over four thousand same-sex couples wed. Other municipalities—Sandoval County, New Mexico, New Paltz, New York, and Multnomah County, Oregon (in which Portland is located)—followed suit by also granting same-sex marriage licenses, in strong support of Mayor Newsom's actions.[74]

The same year that Massachusetts legalized same-sex marriage (2003), the US Supreme Court issued a ruling in *Lawrence v. Texas* declaring state sodomy laws unconstitutional. Although states had slowly been repealing sodomy laws since the 1960s, at the time of the *Lawrence* decision, thirteen states still had them on the books (and in four of these states—Kansas, Missouri, Oklahoma, and Texas—the laws applied only to same-sex behavior).

Seventeen years earlier, the court had affirmed the legitimacy of these laws in *Bowers v. Hardwick*, but with *Lawrence* the court stated, "*Bowers* was not correct when it was decided, and it is not correct today."[75] Once again, as with *Romer v. Evans*, Justice Kennedy wrote the majority opinion; he wrote, "The petitioners are entitled to respect for their private lives. The State cannot demean their existence or control their destiny by making their private sexual conduct a crime."[76]

The tide of public opinion regarding homosexuality was beginning to turn, although some regions and subcultures were more accepting than others and this acceptance often did not extend to gender crossing. In many high schools throughout the United States, students with alternative sexuality or gender expression faced particularly difficult social environments. Throughout the first decade of the twenty-first century, concern grew about the bullying LGBT students faced and its role in many teen suicides. In 2010, author Dan Savage and his partner Terry Miller launched the *It Gets Better* campaign, which includes a book, a website, and a series of videos aimed at giving queer youth assurance that they can live happy lives. President Barack Obama lent his support to the effort a month after its inception by starring in one of the videos.[77]

In general, the Obama administration acted supportively with regard to LGBT issues. In the first hundred days of his 2008 term, the president appointed thirty-five openly gay/lesbian/bisexual people to federal posts, including nine to positions requiring Senate approval, which was a first. In early 2010, he appointed Amanda Simpson to the US Commerce Department; she is believed to be the first-ever transgender person to receive a presidential appointment. President Obama signed two key pieces of legislation on LGBT issues: the Hate Crimes Prevention Act of 2009 and the repeal of Don't Ask, Don't Tell in 2010. In addition, the Obama administration required hospitals receiving Medicare and Medicaid funding to grant visitation rights and honor medical decision-making authority within LGBT families, added gender identity to the federal government's equal employment opportunity policy, and stopped defending DOMA in federal courts.[78] And in his second inaugural address in January 2013, President Obama included special mention of LGBT issues when he said:

> We, the people, declare today that the most evident of truths—that all of us are created equal—is the star that guides us still; just as it guided our forebears through Seneca Falls, and Selma, and Stonewall. . . . Our journey is not complete until our gay brothers and sisters are treated like anyone else under the law—for if we are truly created equal, then surely the love we commit to one another must be equal as well.[79]

A sympathetic executive branch has certainly assisted with the extension of LGBT protections, but as is common with civil rights issues, the judiciary branch has also been a leader in safeguarding equal protection of LGBT people in the United States. This was demonstrated in June 2013, when the Supreme Court ruled in *United States v. Windsor* that the federal government's refusal to recognize same-sex marriages was unconstitutional. The case was brought by Edith Windsor, who was forced to pay over $360,000 in federal inheritance tax upon the death of her female spouse, whom she had legally married in the state of New York. Had the federal government recognized Windsor's marriage, she would have been

Figure 6.5. In the past twenty-five years, trans people have become an increasingly visible part of the LGBT community. Here, Chaz Bono, a transgender activist, speaks at Tulane University.
Courtesy of Tulane University Public Relations

exempt from these taxes. By ruling as it did, the Supreme Court dismantled a significant section of the Defense of Marriage Act (1996) while leaving in place DOMA's stipulation that states did not have to recognize same-sex marriages performed in other states.[80]

The *Windsor* decision was immediately hailed by LGBT activists as a watershed victory—and it certainly did set into motion a sweeping set of changes—but the victory was diluted by other decisions made by the court in the same session. The same day as the *Windsor* decision, the court opted not to rule on a case (*Hollingsworth v. Perry*) concerning the legality of California's marriage ban called Proposition 8. While the immediate impact of this decision was that a lower court ruling throwing out the ban remained in effect, making same-sex marriage legal in California, ultimately the court sidestepped a decision on the constitutionality of state bans on same-sex marriage. In addition, the day before the *Windsor* decision, in *Shelby County, Alabama v. Holder*, the court chose to dismantle a key section of the Voting Rights Act. Many progressives feared that this ruling would reopen the door to discrimination against African Americans at the voting booth. Thus, to those committed to the civil rights of all citizens, June 2013 brought losses as well as gains.[81]

Nearly fifty years have passed since LGBT activists took to the streets to demand equal protection under the law. Those decades have witnessed drastic change. Gay liberation's critique of society's morals and institutions has given way to a movement that is more focused on obtaining the benefits of full participation in that larger society. The AIDS epidemic continues to rage, though it has shifted from being a "gay disease" to a world pandemic, raising more questions about unequal access to healthcare than about God's punishment of "sexual perverts." At this point, multiple generations of LGBT people have chosen to live openly, leading to a growing cultural familiarity that is credited with changing popular opinion concerning queer issues. The pace of change has accelerated even more in recent years. With LGBT issues a fundamental component of our national conversation, the need for historic context becomes even greater. Museums can play an important role in placing current events into larger historical perspective.

Notes

1. Gail Dubrow, "Deviant History, Defiant Heritage," *Friends of 1800*, 2002, http://www.friendsof1800.org/VIEWPOINT/dubrow.html; Division of Cultural Resources, Partnerships, and Science, "Lesbian, Bisexual, Gay and Transgender Heritage Intiative," *National Park Service*, April 16, 2014, http://www.nps.gov/heritageinitiatives/LGBThistory/. See also Gail Dubrow, "Blazing Trails with Pink Triangles and Rainbow Flags: Improving the Presentation and Interpretation of Gay and Lesbian Heritage," in *Restoring Women's History through Historic Preservation*, ed. Jennifer B. Goodman and Gail Dubrow (Baltimore: Johns Hopkins University Press, 2003), 281–300.
2. Michael Bronski, *A Queer History of the United States* (Boston: Beacon, 2011), 210.
3. Todd Gitlin, *The Sixties: Years of Hope, Days of Rage*, rev. trade ed. (New York: Bantam, 1993), 192; Molly McGarry and Fred Wasserman, *Becoming Visible: An Illustrated History of Lesbian and Gay Life in Twentieth-Century America* (New York: Penguin Studio, 1998), 4–10. By 1965, over half of high school graduates—57.3 percent of males and 45.3 percent of females—were entering college.
4. John D'Emilio and Estelle B. Freedman, *Intimate Matters: A History of Sexuality in America*, 3rd ed. (Chicago: University of Chicago Press, 2012), 302–8, 341; Bronski, *A Queer History of the United States*, 206–7; Marc Stein, *Sexual Injustice: Supreme Court Decisions from Griswold to Roe* (Chapel Hill: University of North Carolina Press, 2010), 27–34.
5. Bronski, *A Queer History of the United States*, 205–8, quotation from 207.
6. Ibid., 206.
7. Marc Stein, *Rethinking the Gay and Lesbian Movement* (New York: Routledge, 2012), 70.
8. Quoted in David Carter, *Stonewall: The Riots That Sparked the Gay Revolution* (New York: St. Martin's, 2004), 119. See also Bronski, *A Queer History of the United States*, 208–9; Ian Lekus, "The Long Sixties," *OAH Magazine of History* 20, no. 2 (March 1, 2006): 32–38.
9. Stein, *Rethinking the Gay and Lesbian Movement*, 66, 71; Marc Stein, *City of Sisterly and Brotherly Loves: Lesbian and Gay Philadelphia, 1945–1972* (Philadelphia: Temple University Press, 2004), 231–40; Leila J. Rupp, *A Desired Past: A Short History of Same-Sex Love in America* (Chicago: University of Chicago Press, 1999), 166–67.
10. Josh Sides, *Erotic City: Sexual Revolutions and the Making of Modern San Francisco* (New York: Oxford University Press, 2009), 90, full discussion 90–97. See also Stein, *Rethinking the Gay and Lesbian Movement*, 71; Carter, *Stonewall*, 117–18.
11. Quoted in Sides, *Erotic City*, 92.
12. Ibid., 97–101; Carter, *Stonewall*, 55–66; Susan Stryker, *Transgender History* (Berkeley: Seal, 2008), 65–70; Joey Plaster, "Imagined Conversations and Activist Lineages," *Radical History Review*, no. 113 (Spring 2012): 99–109.

13. Sides, *Erotic City*, 97–101.
14. Stryker, *Transgender History*, 63–75, quotation from 72; Susan Stryker, "Transgender History, Homonormativity, and Disciplinarity," *Radical History Review*, no. 100 (Winter 2008): 144–57.
15. McGarry and Wasserman, *Becoming Visible*, 4–13; D'Emilio and Freedman, *Intimate Matters*, 318–19; David Eisenbach, *Gay Power: An American Revolution* (New York: Carroll & Graf, 2006), 84–100; Martin B. Duberman, *Stonewall* (New York: Plume, 1994); Carter, *Stonewall*.
16. Carter, *Stonewall*, 94.
17. Bronski, *A Queer History of the United States*, 209; McGarry and Wasserman, *Becoming Visible*, 83–85; Eisenbach, *Gay Power*, 113; Stein, *Rethinking the Gay and Lesbian Movement*, 84–90. The phrase "come out" was common before the 1970s, but before this decade, it more commonly referred to coming out into gay society as opposed to revealing one's identity to the larger straight world.
18. Bronski, *A Queer History of the United States*, 210.
19. Ibid., 210–12; Stein, *Rethinking the Gay and Lesbian Movement*, 81–91; Carter, *Stonewall*, 223–32.
20. McGarry and Wasserman, *Becoming Visible*, 16–17; Eisenbach, *Gay Power*, 114–15; Stein, *Rethinking the Gay and Lesbian Movement*, 111–14.
21. Michael McElderry, *Finding Aid, Frank Kameny Papers* (Washington, DC: Library of Congress, 2008), 4, http://lcweb2.loc.gov/service/mss/eadxmlmss/eadpdfmss/2009/ms009068.pdf.
22. Eisenbach, *Gay Power*, 240–51; Vicki Lynn Eaklor, *Queer America: A GLBT History of the 20th Century* (Westport, CT: Greenwood, 2008), 153; Jennifer Terry, *An American Obsession: Science, Medicine, and Homosexuality in Modern Society* (Chicago: University of Chicago Press, 1999), 367–73.
23. Stryker, *Transgender History*, 92–101, 13–16; Terry, *An American Obsession*, 372–73; Camille Beredjick, "DSM Replaces Gender Identity Disorder with Gender Dysphoria," *Advocate.com*, July 23, 2012, http://www.advocate.com/politics/transgender/2012/07/23/dsm-replaces-gender-identity-disorder-gender-dysphoria.
24. Carter, *Stonewall*, 238–43; Eisenbach, *Gay Power*, 104–7.
25. Bronski, *A Queer History of the United States*, 212–13; Stein, *Rethinking the Gay and Lesbian Movement*, 91–92; Lillian Faderman, *Odd Girls and Twilight Lovers: A History of Lesbian Life in Twentieth-Century America* (New York: Columbia University Press, 1991), 204–9.
26. Wini Breines, "What's Love Got to Do with It? White Women, Black Women, and Feminism in the Movement Years," *Signs: Journal of Women in Culture & Society* 27, no. 4 (Summer 2002): 1095.
27. Faderman, *Odd Girls and Twilight Lovers*, 215–45; Alice Echols, *Daring to Be Bad: Radical Feminism in America, 1967–1975* (Minneapolis: University of Minnesota Press, 1989), 210–41.
28. Marc Stein argues for a different organization in Stein, *Rethinking the Gay and Lesbian Movement*, 79–114.
29. Rupp, *Desired Past*, 189–94; Eaklor, *Queer America*, 131–48; Anne Enke, *Finding the Movement: Sexuality, Contested Space, and Feminist Activism* (Durham, NC: Duke University Press, 2007), 217–51.
30. Faderman, *Odd Girls and Twilight Lovers*, 232–34; Eaklor, *Queer America*, 185; George Chauncey, *Why Marriage? The History Shaping Today's Debate over Gay Equality* (New York: Basic, 2004), 93–94.
31. Stryker, *Transgender History*, 95–111.

32. Emanuella Grinberg, "Wisconsin's Tammy Baldwin Is First Openly Gay Person Elected to Senate," *CNN*, accessed April 10, 2014, http://www.cnn.com/2012/11/07/politics/wisconsin-tammy-baldwin-senate/index.html; Eaklor, *Queer America*, 153–54, 213. In addition, Barbara Jordan, an African American woman, was elected to represent Texas in 1972. Jordan spent thirty years in close partnership with another woman, although she never claimed a queer identity.
33. "A Queer Timeline for Michigan/Ann Arbor/University of Michigan" (Bentley Library, University of Michigan, 2013), http://bentley.umich.edu/exhibits/queer/timeline.pdf; Eaklor, *Queer America*, 154.
34. Eaklor, *Queer America*, 155–56; Stein, *Rethinking the Gay and Lesbian Movement*, 126–38.
35. Sides, *Erotic City*, 155–65; Eaklor, *Queer America*, 154–55, 170–71.
36. Sides, *Erotic City*, 164–65; Eaklor, *Queer America*, 171; Rupp, *Desired Past*, 179; Stein, *Rethinking the Gay and Lesbian Movement*, 141; Susan Stryker, *Gay by the Bay: A History of Queer Culture in the San Francisco Bay Area* (San Francisco: Chronicle, 1996), 78–81.
37. D'Emilio and Freedman, *Intimate Matters*, 346–47.
38. Ibid.
39. Ibid., 345–47, quotation from 345.
40. Bronski, *A Queer History of the United States*, 224; Eisenbach, *Gay Power*, 291–92.
41. D'Emilio and Freedman, *Intimate Matters*, 354.
42. Ibid.; Bronski, *A Queer History of the United States*, 228.
43. Bronski, *A Queer History of the United States*, 224–26; Stein, *Rethinking the Gay and Lesbian Movement*, 143–44; Victoria Angela Harden, *AIDS at 30: A History* (Washington, DC: Potomac, 2012), 6–7.
44. Stein, *Rethinking the Gay and Lesbian Movement*, 155–56; Eisenbach, *Gay Power*, 292–93; Jennifer Brier, *Infectious Ideas: U.S. Political Responses to the AIDS Crisis* (Chapel Hill: University of North Carolina Press, 2009), 45–77; Ian K. Lekus, "Health Care, the AIDS Crisis, and the Politics of Community: The North Carolina Lesbian and Gay Health Project, 1982–1996," in *Modern American Queer History*, ed. Allida Mae Black (Philadelphia: Temple University Press, 2001), 227–52.
45. Eaklor, *Queer America*, 179–80; Terry, *An American Obsession*, 389–93; Sides, *Erotic City*, 175–91; Stryker, *Gay by the Bay*, 95.
46. Harden, *AIDS at 30*, 109–10; Sides, *Erotic City*, 178–81; statistic from 178–79; quotation from 180.
47. Stein, *Rethinking the Gay and Lesbian Movement*, 144–48; Harden, *AIDS at 30*, 98–106. Statistic from Eisenbach, *Gay Power*, 292.
48. Harden, *AIDS at 30*, 104–5.
49. D'Emilio and Freedman, *Intimate Matters*, 354–55; Brier, *Infectious Ideas*, 78–121.
50. McGarry and Wasserman, *Becoming Visible*, 27–29; Joyce Murdoch and Deb Price, *Courting Justice: Gay Men and Lesbians v. the Supreme Court* (New York: Basic, 2001), 317; David A. J. Richards, *The Sodomy Cases: Bowers v. Hardwick and Lawrence v. Texas* (Lawrence: University Press of Kansas, 2009), 72–107; Stein, *Rethinking the Gay and Lesbian Movement*, 157.
51. Brier, *Infectious Ideas*, 156–68; Stein, *Rethinking the Gay and Lesbian Movement*, 157–63.
52. Stein, *Rethinking the Gay and Lesbian Movement*, 163, 184; Brier, *Infectious Ideas*, 168–79; quotation from Chauncey, *Why Marriage?*, 44.

53. Rupp, *Desired Past*, 185–89; Faderman, *Odd Girls and Twilight Lovers*, 246–70; Claire Bond Potter, "Taking Back Times Square," *Radical History Review*, no. 113 (Spring 2012): 67–80.
54. Rupp, *Desired Past*, 185–89; Faderman, *Odd Girls and Twilight Lovers*, 246–70; Sides, *Erotic City*, 216–25; Stryker, *Transgender History*, 129–31.
55. Sides, *Erotic City*, 216–25.
56. Chauncey, *Why Marriage?*, 47–48; D'Emilio and Freedman, *Intimate Matters*, 373–74.
57. Chauncey, *Why Marriage?*, 47–48.
58. Brier, *Infectious Ideas*, 187–89; Harden, *AIDS at 30*, 149–51, 213–32; Stryker, *Transgender History*, 113–14.
59. Eaklor, *Queer America*, 216–17; Stein, *Rethinking the Gay and Lesbian Movement*, 172; Chauncey, *Why Marriage?*, 56; Carly S. Woods, Joshua P. Ewalt, and Sara J. Baker, "A Matter of Regionalism: Remembering Brandon Teena and Willa Cather at the Nebraska History Museum," *Quarterly Journal of Speech* 99, no. 3 (2013): 341–63.
60. Eaklor, *Queer America*, 199–202; Beth Bailey, "The Politics of Dancing: 'Don't Ask, Don't Tell' and the Role of Moral Claims," *Journal of Policy History* 25, no. 1 (January 2013): 96.
61. Bailey, "The Politics of Dancing," 96–105, quotation from 105; Nathaniel Frank, "The President's Pleasant Surprise: How LGBT Advocates Ended Don't Ask, Don't Tell," in "Special Issue on Evolution of Government Policy toward Homosexuality in the U.S. Military," *Journal of Homosexuality* 60, no. 2–3 (February 2013): 159–213.
62. Chauncey, *Why Marriage?*, 51.
63. Ibid., 46.
64. Murdoch and Price, *Courting Justice*, 451–82, quotation from 476.
65. Chauncey, *Why Marriage?*, 88–91.
66. Ibid., 89–91.
67. Ibid., 96–105.
68. Ibid., 105–11; D'Emilio and Freedman, *Intimate Matters*, 374.
69. Chauncey, *Why Marriage?*, 111–13; Stein, *Rethinking the Gay and Lesbian Movement*, 169.
70. Chauncey, *Why Marriage?*, 116–25.
71. D'Emilio and Freedman, *Intimate Matters*, 366.
72. Chauncey, *Why Marriage?*, 125–27; D'Emilio and Freedman, *Intimate Matters*, 365–66, statistic from 366.
73. Chauncey, *Why Marriage?*, 127–35.
74. Ibid., 137–38; Sue Rochman, "The Marrying Man," *Advocate*, April 8, 2008, 40–45.
75. Eaklor, *Queer America*, 239–40, quotations from 239 and 239–40; Stein, *Rethinking the Gay and Lesbian Movement*, 191–92.
76. Eaklor, *Queer America*, 239–40; Stein, *Rethinking the Gay and Lesbian Movement*, 191–92.
77. "It Gets Better Project | Give Hope to LGBT Youth," *It Gets Better*, accessed April 22, 2014, http://www.itgetsbetter.org/; "President Obama: It Gets Better," YouTube video, 3:07, posted by "The White House," October 21, 2010, http://www.youtube.com/watch?v=geyAFbSDPVk&feature=youtube_gdata_player.
78. Jen Colletta, "Obama's 100-Day Gay Report Card," *Philadelphia Gay News*, May 2009, 1–17; Timothy Patrick McCarthy, "Sizing Up Obama's GLBT Record," *Gay & Lesbian Review Worldwide*, October 9, 2012, 16–17; Lisa Keen, "A Year in Review," *Between the Lines*, January 2, 2014, 6–8; Russell Goldman, "First Transgender Presidential Appointee Fears Being Labeled 'Token,'" *ABC News*, January 5, 2010, http://abcnews.go.com/Politics/amanda-simpson-transgender

-presidential-appointee-begins-work-commerce/story?id=9477161; Toni Newman, "President Barack Obama and Transgender Rights: The Real Deal," *Huffington Post*, April 12, 2012, http://www.huffingtonpost.com/toni-newman/obama-transgender-rights_b_1420542.html.
79. Keen, "A Year in Review," 6.
80. Adam Liptak, "Justices Extend Benefits to Gay Couples; Allow Same-Sex Marriages in California," *New York Times*, June 27, 2013, final edition; Keen, "A Year in Review"; Meg Wesling, "The Unequal Promise of Marriage Equality," *American Quarterly* 66, no. 1 (March 2014): 171–79.
81. Liptak, "Justices Extend Benefits"; Wesling, "The Unequal Promise of Marriage Equality."

CHAPTER 7

History Coda
What a Strange Year It's Been

IN HIS DISSENTING opinion in *United States v. Windsor*, Justice Antonin Scalia issued what he viewed as a grave prediction. "As far as this Court is concerned, no one should be fooled," he wrote, "it is just a matter of listening and waiting for the other shoe.... The majority arms well every challenger to a state law restricting marriage to its traditional definition."[1] In the year since the *Windsor* decision, Scalia's words have proved prescient. The ruling set into motion an unprecedented series of lower court decisions and actions by state legislatures with regard to same-sex marriage in the United States.

In the first twelve months following the *Windsor* ruling, same-sex marriage bans in thirteen states (Arkansas, Idaho, Indiana, Kentucky, Michigan, Oklahoma, Oregon, Pennsylvania, Tennessee, Texas, Utah, Virginia, and Wisconsin) were ruled illegal in full or in part by federal courts. (At the time of this writing, June 2014, all but two of these decisions—Oregon and Pennsylvania—were being appealed.) All other states that ban same-sex marriage are currently involved in litigation regarding their stance.[2]

As of early June 2014, same-sex marriage was legal in eighteen states (up from nine in March 2013) plus the District of Columbia, while the legality of same-sex marriage in Wisconsin was in flux and two additional states recognized civil unions or domestic partnerships. By late March 2014—nine months after the *Windsor* ruling—an estimated 57 percent of the LGBT population of the United States lived in states that provided some form of legal recognition to same-sex partnerships.[3]

In addition to the *Windsor* decision turning the same-sex marriage issue into a powder keg, it also required the overhaul of the more than 1,100 federal policies that relate to marriage in the United States. Just a few days after the ruling, US Immigration and Citizenship Services granted the first permanent resident visa (or green card) to an immigrant, Traian Popov from Bulgaria, on the grounds of his same-sex marriage to a US citizen. Within months of the *Windsor* decision, the Internal Revenue Service issued a statement that legally married same-sex couples could file joint federal tax returns. In states that did not recognize same-sex marriage, however, each government was allowed to set its own policy with regard to state tax returns. The result, in the words of the *Atlantic*, was "Total Chaos for Same-Sex

Couples," many of whom had to essentially complete their tax returns twice to reflect their inconsistent treatment under various jurisdictions. In February 2014, Attorney General Eric Holder announced that same-sex marriages would be recognized in the federal criminal justice system, with implications for bankruptcy filings, prison visitation rights, and the ability for same-sex spouses to refuse to testify against their partners.[4]

LGBT topics seemed to dominate the news in 2013 and 2014. Soon after the *Windsor* decision, LGBT activists renewed their calls for an executive order from President Obama, prohibiting federal contractors from discriminating on the basis of sexual orientation (a request he had not fulfilled as of spring 2014). In November 2013 the Senate passed the Employment Non-Discrimination Act (ENDA), which banned employment discrimination on the basis of sexual orientation and gender identity, a huge win for transgender people who have been consistently left out of nondiscrimination policies. However, as of spring 2014, the House of Representatives had so far refused to vote on the bill.[5]

In the world of popular culture, numerous high-profile celebrities came out. These included the first (former) contestant in the Miss America pageant to publicly come out, Miss Kentucky 2010, Djaun Trent; the first openly queer *American Idol* participant, M. K. Nobilette; and Sony Music CEO Clive Davis, who discussed his bisexuality in his 2013 autobiography. Actors Jodie Foster, Wentworth Miller, Maria Bello, and Ellen Page have also come out in the last year and a half. The front person for the pop group *Neon Trees*, Tyler Green, recently announced via Twitter, "I am a happy and healthy Mormon Gay Pop Star!"

Figure 7.1. Since the *Windsor* decision, same-sex marriage has become legal in an increasing number of states. San Francisco Pride Parade, 2013.
Courtesy of Quinn Dombroski

And the world of male sports—long stereotyped for its homophobia and hypermasculinity—faced its own coming-out party of sorts. Olympic medal-winning British diver Tom Daley, WWE wrestler Darren Young, and college football star and NFL draftee Michael Sam all publicly declared their LGBT identities.

It will be a few decades before these recent events become the domain of historians, who, with the benefit of emotional and chronological distance, can assess the long-lasting impact and historical significance of these developments. Yet it seems fair to predict that *Windsor* will be remembered as a pivotal turning point in the LGBT history of the United States. The full implications of that turn, however, still lie ahead.

Notes

1. Antonin Scalia, *United States v. Windsor, Dissenting Opinion*, 2013, 24, http://www.supremecourt.gov/opinions/12pdf/12-307_6j37.pdf.
2. "Marriage Equality Impact Map," *Out & About Nashville*, April 2014, 11; Joseph Brownell, "We've Come a Long Way: Marriage Equality in Less Than a Year," *Out & About Nashville*, May 25, 2014, http://www.outandaboutnashville.com/story/weve-come-long-way-marriage-equality-less; Scott Neuman, "N. Dakota's Gay-Marriage Law Challenged; Wisc. Ban Struck Down," *The Two-Way* (blog), *NPR.org*, June 6, 2014, http://www.npr.org/blogs/thetwo-way/2014/06/06/319548157/north-dakotas-gay-marriage-ban-challenged-in-federal-court.
3. "Marriage Equality Impact Map"; Jen Colletta, "SCOTUS Ruling Caps a Momentous Marriage Year," *Philadelphia Gay News*, March 7, 2014, 15.
4. Matt Apuzzo, "U.S. to Give Legal Benefits to Same-Sex Marriages," *New York Times*, February 10, 2014; Emma Green, "This Tax Season: Total Chaos for Same-Sex Couples," *Atlantic.com*, April 2, 2014, http://www.theatlantic.com/business/archive/2014/04/this-tax-season-total-chaos-for-same-sex-couples/360033/; Julia Preston, "Green Card Is Approved for Gay Men in Florida," *New York Times*, July 1, 2013, final edition.
5. Ed O'Keefe, "ENDA, Explained," *The Fix* (blog), *Washington Post*, November 4, 2013, http://www.washingtonpost.com/blogs/the-fix/wp/2013/11/04/what-is-the-employment-non-discrimination-act-enda/; Ed O'Keefe, "Senate Votes to Ban Discrimination against Gay and Transgender Workers," *Washington Post*, November 7, 2013, http://www.washingtonpost.com/politics/senate-set-to-approve-gay-rights-bill/2013/11/07/05717e4a-47c1-11e3-a196-3544a03c2351_story.html; Daniel Reynolds, "John Boehner: 'No Way' ENDA Will Pass This Year," *Advocate.com*, January 30, 2014, accessed April 22, 2014, http://www.advocate.com/politics/politicians/2014/01/30/john-boehner-no-way-enda-will-pass-year.

PART III

INTERPRETING LGBT HISTORY

CHAPTER 8

Trends in LGBT Historical Interpretation

THE PRECEDING chapters provided a broad historical overview of same-sex love and desire in the United States over the past four hundred years or so, but the true stories lie in the details. Every town has its own contribution to make to the larger historical narrative. Every historical actor has experiences that coincide with and diverge from larger cultural trends. Because of this, every organizational attempt to interpret these pasts will follow its own unique paths. Similarly, understanding the historical narrative is only part of the task of interpreting the past. In this section, we turn to the present day to explore the experiences and recommendations of cultural institutions that have begun interpreting LGBT history.

Same-sex love and desire is a relatively new topic for history museums, and there is not yet a substantial body of literature to serve as a guidepost.[1] For this reason, the chapters in this part chronicle the experiences of some relevant organizations and draw from that background to highlight common issues and lessons learned. The next three chapters provide individual case studies of museums and historic sites that have already ventured into interpreting the queer past. Written by museum professionals with firsthand knowledge of the programs they write about, the case studies offer a glimpse into the process and potential—and potential challenges—of interpreting LGBT history. The examples cover a range of organizational structures and interpretive methods. Jill Austin and Jennifer Brier describe the interpersonal and intellectual process by which the Chicago History Museum (CHM) developed its *Out in Chicago* exhibit, which ran from 2011 to 2012. Kenneth C. Turino details a range of interpretive choices made by Historic New England in its various historic house museums. Three Historic New England houses have associations with same-sex love, and each takes a different approach to the topic. Finally, Kyle Parsons and Stewart Van Cleve explore the results of a joint effort between the Minnesota Historical Society (MNHS) and the Special Collections Library of the University of Minnesota to expose local high school students to college preparatory skills using the lens of LGBT history. Theirs is a particularly exciting endeavor, considering the paucity of LGBT interpretive programming aimed specifically at youth.[2]

In selecting examples to use as case studies, I intentionally chose to focus on organizations outside of the coastal troika of San Francisco, New York City, and Los Angeles. To be sure, innovative work is coming out of those locations. San Francisco is home to the GLBT History Museum and the Queer Ancestors Project.[3] New York City boasts the Pop-Up Museum of Queer History, the Museum of Sex, and the Leslie Lohman Museum of Gay and Lesbian Art.[4] And Los Angeles offers the ONE Archives Gallery and Museum and the *Out West* series, curated by Gregory Hinton, at the Autry National Center of the American West.[5] However, the conditions in those cities—with their histories of cultural innovation and their large and often well-positioned LGBT communities—ran the risk of making these examples seem atypical to readers. Instead, I aimed for organizations with missions far broader than simply interpreting LGBT history, located in less obvious geographic locations. With this choice, I hope to make the point that LGBT historical interpretation is a feasible endeavor in organizations of varying sizes and locations. My intention is also to provide more representative examples for readers to explore.

In addition to the three case studies, I incorporate additional real-world examples in the final two chapters of this part. There I suggest some questions to consider in the course of planning interpretive efforts in LGBT history and encapsulate advice garnered from the case studies as well as the reflections of numerous other professionals who have worked on this topic. These frontline lessons can provide a starting point from which your own organization's work can begin. Before moving on to specific experiences, however, I first offer a few observations about the current trends in LGBT historical interpretation generally. These comments draw on extensive research but do not rely strictly on numeric data.[6]

Current Trends in LGBT Historical Interpretation

The longest tradition of exploring queer realities within a museum setting lies with the world of visual art. As a happy result, art museums have produced a small but significant volume of writings on issues related to LGBT interpretation.[7] Such literature is sometimes more evocative than directly applicable, however. Art criticism is by its nature more speculative than historical interpretation; the objects being presented are often more intentionally provocative;[8] and because historical specificity is not its primary objective, art interpretation tends to be more liberal in its use of modern concepts to describe past motivations. Nevertheless, relevant insights are available when including the experiences of museums other than those with an exclusively historical mission.

Perhaps because of the work of art museums—and artists—in interpreting sexual identities, many organizations are interpreting the history of same-sex love and desire through more performative or artistic means. For instance, the Stonewall National Museum and Archives, based in Ft. Lauderdale, Florida, has a mission to "promote understanding through preserving and sharing the proud culture of [LGBT] people and their significant role in American society." Despite the historical reference in its name and its extensive collection of primary documents, Stonewall does not have a specifically historical mission and, indeed, a significant number of its exhibits and programs pertain to creative expressions of LGBT lives.[9] Similarly, the John Q Collective, based in Atlanta, envisions itself as an "idea and art

Figure 8.1. Members of the John Q Collective dressed in police uniforms and handcuffs for their 2011 event, *Policing Ourselves,* which referenced an unlawful 2009 police raid on the Eagle, an Atlanta leather bar.
Courtesy of the John Q Collective

collective." Drawing on primary sources and oral histories related to Atlanta's LGBT communities, John Q creates "discursive memorials" throughout the city, inviting participants to engage with the past in creative ways. The Pop-Up Museum of Queer History and the artist-in-residence program of the GLBT History Museum are other examples of LGBT historical interpretation harnessing the power of art to deliver its message.[10]

With regard to historical organizations, archives have tended to present LGBT history more commonly than museums and historic sites. Exhibits of two-dimensional objects are generally less expensive to produce; exhibit spaces at archives are often quite a bit smaller than museum galleries, and archives usually change their exhibits more frequently than museums, allowing for a greater range of topics to be explored. It is worth noting that the New York Public Library was among the first major institutions in the United States to present an exhibit on LGBT history (*Becoming Visible*, 1994), and this was followed two years later by an exhibit at the Boston Public Library, organized by the History Project (*Public Faces/ Private Lives: Boston's Lesbian and Gay History*, 1996). At the Atlanta History Center (AHC), a staff archivist, Wesley Chenault, curated the exhibit *Unspoken Past: Atlanta's Lesbian and Gay History, 1940–1970* (2005), which ran in the AHC's Kenan Research Center exhibit space. Also, the GLBT History Museum in San Francisco, The ONE Archives Gallery and Museum in Los Angeles, the Leather Archives and Museum in Chicago, and the Stonewall National Museum in southern Florida all began as auxiliaries to archival collections.[11]

Possibly stemming from the leadership that archives and libraries have shown in collecting and interpreting LGBT history, programming in this area also seems to incorporate more two-dimensional items than the average museum exhibit. Of the projects profiled in the case studies, both the Chicago History Museum and the Minnesota Historical Society turned to archival collections to accomplish their interpretive goals.[12] Oral histories are also a common element in exhibits on LGBT history. This is not particularly surprising; in order to incorporate multimedia elements, exhibits of all kinds are using more interview material. Likewise, oral history has also been a long-standing cornerstone in the study of the queer past, due to the relative lack of written and material evidence.[13] A bit more surprising is the lack of three-dimensional objects relating to queer history that are available in museum collections. The reasons for this are probably quite numerous, but I point out four issues that have significantly contributed to this circumstance: cataloging issues; questions of what makes an object queer; the sexual content of some objects; and the need for trust building.

Perhaps the simplest explanation for the difficulty of finding queer artifacts in museum collections lies in issues of cataloging. It is quite likely that the potential queer significance of an object was overlooked when being accessioned into a collection, particularly if it was accessioned decades ago. Yet as a result of such oversights, collections may hold artifacts that could be read as queer without ever being aware of it. To draw an example from women's history, historian Laura Brandon describes a "bosomy 'Mae West' life preserver" in the Canadian War Museum that was cataloged by its function, without any reference to it as a source related to sexuality or men's views about women. Similarly, in their excellent article, "When the Erotic Becomes Illicit," Jill Austin and her coauthors discuss the need to interpret existing holdings in new ways, using the example of a portrait whose original catalog record did not mention its queer significance.[14]

The question of cataloging leads to another issue. What is it, exactly, that makes an object queer? Does the fact that a queer person owned an object qualify it as a queer artifact, or must it relate explicitly to its owner's sexual identity? LGBT people occupy all walks of life, all races and classes, and because of that, their possessions are often indistinguishable from others'. Angela Vanegas captures some of the complicated nature of queer objects when she states, "Certainly, objects are not alive—they have no intrinsic sexuality—however, it is probably fair to say that their users will generally be assumed to have been heterosexual, unless the objects are explicitly connected with lesbian and gay life, such as Gay Pride badges. The history of objects has to be recorded or their real meaning is lost."[15]

Vanegas's point leads us to a third possible explanation for the dearth of LGBT artifacts in mainstream museum collections. If objects are only seen as queer when they are "explicitly connected with lesbian and gay life," and if what makes people lesbian or gay is, by definition, their sexuality, then these objects will tend to be of a sexual nature. Of course, it is possible to overstate the point. Certainly objects pertaining to civil rights efforts (such as political buttons and signs) and community/family formation (a glass from a gay bar, for example, or paraphernalia from a lesbian softball team) are also explicitly connected to lesbian and gay life. LGBT communities are more than simply their sexuality, but at the same time, sex *is* the basis for those communities. As such, it also forms the basis for a significant class of objects that would be understood as explicitly queer. Examples in this category might be objects connected to the International Ms. Leather competition, bawdy costumes from a gay pride parade, or sex toys such as anal plugs or dildos.[16]

One final issue at play regarding LGBT-related artifacts in museum collections involves trust building. There are myriad reasons for LGBT communities to distrust mainstream collecting institutions. As we have seen, there is a long history of same-sex love and desire in the United States, which has only recently captured the attention of museums. For a much longer period of time, these institutions ignored, marginalized, or hid this history, contributing to a general invisibility of LGBT people within the larger culture. Among queer people of color or LGBT members of the working class, that neglect has been even more extreme. Without specific outreach to queer communities and a demonstrated commitment on the part of institutions to respect and care for the artifacts of their lives, LGBT individuals are unlikely to donate their materials. This simple reality provides an explanation for the relative lack of queer objects in museum collections to date.

Ironically, given the issues just discussed, the truth is that the history of same-sex love and desire is being interpreted in a wide variety of ways, in a variety of venues. Organizations with a specifically LGBT mission, museums with a wider historical focus, historic house museums, and even national park units have joined with community centers, libraries, art museums, universities, and performance groups to explore this facet of the past. Some organizations, such as the National Constitution Center, have incorporated LGBT stories into their permanent exhibits. Still more have chosen to present this story through temporary exhibits or special programming, such as LGBT-themed tours or lectures. The acknowledgment and acceptance of LGBT experiences has increased so quickly in recent years that I predict it is only a matter of time before we see queer voices integrated into a wide variety of historical narratives.[17]

Furthermore, sometimes even within one organization, LGBT interpretation can occur through a variety of methods or can change over time. The Alice Austen House, on Staten Island, New York, provides one such example. The house museum, a member of the Historic House Trust of New York City, interprets the life of the turn-of-the-twentieth-century photographer Alice Austen, who challenged gender assumptions in her work and who shared her life with another woman, Gertrude Tate. Twenty years ago, the site was not interpreting these aspects of Austen's life; however, in 1994 a New York Public Library exhibit, *Becoming Visible*, included some of Austen's photographs and identified her as a lesbian. The house museum then became the subject of controversy, with activists demanding that the museum claim Austen as a lesbian and the site's board opposing such representation.[18] In the words of then-director of the site, Carl Rutberg:

> At the core was the word "lesbian." Either she was or she wasn't. To me, the argument wasn't very interesting. What fascinated me was Alice Austen, her work, and her life. And it didn't take much research to conclude that Gertrude Tate was the most important person in Austen's life. This fact, supported by hundreds of photographs, is undeniable. Yet when we stopped debating the "L-word" and started to talk about what we knew of Austen, the disagreements disappeared. Today, we do not claim that Austen was a lesbian,

and we do not hide Gertrude Tate. Instead, we present what we know and let the visitors make up their own minds.[19]

In 2010, the Historic House Trust developed a special program at the site in order to more deeply explore the implications of Alice Austen's work. Photographer Steven Rosen and the drag performance group Switch n' Play restaged some of Austen's more convention-defying pieces in light of contemporary meanings of gender and sexuality, inviting visitors to contemplate the changing nature of social convention. Currently at the museum, Austen's defiance of gender conventions and her relationship with Tate are part of the regular visitor experience, but the site is currently exploring ways to delve more deeply into this aspect of its history. As such, the Alice Austen house represents a trend in LGBT interpretation where an organization's exploration of the topic unfolds in stages and utilizes a variety of methods.[20]

Just as American society is rapidly changing its approach to LGBT communities, so the world of LGBT historical interpretation is building momentum. Without a doubt, many

Figure 8.2. What makes an object queer? In locating queer historical artifacts, questions of cataloging, definitions, sexual content, and trust-building come into play. Here, leather vests on display at the Leather Archives and Museum in Chicago.
Courtesy of Susan Ferentinos

opportunities are still being missed. Yet even while much work remains, exciting examples of innovation and creative approaches to the topic are springing forth. In the chapters that follow, three case studies and two reflective essays look in depth at the process of developing LGBT programming, with all its challenges and rewards.

Notes

1. For recommendations of where to start with the literature, see appendix 2. Early examples of LGBT historical interpretation are explored in Stephanie Lehner, "Becoming Visible: Mainstream Cultural Institutions and the Successful Presentation of LGBTQ History Exhibitions" (MA thesis, State University of New York College at Oneonta, Cooperstown Graduate Program, 2008). See also Jurriënne Ossewold and Paul Verstraeten, *Two of a Kind: A History of Gays and Lesbians in Holland* (Amsterdam: Amsterdams Historisch Museum, 1989); Molly McGarry and Fred Wasserman, *Becoming Visible: An Illustrated History of Lesbian and Gay Life in Twentieth-Century America* (New York: Penguin Studio, 1998); History Project, *Improper Bostonians: Lesbian and Gay History from the Puritans to Playland* (Boston: Beacon, 1998).
2. For other examples of projects aimed at youth, see Joey Plaster, "Imagined Conversations and Activist Lineages," *Radical History Review*, no. 113 (Spring 2012): 99–109; "The Queer Ancestors Project," 2014, http://www.queerancestorsproject.org/.
3. "GLBT History Museum," *GLBT Historical Society*, 2014, http://www.glbthistory.org/museum/; "The Queer Ancestors Project."
4. "The Pop-Up Museum of Queer History," accessed May 23, 2014, http://www.queermuseum.com/; "Museum of Sex | NYC," accessed May 23, 2014, http://museum.museumofsex.com/; "Leslie Lohman Museum of Gay and Lesbian Art," accessed May 23, 2014, http://www.leslielohman.org/.
5. Neal Broverman, "A Night at the Museum," *Advocate*, December 2, 2008, 14; "Out West at the Autry," *The Autry*, accessed May 23, 2014, http://theautry.org/series/out-west.
6. Observations on the trends of LGBT interpretation taking place in the United Kingdom can be found in Maria Anna Tseliou, "Spotlight on Research—Subverting the Heteronormative Museum," *Incluseum* (blog), April 11, 2013, http://incluseum.com/2013/04/11/spotlight-on-research-subverting-the-hetero-normative-museum/.
7. See, for example, Amy K. Levin, ed., *Gender, Sexuality, and Museums: A Routledge Reader* (New York: Routledge, 2010); Jonathan D. Katz and David C. Ward, *Hide/Seek: Difference and Desire in American Portraiture* (Washington, DC: Smithsonian Institution, 2010); Walter M. Kendrick, *The Secret Museum: Pornography in Modern Culture* (New York: Viking, 1987); Stuart Frost, "Secret Museums: Hidden Histories of Sex and Sexuality," *Museums and Social Issues* 3, no. 1 (Spring 2008): 29–40; Patrik Steorn, "Curating Queer Heritage: Queer Knowledge and Museum Practice," *Curator* 55, no. 3 (July 2012): 355–65; Nayland Blake, Lawrence Rinder, and Amy Scholder, eds., *In a Different Light: Visual Culture, Sexual Identity, Queer Practice* (San Francisco: City Lights, 1995); Robin Metcalfe, *Queer Looking, Queer Acting: Lesbian and Gay Vernacular* (Halifax, NS: Mount Saint Vincent University Art Gallery, 1997); ONE National Gay & Lesbian Archives et al., *Cruising the Archive: Queer Art and Culture in Los Angeles, 1945–1980*, ed. Ann Cvetkovich, David Frantz, and Mia Locks (Los Angeles: ONE National Gay & Lesbian Archives, 2011).

8. Two well-known controversies related to US queer art are the outcry concerning the National Endowment of the Arts funding of a Robert Mapplethorpe exhibit in 1989–1990 and the National Portrait Gallery's removal of one of the items in the 2010 *Hide/Seek* exhibit. Jennifer Tyburczy, "All Museums Are Sex Museums," *Radical History Review*, no. 113 (Spring 2012): 202; "Bullying and Censorship," *New York Times*, December 7, 2010, 32; Marc Stein, ed., *Encyclopedia of Lesbian, Gay, Bisexual, and Transgender History in America* (New York: Scribner / Thomson-Gale, 2004), 3:248.

9. "Stonewall National Museum and Archives," accessed May 23, 2014, http://www.stonewallnationalmuseum.org/; David Jobin, Executive Director, Stonewall National Museum and Archives, interview with Susan Ferentinos, May 20, 2014.

10. Julia Brock, "Embodying the Archive (Part 1): Art Practice, Queer Politics, and Public History," *History @ Work* (blog), *Public History Commons*, April 5, 2013, http://publichistorycommons.org/brock-johnq-intro/; Julia Brock, "Embodying the Archive (Part 2): Lineages, Longings Migrations," *History @ Work* (blog), *Public History Commons*, April 12, 2013, http://publichistorycommons.org/tag/queer-history/; Wesley Chenault, Andy Ditzler, and Joey Orr, "Discursive Memorials: Queer Histories in Atlanta's Public Spaces," *Southern Spaces*, February 26, 2010, http://www.southernspaces.org/2010/discursive-memorials-queer-histories-atlantas-public-spaces; Bernard A. Zuckerman Museum of Art *John Q: Projects 2009–2013* (Kennesaw, GA: Kennesaw State University, 2014); Wesley Chenault, curator of *Unspoken Past: Atlanta Lesbian and Gay History, 1940–1970* (Atlanta History Center) and member of the John Q Collective, phone interview with Susan Ferentinos, May 15, 2014; "The Pop-Up Museum of Queer History."

11. McGarry and Wasserman, *Becoming Visible*; Lehner, "Becoming Visible"; Wesley Chenault, "The Unspoken Past: Atlanta Lesbian and Gay History," *Perspectives*, December 2006; Chenault, phone interview with Susan Ferentinos; Robert B. Marks Ridinger, "Sister Fire: Representing the Legacies of Leatherwomen," in *Gender, Sexuality, and Museums: A Routledge Reader*, ed. Amy K. Levin (New York: Routledge, 2010), 172–81; Robert B. Marks Ridinger, "Things Visible and Invisible: The Leather Archives and Museum," *Journal of Homosexuality* 43, no. 1 (March 2002): 1; Jason Baumann, introduction to "1969: The Year of Liberation," online exhibit, *New York Public Library* (2009), http://static.nypl.org/exhibitions/1969/year.html.

12. See also Jill Austin et al., "When the Erotic Becomes Illicit: Struggles over Displaying Queer History at a Mainstream Museum," *Radical History Review* 113 (Spring 2012): 192–93; Ridinger, "Sister Fire: Representing the Legacies of Leatherwomen."

13. As someone with a background in archives, I must make a special plea to the museum community. If you are collecting oral histories with the intention of using them in an exhibit, please record them using methods that meet archival standards so that they become part of the historical record rather than simply filling a short-term exhibition need. Do not assume that your multimedia people know what these standards are. For more information on current standards, see Matrix Center for Digital Humanities and Social Sciences, "Oral History in the Digital Age," *Michigan State University*, accessed May 23, 2014, http://ohda.matrix.msu.edu/. For information on conducting LGBT oral history interviews, see Nan Alamilla Boyd and Horacio N. Roque Ramírez, eds., *Bodies of Evidence: The Practice of Queer Oral History* (New York: Oxford University Press, 2012); Nan Alamilla Boyd, "Who Is the Subject? Queer Theory Meets Oral History," *Journal of the History of Sexuality* 17, no. 2 (May 2008): 177–89.

14. Laura Brandon, "Looking for the 'Total' Woman in Wartime: A Museological Work in Progress," in *Gender, Sexuality, and Museums: A Routledge Reader*, ed. Amy K. Levin (New

York: Routledge, 2010), 110; Austin et al., "When the Erotic Becomes Illicit"; Steorn, "Curating Queer Heritage"; Ridinger, "Things Visible and Invisible"; Darryl McIntyre, "What to Collect? Museums and Lesbian, Gay, Bisexual and Transgender Collecting," *International Journal of Art & Design Education* 26, no. 1 (February 2007): 48–53.

15. Angela Vanegas, "Representing Lesbians and Gay Men in British Social History Museums," in *Gender, Sexuality, and Museums: A Routledge Reader*, ed. Amy K. Levin (New York: Routledge, 2010), 164; Austin et al., "When the Erotic Becomes Illicit," 189–91; McIntyre, "What to Collect?"

16. Austin et al., "When the Erotic Becomes Illicit"; Tyburczy, "All Museums Are Sex Museums"; Ridinger, "Sister Fire."

17. Jenny Ramberg, "'Are Queer Folk the People, Too?' Exhibit Review: National Constitution Center, Philadelphia, PA," *Museums & Social Issues* 3, no. 1 (April 1, 2008): 143–49; Steorn, "Curating Queer Heritage"; Gregory Hinton, "Out West" (keynote address, LGBTQ Alliance Luncheon, American Alliance of Museums, Seattle, May 18, 2014); Jill Austin and Jennifer Brier, eds., *Out in Chicago: LGBT History at the Crossroads* (Chicago: Chicago History Museum, 2011).

18. Tatum Taylor, "Undeniable Conjecture: Placing LGBT Heritage" (Fitch Prize winning paper, Columbia University, 2011), 2–5, http://preservationalumni.org/Default.aspx?pageId=785573.

19. Lillian Faderman and Phyllis Irwin, "Alice Austen and Gertrude Tate: A Boston Marriage on Staten Island," *Historic House Trust Newsletter*, Fall 2010, 6.

20. Faderman and Irwin, "Alice Austen and Gertrude Tate"; Frank D. Vagnone, "A Note from Franklin D. Vagnone, Executive Director," *Historic House Trust Newsletter*, Fall 2010; Taylor, "Undeniable Conjecture," 2–6.

CHAPTER 9

CASE STUDY
Displaying Queer History at the Chicago History Museum
Lessons from the Curators of *Out in Chicago*

JILL AUSTIN AND JENNIFER BRIER

How *Out in Chicago* Came to Be

The exhibition *Out in Chicago*, which opened at the Chicago History Museum (CHM) in May 2011 and closed in March 2012, was a long time coming. In 2003, the museum launched "Out at CHM," one of the first public programs about LGBT history in the country.[1] When Lonnie Bunch was at the helm of CHM in the early 2000s, he forged a practice of inclusive and varied public history. Bunch strengthened curatorial investment and research in high-quality exhibitions that looked at histories considered to be risky or outside of mainstream expectations. To achieve this goal in part, Bunch embarked on an ambitious course to create a platform for telling LGBT history and presenting current LGBT scholarship at the museum. He invited gay historian George Chauncey, then at the University of Chicago, and several of the founding board members of the Center on Halsted, Chicago's LGBT community center also in development during this time, to join him. This initial collaboration of academics, museum professionals, community leaders, and philanthropists formed a new group, the "Out at CHM" committee, dedicated to the notion that building an audience through several years of annual programming was critical to growing external and internal support for an exhibition. The building blocks for *Out in Chicago* and its communities of funders and content partners (potential lenders, advisors, and interviewees) were established nearly five years prior to the exhibition opening. In the interim, a multidisciplinary team of historians, designers, filmmakers, community members, and artists produced an award-winning exhibition that pushed the boundaries of CHM. What follows is an account of how and what we did as well as the challenges we faced while undertaking this work.

Out in Chicago explored the lesbian, gay, bisexual, and transgender history of Chicago from the mid-nineteenth century through the present day. It traced the emergence of diverse LGBT communities, emphasizing the everyday lives of these Chicagoans as well as their activist struggles for equality and against homophobia and the fear of gender difference. One of our guiding curatorial principles was that *Out in Chicago* should strive to be in conversation with CHM's permanent exhibitions, most notably *Chicago: Crossroads of America*. *Crossroads*, as it is affectionately named, was the star of the museum's rebranding in 2006. The twenty-thousand-square-foot exhibition centers Chicago's history in the arc of nineteenth- and twentieth-century US history and tells a critical story about the development of urban America but does so in ways, not surprisingly, given its drive toward mass appeal, that ignore questions of sexuality in Chicago's past. We saw *Out in Chicago* as a way to address this absence, hence our decision to create a thematic exhibition that addressed key issues in urban history and the history of sexuality.

The exhibition's first section, "LGBT at the Crossroads," described the fluidity of gender and sexuality and how the relationship between the two has changed over time. Building on this, three subsequent sections addressed the making of families and homes ("Are You Family?"); role of communities and social spaces ("In the Life"); and diverse forms of activism ("Queers Mobilize Chicago"). The gallery was, in essence, a queer history of Chicago as an urban center. "Queer" served as shorthand for LGBT but also signified a rejection of the normal or normative in relation to sexuality and gender. The exhibition was populated with personal stories made palpable to visitors through audio, video, interactive elements, tokens of affection, remnants of material culture, and examples of defiance captured on camera and canvas.[2]

Exhibition Development

In order for such an exhibition to happen at the Chicago History Museum, the oldest cultural institution in Chicago, rather than at an LGBT-specific space, the "Out at CHM" committee understood that it was critical to build intellectual consensus around the project and achieve widespread buy-in from as many constituents and audiences as possible. We needed to learn how to nurture myriad interests from the ground up. We also realized the importance of letting people use their expertise in ways that made sense to them while at the same time advancing the larger project.

Chicago History Museum exhibitions are often cocurated by a curator on staff and an academic content expert. CHM curators are practicing public historians and educators who come from diverse disciplines and are sometimes selected for projects outside their area of expertise because of their interpretive skill. In the case of *Out in Chicago*, the curatorial team was particularly critical, in part because the museum felt it needed to prevent the appearance of "advocating" sexual freedom and expression.

Soon after she joined the museum staff in 2005, Jill Austin was asked to serve as cocurator for the LGBT project. Her art background and expertise in social history added to her track record of taking on difficult history exhibitions. Museum leadership knew that diplomacy and relationship building were essential to Jill's curatorial approach, principles that guided her through the complex and challenging field of the *Catholic Chicago* exhibition, which was on the cusp of opening at the time she and Jennie were brought together. Coming to Chicago from the Detroit Historical Museum and only vaguely familiar with the burgeoning "Out at CHM" series, Jill had previously viewed an LGBT history exhibition as a pipe dream. A few months prior to the *Out in Chicago* opening, she came out as queer to friends and colleagues, an action prompted by her own personal journey as well as the research, interview, and outreach processes of the project. As a curator of the exhibition, she also wanted to serve as a more open role model for students who came to the museum to learn about LGBT history.

Jennie Brier, meanwhile, as an expert on the history of gender and sexuality and a lesbian who has always been out in professional circles, had joined the faculty of the University of Illinois at Chicago (UIC). She reconnected with Bunch, with whom she had prior exhibition experience at the Smithsonian Institution, and he invited her to join the "Out at CHM" committee as a scholarly advisor with Chauncey and Jay Grossman, an American studies professor at Northwestern University. As an accomplished scholar in the field and someone familiar with creating exhibitions for public audiences, Jennie was an ideal choice for cocurator. During this process, she received tenure, which afforded her a protective cover to push the boundaries of the kinds of LGBT history and experiences featured in the gallery, an important advantage that Jill did not have when it came to justifying curatorial decisions.[3] We strongly recommend the strategy of looking to local colleges and universities to yield the kind of expertise needed to do LGBT museum work.

As cocurators, we set about forming our curatorial team of researchers, including Anne Parsons (a PhD student with a master's degree in public history) and Jessica Herczeg-Konecny (who began as a master's-level intern through her public history program), and realized almost immediately that we could not move forward without building greater support from other museum staff in the exhibitions, marketing, and development departments. For example, we arranged a meeting between UIC researcher Peter Ji and Melissa Hayes Cherry, then vice president of institutional advancement at CHM. Melissa was a key supporter of our fund-raising and promotional efforts but appeared to see herself as an outsider to the project. Peter was a straight ally who led Chicago's PFLAG (Parents and Friends of Lesbians and Gays) organization and felt strongly about playing an active role in LGBT and ally communities. During our informal lunch, we saw Melissa begin to understand herself as an ally. It was a linchpin in the momentum building for the exhibition and audience awareness. From her experience, we came to understand how important it was for museum colleagues to be able to recognize themselves as active participants in the process, even if they didn't see a personal connection to the historical content. Melissa, for example, was inspired to reach out to untapped LGBT audiences, starting with a four-day "save-the-date" display at the International Mr. Leather competition, a first for CHM.

Museums often begin with the assumption that people with particular identities will do work related to those identities and the rest of the staff will come along when they want or need to become involved. For better and for worse, this is as true for LGBT history as it is for any other historical subject. We tried to intervene and make it possible for straight people to see their stake in this history and experience. Through many collaborative discussions, our designer Daniel Oliver, a straight man, came to a place of understanding how heteronormativity (defined as assuming that heterosexuality is the norm and that any sexual or gender model that deviates from that is problematic) in Chicago's past had a place in the telling of LGBT history in the exhibition, particularly in regard to the question of families, housing, and postwar urban development. In a stroke of brilliance, Dan took line drawings from a 1960s housing development proposal aimed at attracting white, middle-class, heterosexual nuclear families (think Don and Betty Draper from *Mad Men*) and cast it as a large mural of an idealized family type which pushed out queer and low-income people from a neighborhood near the museum. This historically desired demographic introduced a section about displacement and looked over the space where visitors watched videos about how contemporary LGBT people form their own kinds of family (figure 9.1). We saw this as Dan's "aha" moment of "getting" the pervasiveness of heteronormativity in the city's history and recognizing his role as an ally in crafting the experiences for the content. He championed

Figure 9.1. Mural depicting the ideal heterosexual family, c. 1965, based on an original brochure by the Chicago Department of Urban Renewal.
Courtesy of the Chicago History Museum, gift of the Lake View Citizens' Council, 1967.0645; Daniel Oliver, designer

the mural when its large-scale presence was questioned as out of proportion to its relevance as subject matter. The mural stayed, to our delight.

Even as we built widespread support for the project within the institution, we struggled to think about how the exhibition would present arguments about the links between Chicago's history and queer history. As museum people and curators, we often enter into a project with many visions and assumptions of what the final product will or should be. Sometimes that is because leaping to the end of a project gives us a sense of possibility; other times it might be that we know how history has been written and let that perspective overdetermine our sense of what the final product should be. Either way, it is a natural part of the creative process, particularly when you are passionate about the topic. Since we came to *Out in Chicago* from different perspectives and work histories, we pushed each other to let go of our assumptions about the exhibition's direction. We made space for the collaborative process to function fully so that we could produce an exhibition that honored our experiences with public history, the history of sexuality, and urban history. But things needed to get a bit messy before coming into focus.

Over the course of several years, we sustained an extended conversation about what we did not want to do. While this had the potential to derail us, in the end it allowed us to imagine new methods for detailing a queer urban historical narrative. We knew that the impulse to research the museum's collection to find "gay" material would not work. While this method might have pleased some, it seemed to hew toward a popular history model of gay hagiography, one that seeks famous LGBT people in the past—who may or may not have understood themselves in this way and may or may not have done anything to advance sexual and gender autonomy—and makes them visible in the present.

Instead of a model that looked for individuals from the past whom we read as gay today and who have had their gayness transferred to material objects (e.g., including a design by Halston merely because you have access to it), we chose to emphasize and utilize the idea that LGBT could be a method for thinking about the past. We tried to use queerness as an interpretive strategy to help us figure out what happened when the history of sexuality met urban history. How does attention to nonnormative gender expression and sexuality allow us to reinterpret objects, images, and archival materials of the city? We were looking for practices, not necessarily identities. How did sexuality, both normative and nonnormative, play out in historical spaces like bars and balls, homes and doctor's offices? By contextualizing the stories of individual LGBT people with discussions of how sexuality and gender suffused the emergence of the city, we forestalled the possibly problematic representation of LGBT as always white and middle class and also gained an interpretive freedom to look to the cultural and social history of Chicago that has detailed how the city addressed transgressions related to gender and sexuality. We took the opportunity to deploy creative interpretive strategies that are typically outside the tried-and-true approaches, because we knew that doing LGBT history meant challenging ourselves to propose new ways of thinking historically. For example, we displayed five video labels, one at the beginning of each section of the exhibition and one that featured Chicago's preeminent historian of sexuality, John D'Emilio. In each video section label, LGBT folks from around the city greeted visitors and introduced the upcoming content. D'Emilio's two-minute video was a distillation of "Capitalism and Gay Identity," one of the seminal historical essays in LGBT scholarship, in which he argues that the history of capitalism in urban environments transformed same-sex desire and behavior into an identity. D'Emilio narrated the article's argument and in so doing created a cornerstone of the exhibition's approach to Chicago's queer past.[4]

The need to illustrate our ideas, of course, forced us into the collection, but we entered with eyes trained on mining the museum for context. We searched every primary source database we could (CHM's collection database, Proquest-Newspapers, Archive Grid) with lists of keywords culled from historical research and including terms like "man/woman," "sexology," "sexual invert," "she was a he," "he was a she," "masquerade," and so on. This made it possible to find needles in the haystacks, and then we used the materials in ways that fit into the larger themes we were building. Keyword discoveries of nineteenth-century sexologists, who happened to be in Chicago blazing a trail to understand sexual inversion and homosexuality, led us to crack rarely opened Chicago Medical Society minutes in the museum archives. The ledgers, dating to the 1880s and 1890s, documented the earliest medical lectures on the topic in the country. This section led us to craft an interactive panel based on an actual test to prove one's sexual inclinations (figure 9.2). A rich history of early gender nonconformists also emerged from the keyword searches, which ultimately shaped how we opened the exhibition (figure 9.3).

While holdings differ from museum to museum, the practice of making careful choices, based on a notion of mining a museum in a more sophisticated way, will ultimately reveal the untold or unknown history of a city. Be aware of, but don't cling to, the well-known stories so that you dig deeper into the collections. But if a story or object isn't powerful or meaningful enough, or, more importantly, if it doesn't support your argument, cut it. Also consider strategic borrowing and potentially mining other collections. We looked to other institutional and private collections according to this method, borrowing from diverse sources ranging from the International Museum of Surgical Sciences to the Illinois State Archives.

Beyond seeking objects to illustrate and enliven our queer interpretation, we found direction in a sustained process of community engagement. We were able to build on connections with the Center on Halsted in the initial "Out at CHM" programming planning and use the services of Slover Linett Audience Research during story line development. We met with two groups of twelve Chicagoans (one heterosexually identified, one LGBT identified) for three evenings over three months—an invaluable opportunity for our team to work with panels of visitors. The heartfelt conversations during these sessions represented an exciting tipping point for the project team's approach to content, interpretation, and experience.

Through the discussions, we developed a sense of the historical and political significance of the project. The LGBT panel, in particular, shaped the organization of the exhibition. The panelists rejected our proposed chronological organization on the basis that it portrayed a false reality—a march toward progress where all improved with time. Instead, they advocated for a thematic presentation structured to accommodate the progress and setbacks, fits and starts of LGBT history. We agreed and came to see our work as a form of queer shared authority, where we had to grapple with very different notions of what belonged in an LGBT history exhibition. We address the details of this complication below, but in the end, the visitor panels provided a tremendous boost to our curatorial vision. They became, for us, a community-based haven for ideas we had a hard time pitching within the museum, particularly when it came to visual representations of sexuality.

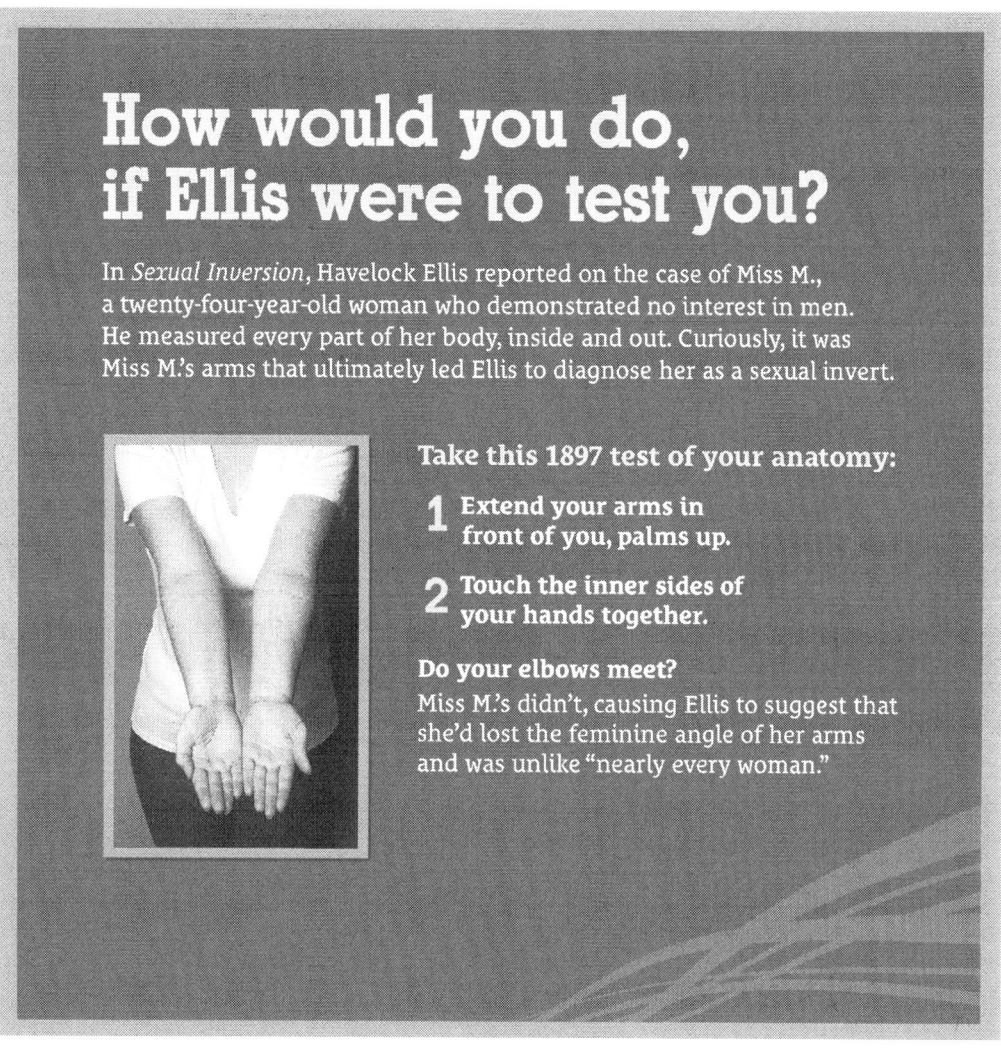

Figure 9.2. Visitors could test how they might measure up by a nineteenth-century sexologist's standards.
Courtesy of the Chicago History Museum; Mark Ramirez, graphic designer

We continued to use the strategy of engaging audiences in the exhibition even after it opened. This expanded the exhibition's audiences and gave us access to people who were working on questions of gender and sexuality in related fields. We worked with K–16 teachers from across our metropolitan area. After *Out in Chicago* opened, we held a Gay-Straight Alliance (GSA) summit with area high school students and served as a venue for a Queer Teacher Mixer, a regular social event for Chicago-based K–16 teachers. By focusing our attention on teachers and students, we were able to provide support to teachers on the frontlines of dealing with bullying and homophobia. But it also gave us new insights into how young LGBT people were at the forefront of thinking about and producing new kinds of historical content. This helped us push the boundaries of who is defined as a contributor to an exhibition and how they participate.

Figure 9.3. We told the story of two early gender nonconformists, Joseph Piatkewicz and Ralph Kerwinieo, exposed in the local press, by finding comparable ensembles in the costume collection to embody them.
Courtesy of the Chicago History Museum; Daniel Oliver and Mark Ramirez, designers

When Our Process Went Awry

Despite our work to create meaningful backing among our various constituencies, we faced a series of challenges in getting our content onto the walls of the gallery as well as into the DVD produced as the exhibition was closing. We have written about a few particular conflicts elsewhere, so here we will reflect on some of the theoretical underpinnings of the debates over what belonged and what needed to be taken out.[5] In hindsight, we found that some of the most vociferous controversy emerged when fear about backlash in the present overwhelmed our evidence from the past. This was put in the sharpest relief, not surprisingly, in the sections of the exhibition that dealt with sex. While many queer historical institutions (Chicago's Leather Archives and Museum, San Francisco's GLBT History Museum) consider it their responsibility to enter into public discussion of sex, addressing sex and sexuality in public spaces that do not identify as queer has long been a challenge. Questions posed to us included: Will talking about sex alienate visitors, funders, or the media? Will it contribute to stereotypes about LGBT people as overly sexualized? Will we be seen as advocates for LGBT activists?

As the curators, we often responded by serving as our own censors, resisting some of our more outlandish desires to figure out ways to make sexuality historically visible and meaningful to audiences that did not necessarily consider it relevant to mainstream public history. When we wanted to justify displaying sexuality, we often turned to our visitor panels, which in turn helped us name the problem and provided a potential solution or course of action. The LGBT participants consistently stressed the importance of addressing sex in the exhibition, making it clear that sexual practice needed to be part of our historical recovery work. But because we worked with two distinct panels, segregated by sexual and gender identity, we also had a group of heterosexual allies who wanted to see similarities between themselves and LGBT Chicagoans. That often meant that they did not want to talk about sex. Using voices from such a diverse group of community members, we were able to lend credence to our historical accounts of why sex mattered for the exhibition. It provided comfort to folks who were concerned about recreating or reifying stereotypes about LGBT people as overly sexualized. For example, the way we represented "family" in the exhibition came directly out of these different conversations. The straight group wanted to see families of origin that welcomed LGBT people serving as examples of how homophobia has diminished over the course of the past thirty years. LGBT folks wanted those kinds of images to be situated in a much larger and sometimes more vexed context, one that showed the violence families of origin can enact on LGBT members, queer homelessness, and how LGBT people have used sexuality to redefine the meaning of family to include families of choice. In the end, we prioritized the LGBT group's requests over those from the straight allies. We did this in part because we wanted to give their voices primacy in the curatorial process. We forged this critical and sometimes difficult consensus about what belonged by steering clear of both heteronormative and homonormative models, for example, ones that centered on struggles for same-sex marriage equality, and instead talked about how imaginative people in the nineteenth century were when it came to family structures that defied gender ideology.

In the end, the process did not go awry. The museum experienced an expanded audience and benefited from great word-of-mouth buzz leading to repeat visitors. In the final weeks of the exhibition, the project team collected exit surveys from ninety-three visitors. The results were highly encouraging. Nearly all of the participants (91.1 percent) were not CHM members, and most (64.6 percent) had heard of the exhibition by word of mouth. The largest age group of those surveyed skewed younger (ages twenty-five to thirty-four) than CHM's typical member population, which does include LGBT families. Just over a quarter of the respondents (26.6 percent) identified as LGBT. A staggering majority (81.6 percent) felt the exhibition met or exceeded their expectations, with 89.2 percent "extremely or somewhat likely" to return to CHM in the future.

The exit survey respondents, in an open-ended question, identified the most memorable component of *Out in Chicago* as its presentation of personal stories using videos. Most visitors were careful readers who took in nearly every piece of the first section and most of the second section, where they gravitated (lingered and sometimes returned) to watch videos about twelve contemporary LGBT families on an old-fashioned TV console. This was the space where the most visitors stopped and where they stayed the longest in the exhibition. Many people took care to explore the entire gallery—a feat at over 4,500 square feet. These results affirmed the casual observations of the team and frontline staff: every day, visitors were making discoveries and personal connections in *Out in Chicago*, particularly through the power of first-person testimony delivered in an appealing and approachable manner. The results of this activity will continue to influence how CHM develops future exhibitions.

Out in Chicago received an Excellence in Exhibitions award and honorable mention for video content from the American Alliance of Museums. We received an honorable mention for an outstanding public history project by the National Council on Public History and were honored with the 2012 Allan J. Bérubé Prize for LGBT history projects awarded by the Committee on LGBT History, an affiliate organization of the American Historical Association.

After the Gallery

Out in Chicago left a significant impression on the Chicago History Museum. Late in the exhibition's run, we received funding to preserve its content through a "curators' cut" video walk-through of the gallery. Ultimately, the DVD included the walk-through, most of the video segments produced for the exhibition, samples of the personal video messages recorded by visitors in the final section of the gallery, and a teacher guide. We distributed more than 250 copies to area high schools with GSA groups, community organizations, and libraries. The DVD came about after a tour with Chicago-area funders and "Out at CHM" committee members who expressed interest in documenting the exhibition and making it accessible for those not able to visit the museum. It was a way to contribute to the overall legacy of *Out in Chicago* and helped us share our curatorial journey with students and other external audiences who did not see the exhibition at CHM.[6]

Now we stand before a different crossroads. The LGBT exhibition has closed and is no longer on view in the museum. Our audiences, however, continue to regard CHM as a place to talk and learn about LGBT history. We are grappling with questions of sustainability: Where do we go from here? Will the emphasis now be on continuing "Out at CHM" programming? We have reverted to three evening programs per year for adults, without further funding sources for GSA groups or other youth program offerings despite requests to collaborate. Does our attention turn instead to strengthening archival and object collections that speak to local gay history? Do we find opportunities for students to help us process these collections and do future collecting?

Now more than ever, different groups and program partners have branched out to create programs independent of the museum. For example, Chicago's Center on Halsted has sponsored a year-long project called the Lavender University (the title of which comes from the Gay Academic Union of the 1970s). This might suggest that it is possible to have a place (city or town) share the collective responsibility of presenting LGBT history.

We continue to advocate for a more permanent and visible LGBT history presence in the museum. A verbal commitment to this kind of work surely exists, but the question remains of how to make it available to a range of visitors. What does it say that the museum does not feature permanent representation of LGBT history in its galleries, that we are essentially back to where we began? Are students to go elsewhere to learn LGBT Chicago history, a history in which they can find themselves? We risk doing a disservice to them by reverting back to the status quo, potentially undoing some of the strides made in audience and stakeholder building as well as sending a potential mixed message to new members who joined CHM as a result of this exhibition.

A possible, sustainable solution could be to tag existing exhibition content as "queer," a method which could test the waters without requiring much permanent physical change to displays. The alternative labeling project undertaken at the Jane Addams Hull-House Museum, for example, addressed questions of Addams's sexuality by generating visitor feedback prior to a new permanent display. It was a successful experiment that led to integrating the topics of sexuality and romantic relationships with long-standing settlement house history. Another approach could be to create an alternative tour of the museum's galleries that utilizes a docent's skills and interests or to produce a cell-phone tour as the Nelson-Atkins Museum of Art in Kansas City and the GLBT History Museum in San Francisco have done via Google Voice and other technologies to provide visitors with new content.

Despite our lament about how little LGBT content remains at the museum, we were truly invigorated by the process of putting together the exhibition and all we did to document its legacy. We would have never envisioned being asked to write for a collection such as this when we first started drafting labels for *Out in Chicago*. The curatorial and historical journey we undertook together, with visitors, and with the entire CHM staff made a lasting impression on us as historians and has provided us with new ways of thinking about and presenting the queer past. We hope it will inspire you to take steps, big and small, toward making LGBT history part of the work you do at your institution.

Notes

1. The Chicago Historical Society (CHS) changed its name to the Chicago History Museum in 2006. At that time, the museum's LGBT program series, originally titled "Out at CHS," was renamed "Out at CHM."

2. For a fuller description of the *Out in Chicago* exhibition, see Jill Austin and Jennifer Brier, "Out in Chicago: Exhibiting LGBT History at the Crossroads," in *Out in Chicago: LGBT History at the Crossroads*, ed. Jill Austin and Jennifer Brier (Chicago: Chicago History Museum, 2011), 1–22.
3. While we cannot go into detail here, we were influenced by the work of Al Young on what museum tenure would look like. See Alfred F. Young, "A Modest Proposal: A Bill of Rights for American Museums," *Public Historian* 14, no. 3 (July 1, 1992): 67–75.
4. John D'Emilio, "Capitalism and Gay Identity," in *Powers of Desire: The Politics of Sexuality*, ed. Ann Barr Snitow, Christine Stansell, and Sharon Thompson (New York: Monthly Review Press, 1983), 100–113.
5. Jill Austin et al., "When the Erotic Becomes Illicit: Struggles over Displaying Queer History at a Mainstream Museum," *Radical History Review* 113 (Spring 2013): 187–97.
6. Unfortunately, the DVD is not available for purchase. Readers interested in obtaining a copy on loan or for use in their institutions should contact Jill Austin at the Chicago History Museum or search WorldCat and arrange for an interlibrary loan.

CHAPTER 10

CASE STUDY
The Varied Telling of Queer History at Historic New England Sites

KENNETH C. TURINO

Historic New England is the oldest, largest, and most comprehensive regional preservation organization in the nation and owns thirty-six historic properties in five of the six New England states. Several of its historic houses have LGBT associations, and the organization has taken various approaches to interpreting these associations, depending on the specific circumstances of each site. This case study examines how, where, and why Historic New England tells or chooses not to tell LGBT stories. To accomplish this, I will look specifically at three of the organization's properties: Beauport in Gloucester, Massachusetts, the Codman Estate in Lincoln, Massachusetts, and the Sarah Orne Jewett House in South Berwick, Maine. The reasons behind Historic New England's decisions encompass the major challenges of interpreting LGBT history that face our field today and demonstrate that even within one institution there can be varying approaches and degrees of success when it comes to interpreting the queer past.

Historic New England has always prided itself on its historic site interpretation, publications, and exhibitions and is known for the depth of its collections and the quality of its programming. We operate five distinct yet interrelated program areas: historic properties, archives and publications, collections, education, and preservation services. Historic New England does not have an official policy regarding overall LGBT interpretation; instead, many factors come into play when deciding what kind of interpretation will be put forth at a property. Peter

Gittleman, team leader for visitor experience, is responsible for the interpretation at all the organization's historic sites. Working with our historian, the collections team, and site staff (including guides), he crafts an interpretive outline that site staff then present at the property.

Beauport

In the case of Beauport (built 1907–1934), one of the organization's most popular properties, the decision was made after many years to interpret Beauport's creator and first owner, Henry Davis Sleeper (1878–1934), as a gay man. Sleeper was one of America's first professional interior designers, and his summer home, Beauport, is a fantasy house of forty rooms overlooking Gloucester Harbor (figure 10.1). The interior and exterior of the house contain Sleeper's lifetime collection of curiosities—colored glass, folk art, china, and silhouettes—in every nook and alcove. Each of the forty rooms (twenty-six of which are shown to the public) is distinguished by a historical or literary figure, theme, color, shape, or object. No two rooms are the same, with each more visually dazzling than the last. The house is framed by restored Arts and Crafts terraces that include intimate garden rooms with dramatic views of the harbor.

Figure 10.1. Henry Davis Sleeper created Beauport, his summer house, as a showcase and as a retreat to entertain his friends.
Courtesy of Historic New England

Visitors to Beauport learn about its architectural evolution, the sources of Sleeper's inspiration, and how he influenced other designers and popular tastes, as well as learning about his longtime housekeepers and Beauport's second owners, the McCanns. They also discover that Sleeper, who never married, spent his summers here with his mother and the house's many colorful guests, who became an integral part of Sleeper's life. Although most of Sleeper's papers were destroyed (not an uncommon situation with gay men of this generation), some correspondence between Sleeper and A. Piatt Andrew (1873–1936), his neighbor and close friend, does survive. The letters, published by Historic New England, show that Sleeper had an infatuation with his neighbor—this handsome man several years his junior, the dashing Harvard professor and United States senator from Massachusetts—but the letters do not contain evidence of a sexual relationship between the two.[1]

For years, visitors commonly asked our guides, "Was Sleeper gay?" The response was simply that he never married and we had no information about his intimate relationships. Having no documentary proof, the team leader felt there was no rationale to address his sexuality in the interpretation. In 2008, team leader Gittleman changed this, making it a requirement to mention that Sleeper was a gay man on every tour. The reason for this development was that new evidence had surfaced. In an oral history conducted by historian Phillip Hayden, the lover of Sleeper's cousin identified Sleeper as a gay man. This addition to the tour was made not to define Sleeper but to contextualize him.

Once it was decided that Sleeper's sexuality would be presented on the tour, Gittleman and site manager Pilar Garro held a "therapy" session with the guides, many of whom had a long history with the organization. (Their average age was sixty; several were in their seventies, and one was in her eighties.) During the session, which was intended to increase the guides' comfort with speaking about Sleeper's sexuality, staff gave the guides several approaches to integrating this fact into the tour. Garro recommends that it be discussed in the introduction, but there is some fluidity as to where and how the guides discuss Sleeper's sexuality. For instance, in the pine kitchen, guides point out a Chase and Sanborn coffee ad that features Sleeper along with Gary Cooper (figure 10.2). In this ad, both men are called "well known Bachelors," and this is often used as an entry point to discussing Sleeper's sexuality. One guide I interviewed said, "By giving this contextual evidence of his life, I believe that the entire tour takes on a different light, starting with his relationship with his mother all the way to the advertisement of Chase and Sanborn coffee that we show in the pine kitchen, as well as everything in between. He just becomes a much more three-dimensional character because of it."

Although many guides were initially reluctant to talk about sexuality, through training they grew more comfortable. In addition, as older guides have left and younger guides have come on staff, discomfort has become less of an issue. It is telling that in the six years since this information has become part of the tour there has been no negative feedback from visitors. Many simply don't respond or they say, "Oh, of course." On one tour with an older married couple, after being told about Sleeper's sexuality, the husband said he was happy to hear this discussed and actually broke down and cried because his son was gay and had died of AIDS. While many museums have been afraid of offending people, we should not underestimate the fact that many people want to hear this information.[2] It can have a personal and deep meaning for visitors and staff alike. In the words of one guide:

Figure 10.2. Staff at Beauport use this Chase and Sanborn advertisement as an entry point to talk about Henry Davis Sleeper as a gay man.
Courtesy of Historic New England

As people, I think we are all attracted to something that we can individually relate to. For me, every tour I give at Beauport is an affirmation of how far we have come in society in terms of acceptance and understanding. Especially because I am gay myself, to be able to even mention that Sleeper was gay is a triumph, but to talk about it so openly that now I get questions from visitors like, "Was he openly gay? Why wasn't he openly gay?" that I have to explain that once upon a time (not so very long ago), being gay was not a socially acceptable thing. No wonder why I love my job!

Recently, site manager Garro has focused on marketing efforts, programming, and partnerships specifically aimed at reaching out to LGBT communities. In 2010, Historic New England began an initiative called "100 Years, 100 Communities," which I am overseeing in my capacity as manager of community outreach and exhibitions. Now called "Everyone's History," this initiative has included a successful partnership with the Boston-based History Project, whose mission is "to document and preserve the history of Boston's LGBT community, and to share that information with the public."[3] We collaborated on a series of sold-out tours of Beauport, lectures, and walking tours of the neighborhood, all with an LGBT theme. These programs culminated on the patio terrace for a reception and time for participants to socialize. In addition to special programming, Garro has reached out to groups like the North Shore Elder

Services' "Over the Rainbow" group as well as the Gay Men's Art & Architecture MeetUp, and she plans to continue her efforts by reaching out to LGBT groups at local colleges.

She is committed to expanding the site's programming as well. One program, "Private Lives, Public Faces: A Conversation about Sexuality and Beauport in the Early 20th Century," is scheduled for summer 2014. She describes it as follows:

> For some time I have wanted to create a program to further engage the LGBT community and spark conversation. This program is aimed to do so and will take on a salon-style conversational format led by historian Phillip Hayden, who has researched, lectured, and written on Beauport and Sleeper extensively. The conversation will begin on the terrace followed by a tour of the house or vice-versa.

Staff members also connect to LGBT visitors through print media. Garro has advertised Beauport as an LGBT site in the Massachusetts Travel and Tourism publication and featured the site in the New England Gay and Lesbian Travel Map. She also worked with *Boston Spirit*, the premier LGBT publication in New England, on a feature article that came out in 2011. In 2014, the Historic New England marketing team was considering the best way to promote Beauport as a wedding ceremony site for same-sex couples. On the whole, the powers that be at Historic New England have embraced the LGBT interpretation and programming at Beauport, demonstrating the institution's commitment to LGBT history in this case.

The Codman Estate

The Codman Estate, in Lincoln, Massachusetts, offers more of a challenge to Historic New England staff. Overlooking a prospect of farm and pleasure grounds, this country seat, also known as "The Grange," was a powerful force in the lives of five generations of the Codman family. Each generation who lived there left its mark, and the estate came to symbolize the family's fascinating past. In the 1790s, John Codman carried out extensive improvements to the original Georgian house and surrounding grounds. Sixty years later, his grandson updated the house in keeping with Victorian taste and filled the house with the finest New York furnishings. Today, the interiors are richly furnished with portraits, memorabilia, and artworks collected in Europe, showing the decorative schemes of every era, including those of noted early twentieth-century interior designer Ogden Codman Jr. (1863–1951). The grounds feature a turn-of-the-century Italian garden with perennial beds, statuary, and a reflecting pool filled with water lilies, as well as a 1930s English cottage garden.

Ogden Codman Jr. is best known for his and coauthor Edith Wharton's influential publication, *The Decoration of Houses* (1897).[4] Although he was happily married to a wealthy widow for a brief time, there is clear evidence that Codman had sexual relations with men. His correspondence survives, as does a photographic collection of mainly male erotica, which was found hidden in the Codman House. At one time this collection was sealed to protect the family's feelings, a relatively common practice at museums and libraries. The restrictions on the collection were well known in the history community. When researching the exhibition *Public Faces/Private Lives: Boston's Lesbian and Gay History* and its follow-up publication,

Improper Bostonians, History Project board members knew better than to ask for access.⁵ More recently, Codman's letters and images have been opened to the public and have become the basis for a number of scholarly articles. In "'A Very Proper Bostonian': Rediscovering Ogden Codman and His Late-Nineteenth-Century Queer World," historian David D. Doyle Jr. goes into detail about Codman's same-sex relationships and those of his circle, concluding that the "correspondence is significant for historians on a number of levels: first and most important, it shows how gender, same-sex attractions, and social class were interrelated."⁶

The question remains how Historic New England should address the topic of Ogden Codman's sexuality, if at all, and how this fits into the overall interpretation at the site. Since the institution interprets five generations of the family's use over time, we do not as part of the typical forty-five minute tour discuss any of the Codmans' sexuality. Peter Gittleman, when speaking on this issue, told me, "Unlike at Beauport, where Sleeper is the real protagonist, Ogden Codman Jr. is one of more than a dozen people whose lives play out on the tour." The site manager, Wendy Hubbard, feels guides have to walk a fine line between telling a holistic story of the Codman family and being honest about Ogden Codman Jr.'s personal life. Should visitors specifically ask about Ogden Codman Jr.'s sexuality, guides are instructed to explain that he was married but known to have relations with men. They can also refer people to the Doyle article mentioned above. By taking this reactive approach, some staff feel they can maintain historical accuracy while also responding to the wishes of older and more conservative stakeholders. However, others may feel that by not explicitly discussing this aspect, the opportunity for a meaningful discussion of sexuality and class is being lost.

On the positive side, over the past twelve years, Historic New England has offered a number of programs specifically dealing with Ogden Codman Jr.'s sexuality and LGBT history generally. One example was an event with Douglas Shand-Tucci, author of *Boston Bohemia, 1881–1900*, the first major biography of renowned church architect Ralph Adams Cram (1863–1942).⁷ This book offers a portrait of America's early avant garde, a world Ogden Codman Jr. moved in and out of, and discloses for the first time the pivotal contribution of Boston's emerging gay subculture to New England's intellectual and cultural history. The event was sold out and received wide press coverage. Another program stemmed out of our "Everyone's History" partnership with the History Project. Working with site manager Hubbard, I organized a house tour, reception, and presentation on Codman's sexuality by historian David D. Doyle Jr., and this event also sold out. In 2011, the Codman Estate hosted the Gay Men's Art & Architecture MeetUp, and Hubbard would like to arrange more LGBT-themed programs in the future. For the reasons stated above, at this time there are no plans to change the general tour outline. However, programming and specialty tours (which the site's staff is considering) do offer an opportunity to keep this discussion going.

The Sarah Orne Jewett House

The challenge of the Sarah Orne Jewett House in South Berwick, Maine, is of another sort. Regional author Sarah Orne Jewett (1849–1909) was born in her grandparents' eighteenth-century house, where she lived with her family until 1854, when a Greek Revival house was built next door. As Jewett gained attention as an author, she and her family continued to live in the two homes in the center of South Berwick. She and her older sister Mary inherited their grandparents' house in 1887. Decorating the house for their own use, the sisters expressed both a pride in their family's past and their own independent, sophisticated tastes. The result is an eclectic blend of eighteenth-century architecture and antiques, with wallpapers and furnishings showing the influence of the Arts and Crafts movement.

Throughout much of her life, Jewett shared a complex, supportive, and loving relationship with Boston author and hostess Annie Adams Fields (1834–1915), the widow of author and publisher James Thomas Fields. Scholars agree that the existing letters between Jewett and Annie Fields, as well as poetry by Jewett, reveal the depth of their commitment to each other. Yet although the two women clearly shared an emotional partnership, there is no documentation of a sexual aspect to their union (figure 10.3).

The Jewett-Fields partnership mirrors a common style of female relationships in the late nineteenth and early twentieth centuries. During this era, unmarried women often paired together in close, loving relationships that allowed them to pool financial resources and maintain respectability during an era when unaccompanied women were considered morally suspect. These unions were clearly romantic in nature, but more often than not the existence of a sexual component was not documented. As such, the Jewett House provides an opportunity to interpret not just the life of one author, but a larger historical context for women's changing positions in society.

The trend of female partnership that existed around the turn of the twentieth century often went by the name "Boston marriage," a reference to the 1886 novel *The Bostonians*, by Henry James. Staff at Historic New England began interpreting the Jewett-Fields relationship within the context of Boston marriage in the 1990s, when Peter Gittleman worked with curators, site managers, and women's historians to craft a tour outline that included discussion of the two women's relationship. In this way, the Sarah Orne Jewett House led the way for interpreting LGBT history at Historic New England and laid the groundwork for the interpretation at Beauport.

Former site manager Peggy Wishart openly discussed with guides the need to talk to visitors about the importance of the Jewett-Fields relationship and to understand Boston marriage within historical context. Wishart felt her "work with the guides was unofficial and could easily backslide into old habits without institutional acknowledgment, implementation, and training." Sadly, this appears to be what actually happened, as over time discussion of Boston marriage disappeared from the tour outline.

Recently a new site manager, Brooke Stienhauser, has come on board, and she is making the interpretation of the Jewett-Fields relationship a priority. Gittleman is now aware that Boston marriage was inadvertently cut from the tour outline and will see to it that an even more up-to-date interpretation of Jewett's relationships with women enters into the conversation. He will work with the site manager and others to review what message we want to get across to the public and to deliver the message consistently in a revised tour outline. With a new site manager and new guides coming on in the spring of 2014, there is an opportunity to include a more open discussion with visitors about Jewett's same-sex relationships and to contextualize them within the broader outline of the tour.

The administration at Historic New England looks at each of its sites individually in terms of interpretation and is actively looking to tell untold stories, such as those involving servants, immigrant tenant farmers, and free and enslaved African Americans. Clearly LGBT

Figure 10.3. Interior view of the James T. Fields House at 148 Charles Street, Boston, with Annie Fields and Sarah Orne Jewett. Staff at the Sarah Orne Jewett House will use images like this to discuss the relationship between Sarah Orne Jewett and Annie T. Fields.
Courtesy of Historic New England

stories fall under this effort, and the results of this initiative are apparent, to varying degrees, at the sites profiled in this case study. At Beauport, discussion of Sleeper as a gay man occurs on the tour, through public programs, and in targeted marketing to LGBT groups. Brooke Stienhauser is developing interpretation at the Sarah Orne Jewett House to follow the example of the tour at Beauport. Organizational leaders are clearly open to wider discussions about Jewett's same-sex relationships, but at the same time, the site's inconsistent inclusion of this element illustrates the need for an institution-wide commitment to telling underrepresented perspectives. At the Codman Estate, we have decided not to discuss Ogden Codman Jr.'s complex sexual identity because he is only one of the family members interpreted at that site. For some, this is a missed opportunity. At all three sites, programming seems to be the key to offering a fuller discussion of same-sex relationships. Perhaps this is because with special programs, visitors can choose to attend or not based on the topic, whereas with a tour they will not necessarily know the full content of what lies ahead.

There is no denying that Historic New England has made great strides. In the summer of 2013, representatives from the Pew Center for Arts & Heritage in Philadelphia visited

Beauport to learn about its LGBT interpretation. The staff of Pew looked at what Historic New England is doing at that site and characterized it as "groundbreaking." Yet, as I have tried to show in this case study, even within the same institution, there are a number of factors that must be considered when moving into LGBT historical interpretation. In a recent article discussing authenticity at sites overseen by the Historic House Trust of New York City, Franklin D. Vagnone posed the question, "Is it authentic to tell the whole story, or is it better to frame the story in a way that may exclude conjectural or controversial aspects?"[8] Staff at museums and historic sites are still arguing this question.

Notes

1. Henry Davis Sleeper et al., *Beauport Chronicle: The Intimate Letters of Henry Davis Sleeper to Abram Piatt Andrew, Jr., 1906–1915* (Boston: Society for the Preservation of New England Antiquities, 1991).
2. On the public's willingness to learn about inclusive histories, see Reach Advisors, "Difficult Issues, Inclusive History," *Museum Audience Insight* (blog), July 8, 2008, accessed March 3, 2014, http://reachadvisors.typepad.com/museum_audience_insight/2008/07/difficult-issues-inclusive-history.html.
3. The History Project, accessed February 13, 2014, www.historyproject.org.
4. Edith Wharton and Ogden Codman Jr., *The Decoration of Houses* (New York: Scribner, 1897).
5. History Project, *Improper Bostonians: Lesbian and Gay History from the Puritans to Playland* (Boston: Beacon, 1998).
6. David D. Doyle Jr., "'A Very Proper Bostonian': Rediscovering Ogden Codman and His Late-Nineteenth-Century Queer World," *Journal of the History of Sexuality* 13, no. 4 (October 2004): 476.
7. Douglass Shand-Tucci, *Ralph Adams Cram: Life and Architecture. Volume I: Boston Bohemia, 1881–1900* (Amherst: University of Massachusetts Press, 1995).
8. Frank D. Vagnone, "A Note from Franklin D. Vagnone, Executive Director," *Historic House Trust Newsletter*, Fall 2010, http://www.historichousetrust.org/assets/attachments/HHTnewsFall10.pdf.

CHAPTER 11

CASE STUDY
Interpreting for the Next Generation
The Summer History Immersion Program (Minnesota)

KYLE PARSONS AND STEWART VAN CLEVE

IN SUMMER 2013, eleven high school students sat nervously in a large conference room in Elmer L. Andersen Library, a vast archival facility on the University of Minnesota's West Bank, with their friends, family members, and representatives of the University of Minnesota and the Minnesota Historical Society (MNHS). After a brief introduction, students walked one by one over to a trifold poster that they had created, brought it to a table in front of the audience, and used it for a well-rehearsed speech that outlined a historic event they had carefully researched over the previous two weeks. Near the end of the presentations and as one student, a young black woman, grabbed her poster, her mother readied a camcorder and beamed as she captured every moment of her daughter's presentation. While many parents have proudly captured many high school presentations, this presentation night at Andersen Library was unique. The young lady presented her research on Reed Erickson, a philanthropist who financed the first sex-reassignment programs in the United States. While the mother filmed, her partner, a transgender man, kept his arm around her shoulders. He and other members of the audience had already listened to presentations about the 1969 Stonewall riots, Dr. Alfred Kinsey, and lesbian feminism in sports. They were attending the last night of Tretter SHIP, a groundbreaking project that was about to finish its second successful year.

Minnesota's first LGBT history course for high school students began as a two-and-a-half-week session of the Summer History Immersion Program (SHIP), a summer program offered annually by the Minnesota Historical Society in partnership with the University of Minnesota. SHIP invited high school students to interface with historical figures and events that they are not traditionally exposed to, in the safety of a supportive environment, and it introduced them to the critical thought processes and research skills they needed to succeed in a college classroom. With primary sources from the Tretter Collection in GLBT Studies at the University of Minnesota's Elmer L. Andersen Library, the LGBT[1] history session offered students a rare opportunity to handle historic materials as they learned about the overlooked figures and events that produced them.[2] In this case study, Kyle Parsons, the MNHS diversity outreach specialist, and Stewart Van Cleve, a local author and the Tretter Collection's former assistant curator, overview the LGBT session of the summer program, Tretter SHIP, and gauge its success.[3]

SHIP began in 2011, when Kyle worked with his department director, Tim Hoogland, and Ryan Bean, a reference and outreach archivist at the University of Minnesota's Kautz Family YMCA Archives, to create a summer program that sought to make college-level archival research possible for high schoolers from underrepresented communities in the Minneapolis-St. Paul area.[4] The program emulated an educational model created by National History Day, an annual competition that requires middle school and high school students to conduct primary and secondary research on a historical topic in relationship to a nationally assigned theme. National History Day resembles a science fair or academic conference, as students are asked to simulate a museum exhibit by creating a poster that highlights their research and use it as a visual aid for discussing the topic to interested visitors. SHIP students were asked to inquire, analyze, interpret, and draw conclusions about a topic's historical significance just as they would when completing a History Day entry.

SHIP's first session took place in summer 2011 at Andersen Library, where the first cohort researched topics rooted in the YMCA Archive. The pilot targeted students from communities of color who selected stories and groups that were unfamiliar to them; their selections related to historic events surrounding communities of color but did not necessarily relate to their own backgrounds or the narratives that their peers were researching. In the course of evaluating the successful pilot, MNHS staff inquired about the possibility of expanding SHIP in summer 2012 to include a second cohort. Ryan expressed interest in expanding the program to the Jean-Nickolaus Tretter Collection in Gay, Lesbian, Bisexual, and Transgender Studies, a separate archival collection located in Andersen Library. The Tretter Collection, he noted, had the potential to let students delve into a completely unfamiliar subject matter and foster their self-understanding.

Kyle and Ryan encountered an immediate problem in identifying participants for Tretter SHIP during the initial planning meeting. Though students from LGBT communities stood to benefit the most from the program, local high schools had no means of reporting who those students were. Difficulties in selecting LGBT-identified students especially hinged on identifying those from communities of color—a principal demographic that SHIP sought to connect with. The problem of selecting LGBT-identified students posed a question of exclusivity: Did Tretter SHIP need to specifically recruit those students in order to be a successful LGBT history program? Organizers decided the program did not need such a

Figure 11.1. This SHIP program teaches college prepatory skills through the lens of LGBT history. Courtesy of the Minnesota Historical Society

stipulation, but they created an opportunity for students to self-identify as LGBT if they wished; the application included a "statement of interest" question that multiple students used to express their interest in what they referred to as "my [LGBT] history." By combining students who expressed LGBT identities with those who did not, the program had an unprecedented potential to serve as a paradigm shift for students who did not identify as LGBT and had little exposure to that community while also assisting LGBT students in discovering the history of a community with which they identified. While MNHS staff recruited through Gay-Straight Alliances in high schools throughout the Minneapolis-St. Paul metropolitan area, they also connected to schools with strong ties to National History Day. In Tretter SHIP's two-year history, approximately 90 percent of participants were students of color, and many were preparing to become first-generation college students.

After Kyle selected ten students from a large pool of interested applicants, he coordinated a team of undergraduate MNHS interns (Amber Jones, Lawrence Karongo, Sam Ndely, and Mela Still), all of whom were people of color, which remained consistent with the original goal of SHIP. The interns offered fresh observations and advice on college life that Tretter SHIP participants may have had little exposure to in their homes or communities. In addition, interns gave critical assistance to ensure that the day's split programming ran smoothly. Each day of Tretter SHIP offered students topic research and "immersive campus experience" components. The immersions ranged from financial aid advising to mock lectures, learning about cultural groups and fraternities that reflect their backgrounds, and campus tours, but they always highlighted opportunities for students to build a sense of community on a college campus, prepare for college, and increase their understanding of different cultures and communities.

In general, the research component followed the National History Day model of historical research, inquiry, and critical analysis. After students became oriented to the program, they selected a research topic; they used primary and secondary sources to conduct extensive archival research on a diverse historical narrative; they wrote a five-section, five-hundred-word report, complete with a thesis statement that made an argument about their topic's historical significance; they created a trifold panel that highlighted their report; and they presented their panel to an audience of their friends, family, and peers. Students received free bus cards, breakfast, and lunch, and, at the end of the program, they received a stipend of $500 to offset the income they would have otherwise sought in part-time summer employment. More than 50 percent of students evaluated after participating in the program reported they would not have been able to participate without the stipend.

Tretter SHIP needed the stipend and other unique modifications to the National History Day model in order to ensure that students had the best opportunity to study gender and sexuality in a university setting. Stewart Van Cleve's participation in SHIP can be understood in terms of these modifications, as Kyle and Ryan contacted Stewart to join as the project's "content lead" and offer his extensive knowledge of the Tretter Collection's holdings. To orient students to LGBT history on Tretter SHIP's first day, he gave a lecture on studying LGBT history that highlighted two main points. The first part of the lecture offered a brief overview of LGBT or queer studies. It outlined that sexuality and gender are socially interpreted and enforced, not biologically innate; that our ideas about sexuality and gender are the products of historical changes; and most important, that our own concepts of sexuality and gender tint our worldview and trouble our ability to understand others' identities and perspectives. He noted that a central tenet of queer studies, and especially the study of queer history (if not history as a whole), is that wholesale judgments are unacceptable in historical interpretation, regardless of any personal revulsion or objections. In short, we impressed upon students our college-level expectations and operated under the assumption that they would meet them immediately.

In the second part of the lecture, Stewart opened a brief discussion on popular stereotypes that surround lesbian, gay, bisexual, and straight identities, as well as those that form our understanding of what purportedly differentiates men, women, and transgender people. That discussion elicited a few tense moments—a lesbian-identified young woman rejected that lesbians were "mannish" and questioned what that even meant—but those moments paled in comparison to what the students learned: that stereotypes are historically rooted, that one person's "truth" is not necessarily shared, and that even supposedly positive attributes (a gay man's purported fashion sense, a lesbian's sports prowess) become negative stereotypes when they are imposed on unwilling subjects. While the introductory discussions of stereotypes gave the Tretter SHIP cohort exposure to a college-level exchange of ideas, they also served as a perfect icebreaker. Such an immediate, open, and constructive discussion of sexuality and gender—possibly a first for many students—established an automatic intimacy among them.

Another departure from the History Day model involved the students' research topics. Stewart created eleven research topics for the students to choose from: the Native American Two-Spirit movement (year one only); the history of drag (year two only); the Harlem Renaissance; Magnus Hirschfeld and interwar Berlin; trans* history; the Mattachine Society and the Daughters of Bilitis; the Stonewall riots; lesbian feminism; Anita Bryant and the "Save Our Children" campaign; the bisexual movement; Twin Cities Pride; and the military ban on homosexuals known as "Don't Ask, Don't Tell." Each topic was broad enough for a student to experience a feeling of submersion before discovering a manageable subtopic. By the second year, we discovered that students could find different areas of interest, subtopics, within the same topic. Two young women, for example, chose lesbian feminism in the two summers: the first focused on the Lesbian Resource Center, a pioneering women's space in 1970s Minneapolis, while the second researched Martina Navratilova, whose "coming out" made her one of the world's first openly lesbian sports figures. The selection process exposed students, under careful guidance, to the struggles that first-year undergraduates often encounter when they must conceptualize a research paper—on a topic that may or may not line up with their immediate interests—for the first time. We also chose topics that we were familiar with, at least to the extent that we could ensure the students avoided "dead-end" topics that could only be explored with extensive study and distant resources.

Our respective areas of expertise delineated our responsibilities and gave students clear direction. Kyle, who took the lead in SHIP's overall organization, was responsible for answering program-related questions, overseeing interns, and directing students as they crafted their displays, while Stewart created a list of research subtopics that students chose from and guided them through the research process. In spite of our respective areas of expertise, Tretter SHIP challenged both of us in unanticipated and unfamiliar ways. Stewart found working with high school students required a vigilant brand of patience and mandated effortless transitions from one student to the next. Kyle, a programmer who had worked with students extensively, had almost no working knowledge of the topics students studied in Tretter SHIP. Knowledge of the topic was important, but the ability to communicate that knowledge in a friendly and supportive manner was key. In general, we discovered that guiding students through an LGBT history course required everyone—students and staff—to demonstrate flexibility and a willingness to learn new things.

Our familiarity also helped us guide students through the labyrinth of available resources. We conceptualized the topics with the holdings of local institutions in mind, including the Tretter Collection, local lending libraries, and reference websites, especially GLBTQ.com and OutHistory.org. The topic "bisexual movement," for example, was clearly too broad for one student research project. We supported focus on the landmark Bisexual Center in San Francisco (1976–1985) and on the work of Dr. Alfred Kinsey, but we advised against more contemporary subtopics with limited historical impact, such as the bisexuality of reality television star Tila Tequila, despite her pervasive web presence.[5] Finally, and perhaps most important, we selected topics that offered possibilities for focus on minorities within the queer population, especially those that pertained to nonwhite and gender-nonconforming people.

Our focus on queer minority narratives revealed a few problems that we did not anticipate. We created the "Two-Spirit movement" topic as an exciting opportunity for a student to confront the limits of popular ideas about sexuality and gender. Two-Spirit people often avoid labels like "man," "woman," "gay," "straight," and—depending on the person or community—"queer" or "trans" (even "Two-Spirit" is the subject of debate); their "orientations" and "genders" are instead intrinsically folded into rich cultural identities. Simply put, there are as many interpretations of Two-Spirit as there are Two-Spirit people to interpret them. This necessary complexity, coupled with an aversion to expansive labels, made the Two-Spirit movement a difficult topic for the student who selected it during the program's first year. Further, as a matter of course for anyone who begins historical study of gender and sexuality, the student interpreted materials incorrectly. For other students, such errors were an understood step of the learning process, but in the case of the Two-Spirit topic, the student's errors had the capacity for adding unintentional offense to a marginalized group. In light of this, in the second year, we changed the "Two-Spirit movement" topic to the nonequatable "history of drag" topic. Our experience helped us conclude that a Two-Spirit topic requires a member of the Two-Spirit community for guidance and instruction that a nonmember cannot emulate, regardless of academic familiarity or professional experience.

The Two-Spirit topic was the most dramatic example of a sharp learning curve that staff and students became accustomed to within hours of the first day of the two-week program. After we introduced students to ourselves and other staff, we used the first several hours

Figure 11.2. High school students in the Tretter SHIP program conduct individualized research in a topic related to LGBT history.
Courtesy of the Minnesota Historical Society

to outline the topic list. Beyond establishing the "rules" of studying sexuality and gender, Stewart's lecture reflected two SHIP goals: setting a tone of respect among students and staff and setting high expectations for students. In less than two days of work, SHIP students pared their interests to manageable subtopics and used the University of Minnesota Library's catalog, MNCAT, to collect secondary sources. They entered the program with varying degrees of research experience beyond their high schools; some frequented branches of the Hennepin County Library (which serves Minneapolis) for schoolwork, while others had only visited the University of Minnesota by passing through it on a public bus.

As students worked on individual projects in Andersen Library's conference room, SHIP staff circled from one to the next, asking them for general updates about their progress. During those initial days of the first week, staff guided students according to their specific needs. Some needed extensive help with finding a manageable focus, while others needed recommendations for additional sources. One lesbian-identified student, a young woman with a sharp wit, had to confront her own prejudices against (and pointed commentary on) antigay crusader Anita Bryant, while a straight-identified young man struggled to look past the nostalgia that surrounds memories of the 1960s—especially drug culture and popular music—to understand what drove people to riot in front of New York's Stonewall Inn. By midweek, all students were ready to consult primary archival materials located in the Tretter Collection.

Some of SHIP's most memorable scenes took place as the students worked with Tretter Collection material. A straight-identified Latino young man, for example, doodled graffiti lettering on scratch paper as he read from *The Ladder*, a 1950s–1960s periodical published by the Daughters of Bilitis. He learned that *The Ladder* was a critical means for queer women to escape isolation and find community in a hostile time. Two young men, one straight-identified and the other gay-identified, each had the rare opportunity to research the Stonewall riots before they handled a flier distributed at the event. The flier, they learned, was one of the last of its kind; it gave them a sense of the event's gravity and, perhaps, an impression that we respected them enough to entrust them with something so immeasurably valuable. Last, two students with Spanish fluency read about Magnus Hirschfeld's landmark sexology institute in *Voilà*, a 1930s French magazine published before Germany invaded France in World War II. In these and countless other instances, students had to temper their hesitation toward using archival material and turn a critical eye toward the content they read.

During the phase of archival work, staff left students to work on their projects with little unsolicited oversight; this allowed them to experience self-direction and overcome research problems on their own. Staff assistance became more persistent as students moved from research to writing; once again, each SHIP participant entered the program with unique experiences in research and writing. Further, with an average of four rotating staff members reading their work at regular intervals, students had to make choices about which editorial changes to consider and which to ignore, as each staff member advocated for revisions and occasionally contradicted another's advice. Though they expressed frustration at the recommendations of multiple editors, their writing revealed dramatic improvement between their first rough draft and their final project. Every student, regardless of their skill level at the program's onset, created writing pieces that demonstrated the critical thought and time management necessary for college work.

Figure 11.3. Using the National History Day model, students in the SHIP programs prepare a small exhibit as their final presentation.
Courtesy of the Minnesota Historical Society

Despite initial concerns over the controversial potential of an LGBT history curriculum for high school students, we did not encounter resistance of any kind from our colleagues. SHIP was viewed as a small project, which actually helped garner support among MNHS staff. The institutional attractiveness of its relatively small program budget—compared to large exhibits, ongoing conservation initiatives, and other museum projects—allowed MNHS to engage communities that are not traditionally targeted through programming without stressing already limited funding options. "Lobbying" for SHIP's worth or value was thus unnecessary, despite the institution's previous inadvertence to LGBT content. The program's clear success has the potential to inspire MNHS to run more programs centered on LGBT history and culture in the future.

Before SHIP began, we did not question high school students' ability to interpret LGBT history. Instead, we privately wondered whether parents, academicians, and public history professionals would lend their support to the program, which represented an educational initiative that was politically untenable as recently as ten years ago. Though all staff members harbored secret fears of angry parents, protesting mobs, or other catastrophes, we were surprised at the support we received and the enthusiasm parents had for their students' work. After the presentations were over, at the end of Tretter SHIP's second year, the proud mother put her camcorder away and gathered her family to leave. When asked how she felt about her daughter's presentation, she flashed a large smile, looked at her, and said, "We are so proud. So proud." Her daughter smiled back and said goodbye to her new friends, and the family left with the daughter's presentation panel in tow.

Notes

1. While this case study uses "LGBT," the Tretter Collection's formal name uses "GLBT." To avoid confusion, it will be referred to as "the Tretter Collection" or simply as "Tretter."
2. Other SHIP sessions used other archival collections in the Twin Cities area. See "Kautz Family YMCA Archives," Elmer L. Andersen Library, University of Minnesota, Twin Cities Campus, accessed October 27, 2013, https://www.lib.umn.edu/ymca/; Minnesota Historical Society Library, Minnesota History Center, retrieved October 27, 2013, http://sites.mnhs.org/library/; "The Jean-Nickolaus Tretter Collection in Gay, Lesbian, Bisexual and Transgender Studies," Elmer L. Andersen Library, University of Minnesota, Twin Cities Campus, retrieved October 27, 2013, https://www.lib.umn.edu/scrbm/tretter.
3. See Stewart Van Cleve, *Land of 10,000 Loves: A History of Queer Minnesota* (Minneapolis: University of Minnesota Press, 2012).
4. Bean is a reference and outreach archivist at the University of Minnesota's Kautz Family YMCA Archives; Hoogland is the director of Education Outreach Programs at MNHS, and Parsons assists the Diversity Outreach unit of the Education Outreach Department.
5. See Maggi Rubenstein, "A Profile of the San Francisco Bisexual Center," *Journal of Homosexuality* 11, no. 1–2 (1985): 227–30; Biblioqueers (San Francisco Public Library Staff), "Archives: David Lourea and the Bisexual Center," *Queerest. Library. Ever.* (blog), January 18, 2013, http://queerestlibraryever.blogspot.com/2013/01/archives-david-lourea-and-bisexual.html; Kinsey Institute, "Origin of the Institute," *Kinsey Institute for Research in Sex, Gender, and Reproduction*, accessed June 2, 2014, http://www.kinseyinstitute.org/about/origins.html.

CHAPTER 12

Issues to Consider When Interpreting LGBT History

IN THE PREVIOUS three chapters, the authors of the case studies shared their experiences with LGBT historical interpretation, chronicling not only their successes but also their challenges in exploring topics that were new for their organizations. A variety of other museum professionals have written about their own efforts to interpret the history of same-sex love and desire (see the appendix "Recommended Reading" at the end of this volume), and numerous others kindly took the time to talk with me about their experiences. From these cumulative sources, certain trends emerge. In the following pages, I offer a discussion of issues that arise when considering LGBT interpretive projects in the hope that it will assist other institutions with project planning. Issues to consider include stakeholders, staffing, terminology, whether to present LGBT history separately or as part of a larger narrative, and the degree to which sexual content will be included in the interpretation.[1]

In the next chapter, by way of conclusion, I detail a series of recommendations made by those who have firsthand experience interpreting LGBT history.

Stakeholders

First and foremost, as with any interpretive effort, museums should consider their stakeholders. Will your board support the interpretation of LGBT history? How will such a project affect your funding? Is this a topic that is of interest to your current visitors, or, just as importantly, will it bring in new visitors? Is your community ready to examine the questions raised by exploring this history? While I urge museums to stretch their organizational selves and embrace the opportunity to expand beyond the usual interpretive terrain of history museums, I also acknowledge that variant sexuality and gender expression are still extremely controversial in some parts of the United States. Because of the potential for controversy, it is worthwhile to do some initial consensus building among key stakeholders before project planning begins.[2]

Conversations with stakeholders will be more productive if they move beyond the general question of whether or not to include LGBT content in interpretation. As mentioned previously, a general acceptance of same-sex relationships that mirror traditional nuclear families does not necessarily equal comfort with more unfamiliar aspects of LGBT experience. Transgender identities, nonmonogamous relationships, sadomasochism, cruising, legalized discrimination, and ongoing critiques of dominant society are all part of the history of LGBT people. Part of the decision to interpret LGBT experiences should be a consideration of various types of experiences so that stakeholders truly understand the implications of the project.[3]

In addition to boards, staff, donors, and established visitors, LGBT people from various backgrounds and social strata are also very obvious stakeholders who should not be overlooked. In the words of gay Wyoming native Gregory Hinton, curator of the *Out West* programming series, "[M]ake no mistake about it. I love Wyoming. And I love western art museums. And by birthright, I am a stakeholder in the past, present and future of the American West."[4]

Staffing

LGBT interpretative projects require conscientious staffing. It is likely that LGBT staff people will be vocal supporters of the project, but their sexual identity does not necessarily mean they are the best qualified to head the effort. Museums and historic sites should strive to involve all relevant staff in interpreting LGBT history based on expertise rather than assigning only queer staff to the project. To do so would send the message that LGBT history is only relevant to those who identify as such. In addition, because the history of variant sexuality and gender expression is not widely taught in history classes, its interpretation may well require expertise beyond that of in-house employees. For *Out in Chicago*, the Chicago History Museum brought together Jill Austin, a curator on staff with extensive expertise in social history, and Jennifer Brier, a professor at the University of Illinois at Chicago who specializes in LGBT history, to cocurate the exhibit. In their case study in this volume, Austin and Brier discuss the process of creating allies among straight staff and stakeholders. The personal relevance of LGBT history to straight staff was not always immediately apparent, but with assistance they discovered these connections, which in turn strengthened their commitment to the project.

In addition, ongoing efforts, such as the Gay Ohio History Initiative (Ohio History Connection) or the Summer History Immersion Program (Minnesota Historical Society), require long-term designated staffing. As Stacia Kuceyeski points out, these efforts should not just be a "labor of love" for a particular staff person who does the work in addition to assigned job duties. Such a model is simply not sustainable. Rather, responsibility for the program should be written into someone's job description and included in performance goals.[5]

Terminology

Another set of issues to consider revolves around terminology. What language is your organization going to use when describing same-sex desire and gender fluidity? How are you going to ensure that your language represents a diversity of lived experience? As we have already discussed, the concept of homosexuality is only about 125 years old. Before the turn of the twentieth century, people had sex with other people of their same sex; they fell in love with people of their same sex; they transgressed gender roles and sometimes adopted gender identities that did not match expectations. However, the words we use to describe such people—gay, lesbian, bisexual, transgender, queer—did not exist. Nor did other words fill in for the same concepts.

Words change their meanings over time. What's more, in a culture that engages in so much political and religious commentary about the meanings of sexual and gender orientation, one's ability to *self*-define and *choose* one's own labels takes on significant emotional meaning. At this particular historical moment, no single agreed-upon language exists for describing these concepts and their history. Different interpretive efforts have made use of different terminology. Nevertheless, although the specific answers may vary, the fact remains that word choice warrants significant thought.

A distinct generational divide exists within the LGBT community regarding use of the word "queer." Until the 1990s, "queer" was a derogatory term used by outsiders. As such, many older people have a strongly negative reaction to the word, associating it with jeers and violence in their youth. They reject the label of queer and instead prefer LGBT. In addition, many lesbians, bisexuals, and transgender people fought hard to establish a distinct identity rather than be lumped under the label "gay," which, like the word "man," once allegedly applied to everyone while also applying exclusively to one subset of humanity, effectively erasing everyone else. This constituency is proud to have their distinct identities recognized in the acronym and may fear that a return to a single label such as "queer" will signal a return to the assumption that everyone who is queer is a (white, middle-class) male homosexual.[6]

On the other hand, people who came of age in the 1990s or later tend to see the word "queer" as an umbrella word that works to break down strict categories (lesbian, gay, bisexual, transgender) in favor of the common experience of questioning inherited wisdom with regard to sexual and gender expression. Those who identify as queer may reject the binaries inherent in words like "homosexual" and "heterosexual," "male" and "female," and because of this may not feel represented by the acronym LGBT, which relies to a large extent on these either-or categories.

In addition to deciding what contemporary labels to embrace, organizations will also face questions about what vocabulary to use when describing the past. Will you use contemporary categories that the historical agents being discussed would not recognize? Will you instead discuss the circumstances of their lives without recourse to such labels (a more historically accurate but also more cumbersome path)? Organizations have chosen to respond to these questions in a variety of ways. The Library Company of Philadelphia, for example, addressed the issue of terminology in the introduction to their exhibit *That's So Gay: Outing Early America* (2014) by stating:

How can we know whether someone was gay? There are many answers to that question, but ultimately we cannot know whether a person who lived in the past would be called lesbian, gay, bisexual, or transgender today.

That does not mean that we cannot study gay history. Individuals took part in same-sex relationships, wrote poems and novels celebrating such relationships, deviated from gender norms, and suffered for transgressive behavior in ways that are well-documented in the historical record. Gayness can also be considered a shared cultural experience based on an intrinsically gay outlook on the world.[7]

A few organizations have even decided to incorporate into their interpretation an exploration of the issues involving terminology. *Revealing Queer*, at the Museum of History and Industry (MOHAI) in Seattle, dedicated a corner of its one-thousand-square-foot exhibit space to definitions and offered an interactive element where visitors could record the words they use to identify themselves. As a result, visitors had a voice in declaring what labels best described their lived experience and, in the aggregate, the responses revealed the range of possible identities available (figure 12.1).[8]

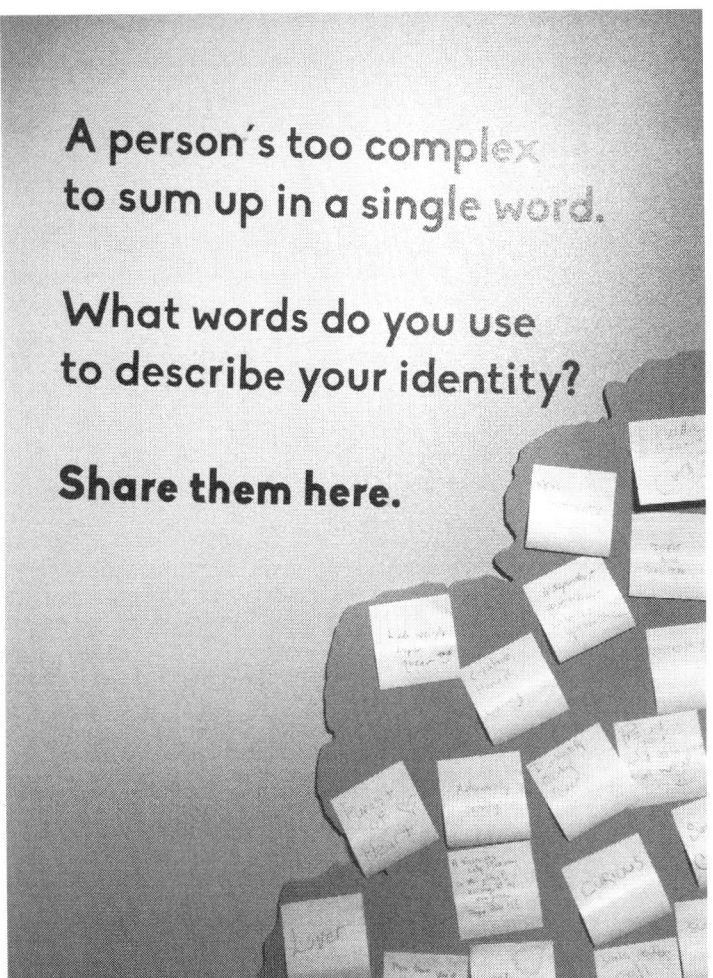

Figure 12.1.
The *Revealing Queer* exhibit at Seattle's Museum of History and Industry invited visitors to share the words they use to describe themselves. Courtesy of Susan Ferentinos

Integration with Larger Themes versus Special Programming

In light of the dominant culture's rapidly growing acceptance of queer experiences, LGBT communities debate the relative merits of assimilation versus maintaining distinct and vibrant subcultures. A parallel set of issues exists for historical organizations, which must decide the most meaningful ways to interpret the LGBT past. Is it best interpreted through special programming (exhibits, tours, events) that highlights the topic, perhaps even celebrates it, or through integration into larger historical narratives (for instance, permanent exhibits or programming on topics other than LGBT history) so that the overall story of the past becomes more richly textured and experiences of variant sexuality and gender expression become "normalized"?

Within a museum setting, we can see this debate illustrated by the Atlanta History Center's *Unspoken Past: Gay and Lesbian Atlanta, 1940–1970* and the Library of Congress's *Creating the United States*. *Unspoken Past* was a special exhibit (2005) that showcased the history of homosexuality in Atlanta and grew out of a specific effort to collect LGBT oral histories. The exhibit provided a space where straight Atlanta residents could learn about a part of their city's past that they likely knew little about and queer Atlanta residents could see themselves represented in the past, an experience that is still dishearteningly rare for this population. The showcasing of gay and lesbian realities in this special exhibit highlighted this part of the city's history and gave potential visitors a new, specific reason to come to the museum. It also provided an opportunity for LGBT visitors to engage with the past in ways traditionally denied to them. In the words of John Fraser and Joe E. Heimlich, "The ghettoizing of the queer story [in special exhibits] is not without its benefits, because a community needs a place to incubate their story."[9]

On the other side of the debate, integration into a larger narrative can send a powerful message of inclusion to groups that have traditionally been shunned and marginalized. Consider the impact of the Library of Congress's decision in 2009 to add LGBT historical documents to its permanent exhibition, *Creating the United States*. This exhibit presented key documents relating to the legal framework of the nation, including its civil rights protections. The LGBT documents on display related to Frank Kameny's 1957 termination from his job with the federal government because of his homosexuality. Kameny challenged his termination, and though he was never reinstated, both his petition and the response letter from the US Civil Service Commission were eventually placed within the larger national narrative by the Library of Congress exhibit, which was seen by approximately two million visitors. In the words of Charles Francis, a founder of the Kameny Papers Project, "This inclusion is an epic milestone in the telling of gay history because it places gay Americans' struggle for equality where it belongs—in the story of the Constitution itself." Sadly, this is a level of inclusion LGBT Americans have rarely experienced.[10]

Interestingly, the question of who is incorporated into the US body politic has been the organizing principle of at least two other exhibits that placed LGBT history into larger narratives. The National Constitution Center in Philadelphia includes intermittent representation of LGBT experiences in its permanent exhibit, and as part of its temporary exhibit, *We the People: The Nebraska Viewpoint* (2010–2011), the Nebraska Historical Society recounted the 1993 rape and murder of Brandon Teena, a trans man living in Humboldt, Nebraska. It is perhaps worth noting that both of these exhibits received some criticism of their LGBT portrayal by observers employing a queer perspective when visiting.[11]

Both integration and segregation carry benefits, so it is fortunate that organizations do not have to choose just one approach. Developing inclusive interpretation is an ongoing effort and will most likely involve a variety of methods undertaken over time.

Interpreting Sexuality

The Museum of Vancouver's exhibit *Sex Talk in the City* (2013) opened with the tantalizing words, "Even Museums Have Sexy Thoughts . . ." Delightful though that line may be, the question remains, how sexy is your discussion of LGBT history going to get? Make no mistake about it, people who engage in same-sex relationships have had their lives defined in many ways by their sexual orientation; sex is a crucial part of the story. Yet, on the other hand, as Stacia Kuceyeski charmingly stated in a recent presentation, "Queer people do a whole lot more than just have sex."[12]

To be sure, the history of sexuality is not the most obvious topic to cover in a public institution, particularly if that venue is an all-ages one and relies on donations or public funding. And in this vast nation of ours, communities vary widely in their level of traditionalism and/

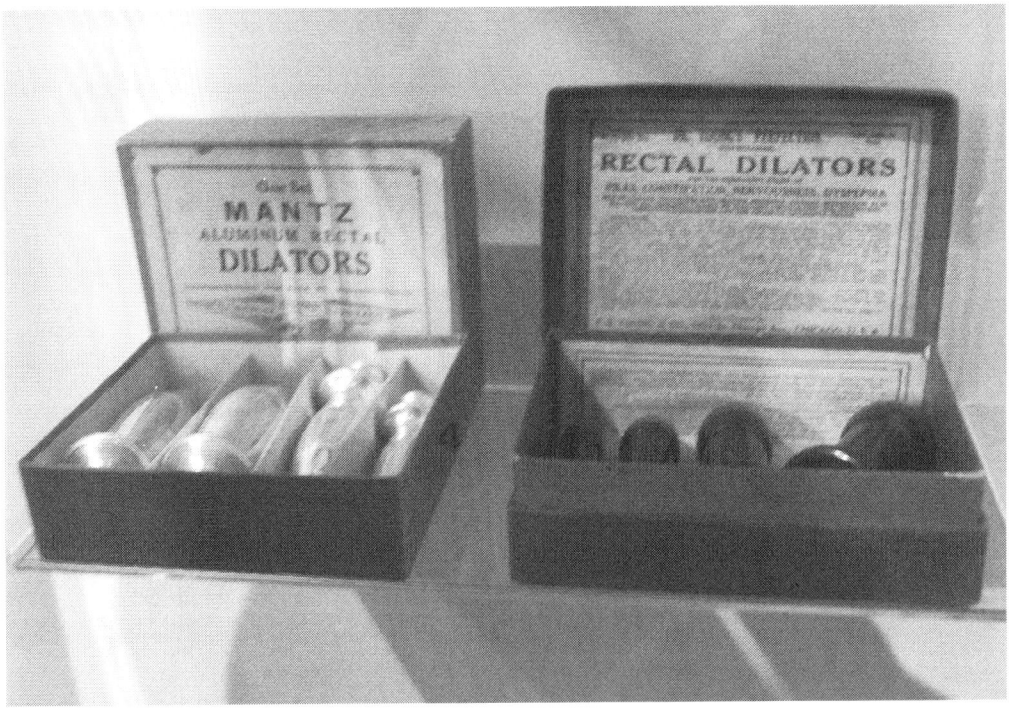

Figure 12.2. Museums need to decide how explicitly to discuss the sexual aspects of LGBT history. Here, rectal dilators on display at the Museum of Sex.
Courtesy of Cleo Leng

or their interest in learning about other cultures. Nevertheless, sexuality is a legitimate lens through which to study the past. Cultures tend to divide sexual behavior into the "normal" and the "abnormal," and these classifications usually intersect with other societal constructs, such as race, class, and gender. By considering who fell into each category at different points in our history, we acquire insight on a given era's values and anxieties. We also gain perspective on the mutability of the seemingly immutable truths of our own age.

Sexuality also, in many cases, provides an express route to issues of power in society. Who defines the sexual norm? Who polices it? Who is free to violate it? Who is punished for violating it? Who is sexually vulnerable? Why? Who are the sexual aggressors, victims, and villains at a given moment? (Or does my very assumption that these roles are universal reveal too much about my own historical moment? My own values?) For nearly fifty years, the historical profession has operated under a shared agreement that race, class, and gender are useful categories of analysis precisely *because* they get to the heart of identity and power in this culture. They draw the lines around who's in and who's out. In more recent decades, growing numbers of historians are realizing that sexuality, too, is a particularly useful category of analysis for the same reasons.

Within museums and historic sites, there is also the simple fact that sexuality is already well represented within interpretation. In reality, it is hard to ignore the role of sexuality in society, past or present. As Fraser and Hemlich put it, "[R]efusing to talk about it does not mean sex is not omnipresent in all social interactions; it's central to the artifacts that define culture, and appears in some form in the collection of almost every museum. Sex and sex roles are socially relevant to everyday experience."[13] Sexuality infuses the museum, but when that sexual content enforces societal norms—in the form of a heterosexual love letter, for instance, or the biographical data of how many children a historical figure had—it is usually not recognized as sexual. In contrast, parallel information about same-sex sexuality—a love letter between two women or the biographical data that this male historical figure joined with another man in life partnership—can sometimes seem challenging to heterosexuals because of its "sexual nature." Interpreters should remain alert to this potential for a double standard to creep into decisions about what materials are and are not appropriate for display. Furthermore, a number of queer museum professionals have commented on the issue of internalized homophobia, whereby LGBT people censor themselves in order to avoid offending the dominant society.[14]

Museums have taken a range of approaches to the question of explicit content. As described in Kenneth C. Turino's case study in this volume, Historic New England tends to avoid commentary that is overtly sexual, choosing *not* to display Ogden Codman Jr.'s collection of homosexual erotica, for example, although the organization does discuss homosexual identities and relationships more generally. The Stonewall National Museum and Archive, on the other hand, embraces sexual expression as a crucial part of LGBT culture. Museum leadership sees it as the museum's function to challenge visitors' established notions, and they have opted against the use of any kind of warning labels concerning explicit content.[15]

Any type of interpretive planning involves a series of decisions. Within the realm of LGBT history, issues of stakeholder buy-in, conscientious staffing, terminology, integration versus segregation, and explicitly sexual content come into play. Final decisions about these issues will depend on a variety of factors—and hopefully the input of stakeholders, particularly representatives of LGBT communities, as well. Nevertheless, careful consideration of these topics will ensure that the resulting interpretation rests on a solid foundation.

Notes

1. For an additional discussion of the issues involved in LGBT historical interpretation, see Kenneth Turino and Susan Ferentinos, "Entering the Mainstream: Interpreting GLBT History," *AASLH History News*, Autumn 2012.
2. Ibid.; Wesley Chenault, curator of *Unspoken Past: Atlanta Lesbian and Gay History, 1940–1970* (Atlanta History Center) and member of the John Q Collective, phone interview with Susan Ferentinos, May 15, 2014; Michael Petry, "Hidden Histories: The Experience of Curating a Male Same-Sex Exhibition and the Problems Encountered," in *Gender, Sexuality, and Museums: A Routledge Reader*, ed. Amy K. Levin (New York: Routledge, 2010), 151–62; Angela Vanegas, "Representing Lesbians and Gay Men in British Social History Museums," in *Gender, Sexuality, and Museums: A Routledge Reader*, ed. Amy K. Levin (New York: Routledge, 2010), 168–69; Stacia Kuceyeski, "The Gay Ohio History Initiative as a Model for Collecting Institutions," *Museums & Social Issues* 3, no. 1 (April 1, 2008): 125–32.
3. For more on this idea, see Kevin P. Murphy, Jason Ruiz, and David Serlin, "Editors' Introduction (Queer Transgressions Issue)," *Radical History Review*, no. 100 (Winter 2008): 1–9.
4. Gregory Hinton, "Out West" (keynote address, LGBTQ Alliance Luncheon, American Alliance of Museums, Seattle, May 18, 2014).
5. Stacia Kuceyeski, Director of Outreach at the Ohio History Connection and liaison to the Gay Ohio History Initiative, phone interview with Susan Ferentinos, April 3, 2014; Kuceyeski, "The Gay Ohio History Initiative as a Model for Collecting Institutions."
6. Paul Gabriel, "Why Grapple with Queer When You Can Fondle It? Embracing Our Erotic Intelligence," in *Gender, Sexuality and Museums: A Routledge Reader*, ed. Amy K. Levin (New York: Routledge, 2010), 71–79; Paul Gabriel, "Embracing Our Erotic Intelligence," *Museums & Social Issues* 3, no. 1 (April 1, 2008): 53–66.
7. "That's So Gay: Outing Early America," *Gay History in the Collections of the Library Company of Philadelphia*, accessed May 30, 2014, http://www.gayatlcp.org/.
8. Erin Bailey, Jill Austin, and Viviane Gosselin, "Revealing Urban Histories through LGBTQ Museum Programming" (paper presented at the American Alliance of Museums Annual Meeting, Seattle, 2014); Lisa Yun Lee, "Peering into the Bedroom: Restorative Justice at the Jane Addams Hull House Museum," in *Routledge Companion to Museum Ethics: Redefining Ethics for the Twenty-First Century Museum*, ed. Janet Marstine (New York: Routledge, 2011), 174–88; Susan Ferentinos, "Lifting Our Skirts: Sharing the Sexual Past with Visitors," *Public History Commons: The Public Historian* (July 1, 2014), http://publichistorycommons.org/tph/.
9. John Fraser and Joe E. Heimlich, "Where Are We?," *Museums & Social Issues* 3, no. 1 (Spring 2008): 11.
10. Associated Press, "Library of Congress Exhibits Gay Rights History," *The Buzz* (blog), *Washington Post*, May 9, 2011, http://www.washingtonpost.com/blogs/the-buzz/post/library-of-congress-exhibits-gay-rights-history/2011/05/09/AFklNtYG_blog.html; Andrew Weber and Brock Thompson, "Gay Rights and the Law: The Library of Congress Displays Gay Rights Documents," *In Custodia Legis: Law Librarians of Congress* (blog), Library of Congress,

June 1, 2011, http://blogs.loc.gov/law/2011/06/gay-rights-and-the-law/; Library of Congress, "'Creating the United States' to Close May 5," news release, April 9, 2012, accessed March 1, 2014, http://www.loc.gov/today/pr/2012/12-071.html.

11. Jenny Ramberg, "'Are Queer Folk the People, Too?' Exhibit Review: National Constitution Center, Philadelphia, PA," *Museums & Social Issues* 3, no. 1 (April 1, 2008): 143–49; Carly S. Woods, Joshua P. Ewalt, and Sara J. Baker, "A Matter of Regionalism: Remembering Brandon Teena and Willa Cather at the Nebraska History Museum," *Quarterly Journal of Speech* 99, no. 3 (2013): 341–63.

12. Viviane Gosselin, "Civic Museography, Porous Narratives and the Choir Effect: Sex Talk in the City at the Museum of Vancouver," *THEMA. La revue des Musées de la civilisation*, 1 (March 24, 2014): 107–15; Susan Ferentinos, Stacia Kuceyeski, and Kenneth Turino, "Sex and Silences: Interpreting LGBT History" (panel presented at the American Alliance of Museums Annual Meeting, Seattle, 2014).

13. Fraser and Heimlich, "Where Are We?," 6. See also Jennifer Tyburczy, "All Museums Are Sex Museums," *Radical History Review*, no. 113 (Spring 2012): 199–211; Gabriel, "Why Grapple with Queer?"

14. Jill Austin et al., "When the Erotic Becomes Illicit: Struggles over Displaying Queer History at a Mainstream Museum," *Radical History Review*, no. 113 (Spring 2012): 187–97; Gabriel, "Why Grapple with Queer?"; David Jobin, Executive Director, Stonewall National Museum and Archives, interview with Susan Ferentinos, May 20, 2014.

15. Jobin, interview with Susan Ferentinos.

CHAPTER 13

Conclusion
Some Suggestions

THE PREVIOUS chapter explored some issues to consider when planning LGBT historical interpretation. The decisions made regarding these issues will vary based on organizational specifics; different institutions have taken different approaches. In this, the final chapter, I highlight some recommendations that appeared repeatedly, both in the literature and in conversations with other museum professionals. Previous chapters have touched on each of these suggestions; here I offer an encapsulated list for easy reference and as a means of summarizing the volume as a whole.

There's More Than One Way to Do This

Kenneth C. Turino's case study of Historic New England provides an excellent illustration of the fact that, even within one organization, there exist multiple effective ways to approach the history of same-sex love and desire. Within historic sites, options include integrating discussion of sexual identity into the standard visitor experience; training staff to answer visitor questions on the subject if asked; and special tours and events designed to appeal to LGBT communities.[1] Museums have also offered special programming, such as the *Out West* series (which began at the Autry and has since spread to other venues) or a tour of the National Museum of Fine Arts in Stockholm given from a queer perspective. In addition, museums have used various types of exhibits to interpret LGBT history. Seattle's Museum of History and Industry (MOHAI) includes LGBT community life and activism in its permanent exhibit on the history of the city. The Museum of Vancouver integrated LGBT experiences into a larger exploration of sexuality with its *Sex Talk in the City* exhibit, an approach similar to that taken by the Museum of Sex. Many museums—Chicago History Museum, Atlanta History Center, and Rosie the Riveter/World War II Home Front National Historical Park among them—have offered or are developing special exhibits on the topic.[2]

Solicit Input from Community Advisors

As is true of other oppressed groups, people with nonnormative sexual and gender identity have a long history of the voices of authority misrepresenting them. Given this historical context, an invitation to participate in the development of LGBT content sends an important message of respect. Oral histories and interviews lend a human face to a community so often vilified, and advisory panels that include diverse representation of LGBT communities can ensure that content is relevant and meaningful. In soliciting such input, however, organizations should remember that a single, monolithic LGBT community does not exist. Advisory groups should represent not only lesbians, gays, bisexuals, and transgender people, but also a diversity of races/ethnicities, classes, ages, and social groups.

Some organizations have expanded on the standard idea of an advisory panel to ensure even richer input. The Chicago History Museum assembled two separate community panels, one comprising people who identified as LGBT/queer and one comprising people who identified as straight, in order to gather a wide range of perspectives on the *Out in Chicago* exhibit. The Museum of Vancouver selected only four people to serve on its advisory panel for *Sex Talk in the City*, empowering those committee members to identify other potential participants for the panel, which eventually included eighteen members. This approach allowed the museum to benefit from a wider network of potential contacts and permitted the committee to identify its own needs. Finally, *Revealing Queer*, at the Museum of History and Industry in Seattle (MOHAI), represents a particularly community-based approach. The product of a larger endeavor called "Queering the Museum," the exhibit was actually cocurated by a committee of representatives from a wide range of LGBT community groups in the Seattle area under the facilitation of Erin Bailey and Nicole Robert, founders of the "Queering the Museum" project.[3]

Get Comfortable Giving Up Control

Related to the idea of soliciting input from LGBT communities, those with experience also encourage museums to prepare to give up some curatorial control. Indeed, this is a larger effort for our field, as museums transition from the role of expert to the role of facilitator. This general trend becomes even more important as interpretation pushes into new territory and utilizes new approaches. For example, the John Q Collective uses historical sources to create "discursive memorials" on the streets of Atlanta. A 2010 effort, *Memory Flash*, took four moments from Atlanta's LGBT past to memorialize at the sites where the events originally occurred, engaging audience members and passersby in an interpretation of past events. Incorporating the public into a real-time memorial performance, however, required the collective to embrace the audience as cocreators of the event, since their reactions to the unfolding narrative could not be predicted ahead of time.[4]

Explore Partnerships

To further expand on the theme of sharing authority, most LGBT interpretive efforts have benefited from making ample use of partnerships. Partnering with other organizations can serve a variety of purposes, among them: enhancing community buy-in and trust; increasing the available sources of artifacts; combining different organizational strengths; and delivering public service information. The Summer History Immersion Program (SHIP) case study featured in this volume provides an example of effective partnering. When developing college preparatory programming for high school students, the Minnesota Historical Society (MNHS) and the Special Collections Library of the University of Minnesota partnered together to deliver content related to LGBT history. MNHS provided the template for the program and the connections with area high schools, having successfully offered SHIPs on other topics previously, while the University of Minnesota—specifically the Tretter Collection in GLBT Studies—offered content expertise in LGBT history and primary materials with which students could practice the research and writing skills they were learning. Likewise, the *Out West* programming series relies on the expertise, community connections, and passion of independent curator Gregory Hinton, who partners with various institutions—including the Autry National Center for the American West, the Buffalo Bill Center of the West, and the Eiteljorg Museum of American Indians and Western Art—to provide the physical location, museum staff, and infrastructure for the program's various projects.[5]

Define Your Terms

Creators of inclusive museum experiences understand that words have power. In the previous chapter, I presented some of the issues involved in selecting vocabulary to describe LGBT realities. The specific words used in interpretation are something to determine in consultation with your stakeholders, both representatives of your local LGBTQ communities and historians knowledgeable about the changing meanings of words over time. Regardless of which words you ultimately use, defining your terms will assist visitors, particularly those who are new to this subject, to engage with the interpretive content. *Out in Chicago* included a "sexicon" throughout the exhibit, which provided definitions of terms used and demonstrated words' changing meanings over time (figure 13.1). One sexicon label, for instance, offered definitions of the word "queer":

> *Queer*
>   1 (1513): strange, odd, peculiar, eccentric
>   2 (c. 1895) *often disparaging*: a male homosexual
>   3 (c. 1980): reclaimed by activists to describe a range of gender and sexual nonconformities[6]

Avoid the Progress Narrative

Those who have studied US history are likely well aware of the caveat against viewing the past as one consistent march toward progress. While traditionally US history was taught this way, for the past half century there has been a growing acknowledgment that previous eras were just as complicated as our own, with societal changes regularly bringing both benefits and challenges and one group's "progress" producing more ambivalent outcomes for others.

queer

1 (1513): strange, odd, peculiar, eccentric
2 (c. 1895) *often disparaging*: a male homosexual
3 (c. 1980): reclaimed by activists to describe a range of gender and sexual nonconformities

Figure 13.1. The *Out in Chicago* exhibit included a "sexicon" that demonstrated the changing meaning of words over time.
Courtesy of the Chicago History Museum

Just as this is true for the nation as a whole, so is it true for the story of any particular group within the nation. As such, commentators urge against employing a "progress narrative," which presents LGBT historical experience as uniform and unerringly one of increasing acceptance and expanding civil rights protection.[7]

As the history section of this volume demonstrates, same-sex desire has carried different meanings in different eras. These shifting meanings have had shifting implications for acceptance, safety, and acknowledgment of those who desire their own sex or whose gender identity does not match their physical body. To name but one example, before the medical profession developed the concept of homosexuality as a mental disorder at the turn of the twentieth century, intense, affectionate female friendships were commonplace among the middle class and did not carry any taint of sexual impropriety. This social acceptance eroded as the twentieth century progressed, and such relationships eventually became cause for consternation. To carry the point into the current era, while many LGBT people view the growing acceptance of same-sex marriage as a watershed political victory, others greet the trend more equivocally. For those who see their sexual and/or gender orientation as a critique of dominant relationship models and gender roles, the adoption of a nuclear family framework within the LGBT community is a setback in the effort to create a world of more fluid and diverse sexual/gender expression.

Understand the Trauma of Oppression

The LGBT past is not an unflinching march of progress, but it *is* a terrain marked by trauma. Words (such as "queer," "dyke," or "fairy") that some LGBT people now embrace carry damaging memories for others. Older LGBT people are survivors of an era when openness about one's sexual orientation and/or transgender identity quite possibly meant ostracism, job loss, violence, dishonorable military discharge, loss of parental custody rights, rejection by church and family, and/or confinement to a mental hospital. Gay men who were sexually active from the 1970s through the mid-1990s likely experienced profound loss of friends, lovers, and associates to the AIDS epidemic. Such experiences necessarily inform individual choices to engage with the past, publicly identify as LGBT, or share artifacts and memories.

In light of this context, engagement with this community requires sensitivity to issues of discretion and to the possibility that historical content might be personally disturbing for some. Staff at Rosie the Riveter/National World War II Home Front National Historical Park, aware that they were dealing with a generation who came of age in the 1930s and 1940s, set up a confidential phone line when soliciting stories of the LGBT home front so that closeted individuals could feel safe sharing their stories. Likewise, in the curators' tour featured in the *Out in Chicago* DVD, cocurator Jennifer Brier movingly describes the active grieving she witnessed as visitors to the exhibit confronted pictures of gay community life in the 1970s and 1980s. Longtime gay Chicago residents recognized many people in the photographs, and they knew that most men pictured—their friends, their partners—were killed by the lack of government response to the epidemic.[8]

Prepare for a Range of Reactions

Interpreters report a range of audience responses to LGBT programming. As discussed in chapter 2, many organizations have received only accolades when presenting LGBT history. Others have faced complaints. Most report both positive and negative feedback, a sign that their interpretive efforts are generating notice, engaging visitors, and prompting reactions. A workshop at the 2014 American Alliance of Museums Annual Meeting asked participants to develop a response to a strongly worded complaint from a gay visitor who felt an exhibit on queer history had not gone deep enough. Lisa Yun Lee reports that some visitors to the Jane Addams Hull-House Museum expressed discomfort with interpretation of Addams's relationship with Mary Rozet Smith, feeling that it was either irrelevant to the story of Hull House or that it was a violation of Addams's privacy. Meanwhile, Lauren Jae Gutterman describes efforts that the staff at OutHistory.org—a wiki-style website designed for public interactivity—took to determine why initial interaction with the site fell far below anticipated levels. As with all public programming, specific audience reactions can be difficult to predict. For this reason, museums should prepare for a variety of feedback so that they can respond promptly and nimbly to visitor comments.[9]

The ToonSeum, in Pittsburgh, received some publicity in 2014 when it became a sponsor of a citywide LGBT pride event. In responding, Joe Wos, the executive director of the museum, framed the organization's decision in terms of ethics, not visitation. In his words:

> We had about 6 people drop from our mailing list. We also had several people make donations or buy memberships. But truthfully none of that matters. You just have to do what is right. Any risk or consequence or any reward is irrelevant because doing right and treating people right is simply the only choice in my mind. It isn't someone's sexuality that matters it's their humanity that requires we treat all people equally and with respect.[10]

Develop a Sustainability Plan

Finally, informants repeatedly stressed the need for long-term planning. Consistently, organizational efforts to interpret LGBT history are met with a great outpouring of enthusiasm from LGBT communities. Such projects send a message of welcome and inclusion that causes LGBT visitors to invest emotionally and perhaps financially in the organizations that are telling this forgotten history. This investment carries expectations. While a museum may feel it has done its part for its LGBT audiences by offering a few special events or a temporary exhibit, LGBT stakeholders want to know that they are an ongoing part of the organization's mission.[11] As one blog writer commented after announcing a small, temporary 2009 exhibit on LGBT history at the National Museum of American History, "This first exhibit is a historical moment itself, but should not be the beginning and end of the conversation about gay Americans."[12]

After the "special" programming is complete, how will LGBT history be incorporated into larger narratives? How will your organization continue to engage with LGBT communities? Will LGBT interpretation be permitted to "queer" the organization, prompting an exploration of the ways discriminatory messages of what is and is not "normal" infuse the wider work of the museum? LGBT stakeholders will want to know the answers to these questions. Museums would do well to have their answers ready.[13]

No single book can comprehensively cover the history of same-sex love and desire in the United States as well as explore all the considerations and examples of interpreting that history to the public. However, I hope this volume has provided a tantalizing glimpse of the possibilities. The changing ways the dominant society has defined "normal" behavior and the fortitude people have employed to live their truths amid those changing definitions make for a fascinating tale. Equally exciting are the creative means that museums and historic sites have utilized in order to share that history with visitors. LGBT history represents a unique opportunity for museums to prove their relevance by providing context to contemporary issues and sharing a narrative of US history that more fully encompasses all its citizens.

Notes

1. Kenneth Turino and Susan Ferentinos, "Entering the Mainstream: Interpreting GLBT History," *AASLH History News*, Autumn 2012; Frank D. Vagnone, "A Note from Franklin D. Vagnone, Executive Director," *Historic House Trust Newsletter*, Fall 2010; Alison Oram, "Going on an Outing: The Historic House and Queer Public History," *Rethinking History* 15, no. 2 (June 2011): 189–207; Lisa Yun Lee, "Peering into the Bedroom: Restorative Justice at the Jane Addams Hull House Museum," in *Routledge Companion to Museum Ethics: Redefining Ethics for the Twenty-First Century Museum*, ed. Janet Marstine (New York: Routledge, 2011), 174–88; Kevin D. Murphy, "'Secure from All Intrusion': Heterotopia, Queer Space, and the Turn-of-the-Twentieth-Century American Resort," *Winterthur Portfolio* 43, no. 2/3 (Summer 2009): 185–228.
2. Gregory Hinton, "Out West" (keynote address, LGBTQ Alliance Luncheon, American Alliance of Museums, Seattle, May 18, 2014); Patrik Steorn, "Curating Queer Heritage: Queer Knowledge and Museum Practice," *Curator* 55, no. 3 (July 2012): 355–65; Viviane Gosselin, "Civic Museography, Porous Narratives and the Choir Effect: Sex Talk in the City at the Museum of Vancouver," *THEMA. La revue des Musées de la civilisation*, 1 (March 24, 2014): 107–15; Jill Austin and Jennifer Brier, eds., *Out in Chicago: LGBT History at the Crossroads* (Chicago: Chicago History Museum, 2011); Wesley Chenault, "The Unspoken Past: Atlanta

Lesbian and Gay History," *Perspectives*, December 2006; Elizabeth Tucker, lead park ranger, Rosie the Riveter/World War II Home Front National Historical Park, phone interview with Susan Ferentinos, April 29, 2014; Erin Bailey, Jill Austin, and Viviane Gosselin, "Revealing Urban Histories through LGBTQ Museum Programming" (panel presented at the American Alliance of Museums Annual Meeting, Seattle, 2014).

3. Jill Austin et al., "When the Erotic Becomes Illicit: Struggles over Displaying Queer History at a Mainstream Museum," *Radical History Review* 113 (Spring 2013): 192; Gosselin, "Civic Museography, Porous Narratives and the Choir Effect," 108; Jana Greenslit, "The Road to Revealing Queer: An Interview with Curator Erin Bailey, Part I," *Incluseum* (blog), March 5, 2014, http://incluseum.com/2014/03/05/the-road-to-revealing-queer-an-interview-with-curator-erin-bailey-part-i/; Jana Greenslit, "The Road to Revealing Queer: An Interview with Curator Erin Bailey, Part II," *Incluseum* (blog), March 14, 2014, http://incluseum.com/2014/03/14/the-road-to-revealing-queer-an-interview-with-curator-erin-bailey-part-ii/; Darryl McIntyre, "What to Collect? Museums and Lesbian, Gay, Bisexual and Transgender Collecting," *International Journal of Art & Design Education* 26, no. 1 (February 2007): 48–53.

4. Wesley Chenault, Andy Ditzler, and Joey Orr, "Discursive Memorials: Queer Histories in Atlanta's Public Spaces," *Southern Spaces*, February 26, 2010, http://www.southernspaces.org/2010/discursive-memorials-queer-histories-atlantas-public-spaces; Wesley Chenault, curator of *Unspoken Past: Atlanta Lesbian and Gay History, 1940–1970* (Atlanta History Center) and member of the John Q Collective, phone interview with Susan Ferentinos, May 15, 2014; Bernard A. Zuckerman Museum of Art, *John Q: Projects 2009–2013* (Kennesaw, GA: Kennesaw State University, 2014); Erin Bailey and Nicole Robert, "An Insider's Look at the Queering the Museum Project" (workshop presented at the American Alliance of Museums Annual Meeting, Seattle, 2014); Bill Adair, Benjamin Filene, and Laura Koloski, eds., *Letting Go? Sharing Historical Authority in a User-Generated World* (Philadelphia: Pew Center for Arts & Heritage, 2011), 13; Lauren Jae Gutterman, "OutHistory.org: An Experiment in LGBTQ Community History-Making," *Public Historian* 32, no. 4 (November 2010): 96–109.

5. Hinton, "Out West."

6. Example from the *Out in Chicago* exhibit, described in the curators' cut DVD, Jill Austin and Jennifer Brier, *Out in Chicago: LGBT History at the Crossroads* (Chicago: Chicago History Museum, Trillium Productions, 2013), DVD.

7. Robert Mills, "Queer Is Here? Lesbian, Gay, Bisexual and Transgender Histories and Public Culture," *History Workshop Journal*, no. 62 (October 1, 2006): 253–63; Robert Mills, "Theorizing the Queer Museum," *Museums & Social Issues* 3, no. 1 (April 1, 2008): 41–52; Austin and Brier, *Out in Chicago: LGBT History at the Crossroads*, 16; Stuart Frost, "Are Museums Doing Enough to Address LGBT History?," *Museums Journal* 111, no. 1 (January 2011): 19.

8. Tucker, phone interview with Susan Ferentinos; Austin and Brier, *Out in Chicago: LGBT History at the Crossroads*, DVD; Anne Clark and Geoffrey Wexler, "Queer Collections Appear: Oregon's Wedding Album," *Museums & Social Issues* 3, no. 1 (April 1, 2008): 115–24; McIntyre, "What to Collect?"

9. Bailey and Robert, "An Insider's Look at the Queering the Museum Project"; Lee, "Peering into the Bedroom"; Gutterman, "OutHistory.org"; Ken Yellis, "Concerning the Telling of Painful Tales: The Case of Masks of the Sacred Bush," *Curator* 55, no. 2 (April 2012): 139–51.

10. Sue Kerr, "Pittsburgh Museum Faces Backlash for Supporting PrideFest, LGBTQ Community," *Gay Voices* (blog), *Huffington Post*, June 5, 2014, http://www.huffingtonpost.com/sue-kerr/pittsburgh-museum-faces-b_b_5452499.html.

11. Joe Heimlich and Judy Koke, "Gay and Lesbian Visitors and Cultural Institutions: Do They Come? Do They Care? A Pilot Study," *Museums & Social Issues* 3, no. 1 (April 1, 2008): 93–104; Donna Mertens, John Fraser, and Joe Heimlich, "M or F? Gender, Identity, and the Transformative Research Paradigm," *Museums & Social Issues* 3, no. 1 (April 1, 2008): 81–92; Bailey, Austin, and Gosselin, "Revealing Urban Histories through LGBTQ Museum Programming"; Chenault, phone interview with Susan Ferentinos; Stacia Kuceyeski, Director of Outreach at the Ohio History Connection and liaison to the Gay Ohio History Initiative, phone interview with Susan Ferentinos, April 3, 2014.
12. Joseph Caputo, "Smithsonian Marks Anniversary of Stonewall Riots," *Smithsonian Magazine*, June 25, 2009, http://www.smithsonianmag.com/smithsonian-institution/smithsonian-marks-anniversary-of-stonewall-riots-10073644/.
13. Heimlich and Koke, "Gay and Lesbian Visitors and Cultural Institutions"; Mertens, Fraser, and Heimlich, "M or F?"; Bailey, Austin, and Goselin, "Revealing Urban Histories through LGBTQ Museum Programming"; Chenault, phone interview with Susan Ferentinos; Kuceyeski, phone interview with Susan Ferentinos.

APPENDICES

APPENDIX 1

Timeline of Key Events in LGBT United States History

As readers have been reminded throughout this book, homosexuality as an established concept did not exist during most of the years covered by US history. The categories of bisexuality and transsexuality developed even later. Without such concepts, it is difficult to identify events of the colonial period or the eighteenth or nineteenth centuries as being specifically LGBT in nature. Because of this reality, my timeline begins with the late nineteenth century.

In addition, LGBT communities, because of their clandestine nature throughout all but the most recent decades, often developed in isolation from each other. As such, LGBT history is quite often a set of local stories, and as a result, some of the most influential events for a particular location might not appear on a national timeline. For instance, the arrest of a (hypothetical) prominent citizen in a 1960s raid on a local gay bar may have had a huge impact on the lives of gays and lesbians in that particular locale. Perhaps it created a citywide panic about homosexuals hiding in plain sight and sparked months of suspicion and surveillance that led to numerous other local citizens in good standing being ostracized and fired from their jobs. Such a chain of events would be crucial to understanding the LGBT history of that particular city but is not something that would appear on my timeline. I suggest this caveat simply so that readers will keep in mind the need to consider both local events and the larger national context when piecing together their narratives.

Timeline

1864	Karl Heinrich Ulrichs, a German, formulates the first theory of same-sex desire that identifies it as an inborn characteristic.
1873	Congress passes the Comstock Law, prohibiting the transport of "obscene" materials through the US mail system; the law is used to suppress information related to same-sex desire until the late 1950s.

1897	*Sexual Inversion*, by British authors Havelock Ellis and John Addington Symonds, is published; it is the first full-length book written in English on the topic of homosexuality.
1924	Henry Gerber forms the Society for Human Rights, the first officially recognized organization for homosexuals in the United States. Based in Chicago, the group receives a charter from the State of Illinois but lasts for less than a year before disbanding in the aftermath of a police raid.
1933	(May 6) Nazi forces in Berlin break into the Institute of Sexual Science, the research center of the internationally acclaimed sexologist Magnus Hirschfeld. They burn the institute's library, destroying decades of research on sexuality.
1947	Edith Eyde, writing under the pseudonym Lisa Ben, begins circulating a mimeographed newsletter called *Vice Versa*, producing what is believed to be the first periodical in the United States aimed at women who desire their own sex.
1948	Alfred Kinsey, Wardell Pomeroy, and Clyde Martin release *Sexual Behavior in the Human Male*, a study of sexual behavior among white males in the United States. Popularly referred to as the Kinsey Report, this study reveals that homosexual behavior among men is significantly more common that previously assumed. A companion volume, *Sexual Behavior in the Human Female*, is published in 1953.
1951	In *Stouman v. Reilly*, the California Supreme Court rules that bars can serve a homosexual clientele "so long as they are acting properly and are not committing illegal or immoral acts." In the next two decades, a handful of other states follow suit.
1951	The Mattachine Society forms in Los Angeles; it becomes the first national organization advocating for fair treatment of homosexuals.
1952	Two issues of the mimeographed newsletter *Transvestia* mark the first US periodical aimed at a gender-variant audience.
1953	In January, *ONE Magazine*, the first publicly distributed periodical focused on issues related to homosexuality in the United States, begins publication.
1953	On April 27, President Dwight D. Eisenhower signs Executive Order 10450, making "sexual perversion" (largely interpreted to mean homosexuality) grounds for being barred from employment in the civil service.
1955	The Daughters of Bilitis, the major lesbian homophile organization, is formed in San Francisco.
1958	In *ONE v. Oleson*, the US Supreme Court rules that homosexual content alone does not warrant "obscenity," paving the way for the greater distribution of information and networking among the LGBT communities.
1961	José Sarria, a well-known Latino camp performer, runs for the San Francisco Board of Supervisors, becoming the first openly gay candidate for public office in the United States. He loses the election but garners six thousand votes.
1964	*Life* magazine publishes a lengthy article called "Homosexuality in America." In subsequent months a number of other magazines also publish articles on homosexuality, thrusting the issue into national consciousness.
1966	Vanguard, an organization of street youth believed to be the nation's first LGBT youth organization, forms in San Francisco.

1966	(August) The Compton's Cafeteria riot in San Francisco marks a pre-Stonewall example of queer people fighting back in the face of police harassment.
1969	(April) The Committee on Homosexual Freedom forms in San Francisco and calls for a "Homosexual Revolution."
1969	(June 28) The Stonewall riots begin in New York City.
1969	Activists organize the Gay Liberation Front in New York City to carry on the momentum of the Stonewall riots.
1970	(May) Lesbians disrupt the Second Congress to Unite Women, demanding that the National Organization for Women (NOW), then the leading feminist organization in the United States, take a stand in support of lesbian rights.
1970	(June) The first Christopher Street Liberation Day parades, the precursors to today's LGBT pride events, are held in New York City, Los Angeles, San Francisco, and Chicago to mark the one-year anniversary of the Stonewall riots.
1970	Couples in Minnesota and Kentucky file the first lawsuits seeking legal recognition of same-sex marriages.
1971	Frank Kameny becomes the first openly gay candidate to run for Congress when he launches a campaign to become the Washington, DC, nonvoting representative.
1973	After a substantial lobbying effort by LGBT activists, the American Psychological Association removes homosexuality from the *Diagnostic and Statistical Manual of Mental Disorders*, the profession's official list of mental illnesses.
1973	Nancy Wechsler and Jerry DeGrieck, both members of the Ann Arbor, Michigan, City Council, become the first public officials in the United States to come out as LGBT.
1974	Kathy Kozachenko and Elaine Noble become the first openly LGBT candidates in the United States to win election to public office when they are voted into the Ann Arbor City Council and the Massachusetts State Assembly, respectively.
1977	Harvey Milk wins election to the San Francisco Board of Supervisors. The following year, he and Mayor George Moscone are assassinated.
1978	Anita Bryant's "Save Our Children" campaign to overturn a Dade County, Florida, ordinance granting civil rights protection to homosexuals gives birth to a conservative religious backlash against the gains of gay liberation.
1981	(June) A newsletter of the US Centers for Disease Control and Prevention runs the first article on a strange syndrome afflicting gay men. The spectrum of symptoms described would come to be known as AIDS.
1986	In *Bowers v. Hardwick*, the US Supreme Court upholds the legality of state sodomy laws.
1987	(March) ACT UP (The AIDS Coalition to Unleash Power) forms and stages its first protest in New York City.
1987	(May) As part of the Second National March on Washington for Lesbian and Gay Rights, two thousand same-sex couples take part in a mass wedding on the steps of the Internal Revenue Service (IRS) building, protesting the lack of legal recognition of their relationships.

1992	Lotus software company becomes the first publicly traded firm in the United States to offer domestic partner benefits to its employees.
1993	Congress passes "Don't Ask, Don't Tell" legislation, allowing gays and lesbians to serve in the US military as long as they conceal their sexual orientation.
1993	(December) Brandon Teena, a transgender man, is raped and murdered in Humboldt, Nebraska, after his transgender identity is revealed. The crime calls attention to the danger that is a regular part of queer lives.
1996	President William Jefferson Clinton signs the Defense of Marriage Act (DOMA), defining marriage as between a man and a woman for the purposes of federal law and allowing states to refuse to recognize same-sex marriages performed in other states.
1998	Matthew Shepard, an openly gay college student, is severely beaten and left to die tied to a fence post in Laramie, Wyoming. The murder receives national attention and eventually leads to the passage of the Matthew Shepard and James Byrd Jr. Hate Crimes Prevention Act in 2009. (James Byrd Jr. was the victim of racially motivated torture and murder, also in 1998.)
1999	Tammy Baldwin (D-WI) becomes the first nonincumbent openly LGBT person elected to Congress when she wins a seat in the US House of Representatives.
2000	Vermont becomes the first state to allow "civil unions" between same-sex couples.
2003	Massachusetts becomes the first state to allow same-sex marriages.
2003	In *Lawrence v. Texas*, the US Supreme Court overturns its earlier decision in *Bowers v. Hardwick* and rules that state sodomy laws are unconstitutional.
2010	(January) Amanda Simpson becomes the first known transgender person to receive a presidential appointment when she is appointed to serve in the US Commerce Department.
2010	(December) Congress repeals "Don't Ask, Don't Tell."
2012	Tammy Baldwin again makes history by becoming the first openly LGBT candidate to win election to the US Senate.
2013	(June) In *United States v. Windsor*, the US Supreme Court strikes down the part of the Defense of Marriage Act that denies federal recognition of same-sex marriages.

APPENDIX 2

Recommended Reading

Introduction

The sources available for interpreting LGBT history vary widely, depending on whether one is seeking information on the queer past or seeking information on how to interpret that history to the public. The literature on the history of same-sex love and desire in the United States is vast; information on discussing that topic within history museums and historic sites is surprisingly scarce. In light of this situation, I have taken a twofold approach to selecting items to include in this list of "Recommended Reading." In order to keep the selection to a manageable size, I have excluded all sources that deal with a focused topic of LGBT history and instead included only historical overviews that provide a synthetic view. This was a painful decision, as so much of the richness of LGBT history lies in books with a narrower focus. To locate these types of sources, I refer readers to my endnotes in each chapter. In contrast, I have taken a more expansive approach to sources concerning LGBT historical interpretation. Although I have, for the most part, excluded articles from the popular press and from blogs, I have included a greater proportion of the available sources that focus specifically on historical interpretation so as to save readers the trouble of tracking them down.

Historical Overviews, Reviews of the Literature, and Methodology

Bronski, Michael. *A Queer History of the United States*. Boston: Beacon, 2011. Bronski's overview of US history integrates sexual and gender variance into the larger picture, highlighting developments that had a particular impact on same-sex love and desire while also emphasizing the influence of these events on the larger population.

Chauncey, George. *Why Marriage? The History Shaping Today's Debate over Gay Equality*. New York: Basic, 2004. Published just as Massachusetts was becoming the first state to legally recognize same-sex marriage, this book offers insight into the history leading up to that momentous event. Readers should be aware, of course, that much has happened in this area since the book was published in 2004.

D'Emilio, John, and Estelle B. Freedman. *Intimate Matters: A History of Sexuality in America*. 3rd ed. Chicago: University of Chicago Press, 2012. A panoramic introduction to the history of sexuality in the United States, this book provides a good sense of the ways same-sex desire fits into the larger national narrative. This book has gone through multiple editions and so relies on older historiography, although the 2012 edition has added two chapters on more recent events and includes a bibliographic essay citing more recent writing on the topic.

Duberman, Martin B. "'Writhing Bedfellows' in Antebellum South Carolina: Historical Interpretation and the Politics of Evidence." In *About Time: Exploring the Gay Past*, rev. and expanded ed., 3–23. New York: Meridian, 1991. Although this essay is twenty-five years old, it provides a useful glimpse into some of the challenges of researching the history of same-sex love and desire.

Eaklor, Vicki Lynn. *Queer America: A GLBT History of the 20th Century*. Westport, CT: Greenwood, 2008. Although Eaklor does not go into much depth, her survey of LGBT life in the twentieth century is quite broad, providing a range of topics that interested parties can then explore further. Her history also ends later than many of the other historical overviews mentioned here.

Freedman, Estelle B. "'The Burning of Letters Continues': Elusive Identities and the Historical Construction of Sexuality." *Journal of Women's History* 9, no. 4 (Winter 1998): 181–200. Using reformer Miriam Van Waters as a case study, Freedman discusses some of the issues involved in deciphering same-sex love and desire in historical sources.

Rupp, Leila J. *A Desired Past: A Short History of Same-Sex Love in America*. Chicago: University of Chicago Press, 1999. Rupp provides an easy-to-read synthesis of the secondary literature on same-sex desire from early America to the 1990s.

———. "What's Queer Got to Do with It?" *Reviews in American History* 38, no. 2 (June 2010): 189–98. This historiographical essay discusses the contributions that the field of LGBT history has made to the wider discipline of history. It can assist readers in thinking about ways of integrating LGBT experiences into wider narratives.

Stein, Marc, ed. *Encyclopedia of Lesbian, Gay, Bisexual, and Transgender History in America*. New York: Scribner / Thomson-Gale, 2004. This three-volume encyclopedia provides articles on a wide range of topics in LGBT history; it also includes a detailed timeline of events relevant to the topic.

———. *Rethinking the Gay and Lesbian Movement*. New York: Routledge, 2012. Focusing specifically on gay and lesbian politics, Stein provides historical context for the contemporary LGBT movement.

Stryker, Susan. *Transgender History*. Berkeley: Seal, 2008. Too often, the specific experiences of transgender people get lost in the larger LGBT historical narrative. With this book, Stryker seeks to rectify that situation by focusing on those with a trans identity.

Vicinus, Martha. "The History of Lesbian History." *Feminist Studies* 38, no. 3 (Fall 2012): 566–96. This historiographical essay reviews trends in the scholarly literature of lesbian history.

Wrathall, John D. "Provenance as Text: Reading the Silences around Sexuality in Manuscript Collections." *Journal of American History* 79, no. 1 (June 1992): 165–78. This article discusses some of the issues involved in LGBT historical research.

LGBT Historical Interpretation

Austin, Jill, and Jennifer Brier. *Out in Chicago: LGBT History at the Crossroads*. Chicago: Chicago History Museum, Trillium Productions, 2013. DVD. Although difficult to locate, this DVD contains a curators' tour of the *Out in Chicago* exhibit at the Chicago History Museum. It thus allows viewers to actually see parts of the exhibit (which is now closed) and experience some of the video components that were included in the exhibit.

———, eds. *Out in Chicago: LGBT History at the Crossroads*. Chicago: Chicago History Museum, 2011. This companion volume to the Chicago History Museum's *Out in Chicago* exhibit includes a curatorial essay plus additional chapters exploring some aspects of Chicago's LGBT history in more depth.

Austin, Jill, Jennifer Brier, Jessica Herczeg-Konecny, and Anne Parsons. "When the Erotic Becomes Illicit: Struggles over Displaying Queer History at a Mainstream Museum." *Radical History Review*, no. 113 (Spring 2012): 187–97. Using the *Out in Chicago* exhibit as an example, this article explores the issues inherent in interpreting the sexual aspects of LGBT history in museum settings.

Bernard A. Zuckerman Museum of Art. *John Q: Projects 2009–2013*. Kennesaw, GA: Kennesaw State University, 2014. A catalog of the "discursive memorials" executed by the John Q Idea Collective, whose intent is to evoke the LGBT heritage of Atlanta.

Farrell, Kelly. "Exposing the Soul: An Unexpected Encounter with Community-Based Interpretation." *Legacy: The Journal of the National Association of Interpretation*, February 2010. Using Freeman Tilden's interpretive method as a framework, Farrell explores the elements that contributed to her powerful response to *Gay Liberation*, a memorial to the Stonewall Riots created by George Segal.

Gosselin, Viviane. "Civic Museography, Porous Narratives and the Choir Effect: Sex Talk in the City at the Museum of Vancouver." *THEMA. La revue des Musées de la civilisation*, 1 (March 24, 2014): 107–15. This article describes the development of the *Sex Talk in the City* exhibit at the Museum of Vancouver (British Columbia), which examined the history of sexuality generally and was inclusive of LGBT history.

Greenslit, Jana. "The Road to Revealing Queer: An Interview with Curator Erin Bailey, Part I." *Incluseum* (blog), March 5, 2014. http://incluseum.com/2014/03/05/the-road-to-revealing-queer-an-interview-with-curator-erin-bailey-part-i/. See next entry.

———. "The Road to Revealing Queer: An Interview with Curator Erin Bailey, Part II." *Incluseum* (blog), March 14, 2014. http://incluseum.com/2014/03/14/the-road-to-revealing-queer-an-interview-with-curator-erin-bailey-part-ii/. This two-part blog post features an interview with Erin Bailey discussing the development of the *Revealing Queer* exhibit at the Museum of History and Industry in Seattle.

Gutterman, Lauren Jae. "OutHistory.org: An Experiment in LGBTQ Community History-Making." *Public Historian* 32, no. 4 (November 2010): 96–109. This article describes OutHistory.org, a website that employs a wiki model to collect LGBT history from the public. The author considers some of the challenges the project faced, along with providing suggestions on what worked well with this type of effort.

History Project. *Improper Bostonians: Lesbian and Gay History from the Puritans to Playland*. Boston: Beacon, 1998. The volume serves as a companion to the 1996 exhibit at the Boston Public Library, *Public Faces/Private Lives: Boston's Lesbian and Gay History*. It offers a brief taste of the exhibit.

Lee, Lisa Yun. "Peering into the Bedroom: Restorative Justice at the Jane Addams Hull House Museum." In *Routledge Companion to Museum Ethics: Redefining Ethics for the Twenty-First Century Museum*, edited by Janet Maistine, 174–88. New York: Routledge, 2011. The former director of the Jane Addams Hull-House Museum in Chicago discusses that organization's alternative labeling project, which explored issues around interpreting Jane Addams's relationship with Mary Rozet Smith.

Lehner, Stephanie. "Becoming Visible: Mainstream Cultural Institutions and the Successful Presentation of LGBTQ History Exhibitions." MA thesis, State University of New York College at Oneonta, Cooperstown Graduate Program, 2008. In this master's thesis, Lehner profiles three early examples of interpreting LGBT history: *Becoming Visible* at the New York Public Library; *AIDS/Brooklyn* at the Brooklyn Historical Society; and *The Nazi Persecution of Homosexuals* at the United States Holocaust Memorial Museum.

Levin, Amy K., ed. *Gender, Sexuality, and Museums: A Routledge Reader*. New York: Routledge, 2010. Levin has compiled a thick volume of essays considering how messages about gender and sexuality inform museum studies. The focus is international and includes different types of museums.

McGarry, Molly, and Fred Wasserman. *Becoming Visible: An Illustrated History of Lesbian and Gay Life in Twentieth-Century America*. New York: Penguin Studio, 1998. Although it ran more than twenty years ago, the *Becoming Visible* exhibit at the New York Public Library represented an early attempt at interpreting LGBT history. This companion volume provides an overview of the LGBT history presented in the exhibit, with a focus on New York City.

McIntyre, Darryl. "What to Collect? Museums and Lesbian, Gay, Bisexual and Transgender Collecting." *International Journal of Art & Design Education* 26, no. 1 (February 2007): 48–53. McIntyre presents an overview of issues to consider when collecting LGBT historical artifacts.

ONE National Gay & Lesbian Archives, ONE Archives Gallery & Museum, University of Southern California, and Pacific Standard Time (Exhibition). *Cruising the Archive: Queer Art and Culture in Los Angeles, 1945–1980*. Edited by Ann Cvetkovich, David Frantz, and Mia Locks. Los Angeles: ONE National Gay & Lesbian Archives, 2011. This book documents the recent exhibit by the same name; it provides an interesting example of interpretation that combines history with visual art.

Oram, Alison. "Going on an Outing: The Historic House and Queer Public History." *Rethinking History* 15, no. 2 (June 2011): 189–207. Using British house museums with some connection to the queer past as her starting point, Oram explores the meaning such houses have for LGBT visitors.

Steorn, Patrik. "Curating Queer Heritage: Queer Knowledge and Museum Practice." *Curator* 55, no. 3 (July 2012): 355–65. Using examples from the Swedish National Museum of Fine Arts and the Nordic Museum, both in Stockholm, Steorn considers issues of collecting, cataloging, and interpreting queer objects.

Tseliou, Maria Anna. "Spotlight on Research—Subverting the Hetero-normative Museum." *Incluseum* (blog), April 11, 2013. http://incluseum.com/2013/04/11/spotlight-on-research-subverting-the-hetero-normative-museum/. This blog post presents a short synopsis of trends in interpreting LGBT topics in the United Kingdom.

Turino, Kenneth, and Susan Ferentinos. "Entering the Mainstream: Interpreting GLBT History." *AASLH History News*, Autumn 2012. The authors explore four issues to consider when interpreting LGBT history.

Tyburczy, Jennifer. "All Museums Are Sex Museums." *Radical History Review*, no. 113 (Spring 2012): 199–211. Tyburczy describes an undergraduate class she teaches that explores the ways museums convey cultural messages regarding sexuality. The article includes a sample syllabus.

"Where Is Queer?" Special issue, *Museums & Social Issues* 3, no. 1 (April 2008). A special issue of the journal *Museums & Social Issues*, this volume contains numerous articles exploring LGBT issues in museums of all types. It is a great starting point for considering this topic.

APPENDIX 3

Bibliography

Abdur-Rahman, Aliyyah I. "'The Strangest Freaks of Despotism': Queer Sexuality in Antebellum African American Slave Narratives." *African American Review* 40, no. 2 (Summer 2006): 223–37.

"About Spelman College." *Spelman College*, 2012. http://www.spelman.edu/about-us.

Abraham, Julie. *Metropolitan Lovers: The Homosexuality of Cities*. Minneapolis: University of Minnesota Press, 2008.

Adair, Bill, Benjamin Filene, and Laura Koloski, eds. *Letting Go? Sharing Historical Authority in a User-Generated World*. Philadelphia: Pew Center for Arts & Heritage, 2011.

Adair, Joshua G. "House Museums or Walk-In Closets? The (Non) Representation of Gay Men in the Museums They Called Home." In *Gender, Sexuality, and Museums: A Routledge Reader*, edited by Amy K. Levin, 264–78 (New York: Routledge, 2010).

Apuzzo, Matt. "U.S. to Give Legal Benefits to Same-Sex Marriages." *New York Times*, February 10, 2014.

Archibald, Robert R. *The New Town Square: Museums and Communities in Transition*. Walnut Creek, CA: Alta Mira, 2004.

Associated Press. "Library of Congress Exhibits Gay Rights History." *The Buzz* (blog), *Washington Post*, May 9, 2011. http://www.washingtonpost.com/blogs/the-buzz/post/library-of-congress-exhibits-gay-rights-history/2011/05/09/AFklNtYG_blog.html.

Austin, Jill, and Jennifer Brier. "Out in Chicago: Exhibiting LGBT History at the Crossroads." In *Out in Chicago: LGBT History at the Crossroads*, edited by Jill Austin and Jennifer Brier, 1–22. Chicago: Chicago History Museum, 2011.

———, eds. *Out in Chicago: LGBT History at the Crossroads*. Chicago: Chicago History Museum, 2011.

———. *Out in Chicago: LGBT History at the Crossroads*. Chicago: Chicago History Museum, Trillium Productions, 2013. DVD.

Austin, Jill, Jennifer Brier, Jessica Herczeg-Konecny, and Anne Parsons. "When the Erotic Becomes Illicit: Struggles over Displaying Queer History at a Mainstream Museum." *Radical History Review*, no. 113 (Spring 2012): 187–97.

Bailey, Beth L. *From Front Porch to Back Seat: Courtship in Twentieth-Century America*. Baltimore: Johns Hopkins University Press, 1988.

———. "The Politics of Dancing: 'Don't Ask, Don't Tell' and the Role of Moral Claims." *Journal of Policy History* 25, no. 1 (January 2013): 89–113.

Bailey, Erin, Jill Austin, and Viviane Gosselin. "Revealing Urban Histories through LGBTQ Museum Programming." Panel presented at the American Alliance of Museums Annual Meeting, Seattle, 2014.

Bailey, Erin, and Nicole Robert. "An Insider's Look at the Queering the Museum Project." Workshop presented at the American Alliance of Museums Annual Meeting, Seattle, 2014.

Barrett, Jennifer. *Museums and the Public Sphere*. Malden, MA: Wiley-Blackwell, 2011.

Baumann, Jason. Introduction to "1969: The Year of Liberation." Online exhibit. *New York Public Library*, 2009. http://static.nypl.org/exhibitions/1969/year.html.

Beemyn, Brett, ed. *Creating a Place for Ourselves: Lesbian, Gay, and Bisexual Community Histories*. New York: Routledge, 1997.

Behling, Laura L. *The Masculine Woman in America, 1890–1935*. Urbana: University of Illinois Press, 2001.

Benemann, William. *Male-Male Intimacy in Early America: Beyond Romantic Friendships*. New York: Harrington Park, 2006.

Beredjick, Camille. "DSM Replaces Gender Identity Disorder with Gender Dysphoria." *Advocate.com*, July 23, 2012. http://www.advocate.com/politics/transgender/2012/07/23/dsm-replaces-gender-identity-disorder-gender-dysphoria.

Bergman, Teresa. *Exhibiting Patriotism: Creating and Contesting Interpretations of American Historic Sites*. Walnut Creek, CA: Left Coast, 2013.

Bernard A. Zuckerman Museum of Art. *John Q: Projects 2009–2013*. Kennesaw, GA: Kennesaw State University, 2014.

Bérubé, Allan. *Coming out under Fire: The History of Gay Men and Women in World War Two*. New York: Free Press, 1990.

Biblioqueers (San Francisco Public Library Staff). "Archives: David Lourea and the Bisexual Center." *Queerest. Library. Ever.* (blog), January 18, 2013. http://queerestlibraryever.blogspot.com/2013/01/archives-david-lourea-and-bisexual.html.

Black, Allida Mae, ed. *Modern American Queer History*. Philadelphia: Temple University Press, 2001.

Black, Graham. *Transforming Museums in the 21st Century: Developing Museums for Visitor Involvement*. Hoboken: Taylor & Francis, 2011.

Blake, Nayland, Lawrence Rinder, and Amy Scholder, eds. *In a Different Light: Visual Culture, Sexual Identity, Queer Practice*. San Francisco: City Lights, 1995.

Boag, Peter. *Re-Dressing America's Frontier Past*. Berkeley: University of California Press, 2011.

———. *Same-Sex Affairs: Constructing and Controlling Homosexuality in the Pacific Northwest*. Berkeley: University of California Press, 2003.

Boyd, Nan Alamilla. "Same-Sex Sexuality in Western Women's History." *Frontiers: A Journal of Women Studies* 22, no. 3 (September 2001): 13.

———. "Who Is the Subject? Queer Theory Meets Oral History." *Journal of the History of Sexuality* 17, no. 2 (May 2008): 177–89.

———. *Wide-Open Town: A History of Queer San Francisco to 1965*. Berkeley: University of California Press, 2003.

Boyd, Nan Alamilla, and Horacio N. Roque Ramírez, eds. *Bodies of Evidence: The Practice of Queer Oral History*. New York: Oxford University Press, 2012.

Bradley, Patricia. *Making American Culture: A Social History, 1900–1920*. New York: Palgrave Macmillan, 2009.

Brandon, Laura. "Looking for the 'Total' Woman in Wartime: A Museological Work in Progress." In *Gender, Sexuality, and Museums: A Routledge Reader*, edited by Amy K. Levin, 110. New York: Routledge, 2010.

Braukman, Stacy Lorraine. *Communists and Perverts under the Palms: The Johns Committee in Florida, 1956–1965*. Gainesville: University Press of Florida, 2012.

Breines, Wini. "What's Love Got to Do with It? White Women, Black Women, and Feminism in the Movement Years." *Signs: Journal of Women in Culture & Society* 27, no. 4 (Summer 2002): 1095.

Brier, Jennifer. *Infectious Ideas: U.S. Political Responses to the AIDS Crisis*. Chapel Hill: University of North Carolina Press, 2009.

Brier, Jennifer, and Anne Parsons. "Gender Crossroads: Representations of Gender Transgressions in Chicago's Press, 1850–1920." In *Out in Chicago: LGBT History at the Crossroads*, edited by Jill Austin and Jennifer Brier, 23–40. Chicago: Chicago History Museum, 2011.

Bright, Deborah, and Erica Rand. "Queer Plymouth." *GLQ: A Journal of Lesbian & Gay Studies* 12, no. 2 (April 2006): 259–77.

Brock, Julia. "Embodying the Archive (Part 1): Art Practice, Queer Politics, and Public History." *History @ Work* (blog), *Public History Commons*, April 5, 2013. http://publichistorycommons.org/brock-johnq-intro/.

———. "Embodying the Archive (Part 2): Lineages, Longings Migrations." *History @ Work* (blog), *Public History Commons*, April 12, 2013. http://publichistorycommons.org/tag/queer-history/.

Bronski, Michael. *A Queer History of the United States*. Boston: Beacon, 2011.

Broverman, Neal. "A Night at the Museum." *Advocate*, December 2, 2008, 14.

Brown, Tracy. "'Abominable Sin' in Colonial New Mexico: Spanish and Pueblo Perceptions of Same-Sex Sexuality." In *Long before Stonewall: Histories of Same-Sex Sexuality in Early America*, edited by Thomas A. Foster, 51–78. New York: New York University Press, 2007.

Brown, Victoria Bissell. "Queer or Not: What Jane Addams Teaches Us about Not Knowing." In *Out in Chicago: LGBT History at the Crossroads*, edited by Jill Austin and Jennifer Brier, 63–75. Chicago: Chicago History Museum, 2011.

Brownell, Joseph. "We've Come a Long Way: Marriage Equality in Less Than a Year." *Out & About Nashville*, May 25, 2014. http://www.outandaboutnashville.com/story/weve-come-long-way-marriage-equality-less.

Bullough, Vern L. *Science in the Bedroom: A History of Sex Research*. New York: Basic, 1994.

"Bullying and Censorship." *New York Times*, December 7, 2010, 32.

Canaday, Margot. "Building a Straight State: Sexuality and Social Citizenship under the 1944 G.I. Bill." *Journal of American History* 90, no. 3 (December 2003): 935–57.

———. *The Straight State: Sexuality and Citizenship in Twentieth-Century America*. Princeton, NJ: Princeton University Press, 2009.

Capote. Directed by Bennett Miller. 2005. Culver City, CA: Sony Pictures Home Entertainment, 2006. DVD.

Caputo, Joseph. "Smithsonian Marks Anniversary of Stonewall Riots." *Smithsonian Magazine*, June 25, 2009. http://www.smithsonianmag.com/smithsonian-institution/smithsonian-marks-anniversary-of-stonewall-riots-10073644/.

Carter, David. *Stonewall: The Riots That Sparked the Gay Revolution*. New York: St. Martin's, 2004.

Carter, Julian B. *The Heart of Whiteness: Normal Sexuality and Race in America, 1880–1940*. Durham, NC: Duke University Press, 2007.

Chauncey, George. *Gay New York: Gender, Urban Culture, and the Making of a Gay Male World, 1890–1940*. New York: Basic, 1994.

———. *Why Marriage? The History Shaping Today's Debate over Gay Equality*. New York: Basic, 2004.

Chenault, Wesley. Phone interview with Susan Ferentinos, May 15, 2014.

———. "The Unspoken Past: Atlanta Lesbian and Gay History." *Perspectives*, December 2006.

Chenault, Wesley, Andy Ditzler, and Joey Orr. "Discursive Memorials: Queer Histories in Atlanta's Public Spaces." *Southern Spaces*, February 26, 2010. http://www.southernspaces.org/2010/discursive-memorials-queer-histories-atlantas-public-spaces.

Chideckel, Maurice. *Female Sex Perversion: The Sexually Aberrated Woman as She Is*. New York: Eugenics, 1938.

Chudacoff, Howard P. *The Age of the Bachelor: Creating an American Subculture*. Princeton, NJ: Princeton University Press, 1999.

"City Life in the Late 19th Century." Online lesson plan. *Library of Congress Teacher Resources*. Accessed June 8, 2014. http://www.loc.gov/teachers/classroommaterials/presentationsandactivities/presentations/timeline/riseind/city/.

Clark, Anne, and Geoffrey Wexler. "Queer Collections Appear: Oregon's Wedding Album." *Museums & Social Issues* 3, no. 1 (April 1, 2008): 115–24.

Clark, Badger. *Sun and Saddle Leather*. Boston: Gorham, 1919, quoted in Jonathan Katz, *Gay American History: Lesbians and Gay Men in the U.S.A.: A Documentary History*. Rev. ed. New York: Meridian, 1992.

Coffee, Kevin. "Cultural Inclusion, Exclusion and the Formative Roles of Museums." *Museum Management & Curatorship* 23, no. 3 (September 2008): 261–79.

Colletta, Jen. "Obama's 100-Day Gay Report Card." *Philadelphia Gay News*, May 2009, 1–17.

———. "SCOTUS Ruling Caps a Momentous Marriage Year." *Philadelphia Gay News*, March 7, 2014, 15.

Contemporary Museum, Baltimore, and Maryland Historical Society. *Mining the Museum: An Installation by Fred Wilson*. Edited by Lisa G. Corrin. Baltimore, New York: The Contemporary, in cooperation with the New Press, 1994.

Coyle, Katy, and Nadiene Van Dyke. "Sex, Smashing, and Storyville in Turn-of-the-Century New Orleans: Reexamining the Continuum of Lesbian Sexuality." In *Carryin' On in the Lesbian and Gay South*, edited by John Howard, 54–72. New York: New York University Press, 1997.

Craighill, Peyton M., and Scott Clement. "Support for Same-Sex Marriage Hits New High; Half Say Constitution Guarantees Right." *WP Politics*, March 5, 2014. http://www.washingtonpost.com/politics/support-for-same-sex-marriage-hits-new-high-half-say-constitution-guarantees-right/2014/03/04/f737e87e-a3e5-11e3-a5fa-55f0c77bf39c_story.html.

Davis, Katharine Bement. *Factors in the Sex Life of Twenty-Two Hundred Women*. New York: Harper & Brothers, 1929.

Dayton, Cornelia H., and Lisa Levenstein. "The Big Tent of U.S. Women's and Gender History: A State of the Field." *Journal of American History* 99, no. 3 (December 1, 2012): 793–817.

De la Croix, St. Sukie. *Chicago Whispers: A History of LGBT Chicago before Stonewall*. Madison: University of Wisconsin Press, 2012.

D'Emilio, John. "Capitalism and Gay Identity." In *Powers of Desire: The Politics of Sexuality*, edited by Ann Barr Snitow, Christine Stansell, and Sharon Thompson, 100–13. New York: Monthly Review Press, 1983.

———. *Sexual Politics, Sexual Communities: The Making of a Homosexual Minority in the United States, 1940–1970*. 2nd ed. Chicago: University of Chicago Press, 1998.

D'Emilio, John, and Estelle B. Freedman. *Intimate Matters: A History of Sexuality in America*. 3rd ed. Chicago: University of Chicago Press, 2012.

Division of Cultural Resources, Partnerships, and Science. "Lesbian, Bisexual, Gay and Transgender Heritage Intiative." *National Park Service*, April 16, 2014. http://www.nps.gov/heritageinitiatives/LGBThistory/.

Doyle, David D., Jr. "'A Very Proper Bostonian': Rediscovering Ogden Codman and His Late-Nineteenth-Century Queer World." *Journal of the History of Sexuality* 13, no. 4 (October 2004): 446–76.

Duberman, Martin B. *Stonewall*. New York: Plume, 1994.

———. "'Writhing Bedfellows' in Antebellum South Carolina: Historical Interpretation and the Politics of Evidence." In *About Time: Exploring the Gay Past*. Rev. and expanded ed., 3–23. New York: Meridian, 1991. Reprinted in *Carryin' On in the Lesbian and Gay South*, edited by John Howard, 15–33. New York: New York University Press, 1997.

Dubrow, Gail. "Blazing Trails with Pink Triangles and Rainbow Flags: Improving the Presentation and Interpretation of Gay and Lesbian Heritage." In *Restoring Women's History through Historic Preservation*, edited by Jennifer B. Goodman and Gail Dubrow, 281–300. Baltimore: Johns Hopkins University Press, 2003.

———. "Deviant History, Defiant Heritage." *Friends of 1800*, 2002. http://www.friendsof1800.org/VIEWPOINT/dubrow.html.

Duggan, Lisa. *Sapphic Slashers: Sex, Violence, and American Modernity*. Durham, NC: Duke University Press, 2000.

Dunlap, David W. "Library's Gay Show Is an Eye-Opener, Even for Its Subjects." *New York Times*, September 6, 1994, sec. Arts. http://www.nytimes.com/1994/09/06/arts/library-s-gay-show-is-an-eye-opener-even-for-its-subjects.html.

Eaklor, Vicki Lynn. *Queer America: A GLBT History of the 20th Century*. Westport, CT: Greenwood, 2008.

Echols, Alice. *Daring to Be Bad: Radical Feminism in America, 1967–1975*. Minneapolis: University of Minnesota Press, 1989.

Edsall, Nicholas C. *Toward Stonewall: Homosexuality and Society in the Modern Western World*. Charlottesville: University of Virginia Press, 2003.

Eisenbach, David. *Gay Power: An American Revolution*. New York: Carroll & Graf, 2006.

Enke, Anne. *Finding the Movement: Sexuality, Contested Space, and Feminist Activism*. Durham, NC: Duke University Press, 2007.

Faderman, Lillian. *Odd Girls and Twilight Lovers: A History of Lesbian Life in Twentieth-Century America*. New York: Columbia University Press, 1991.

———. *Surpassing the Love of Men: Romantic Friendship and Love between Women from the Renaissance to the Present*. London: Women's Press, 1985.

Faderman, Lillian, and Phyllis Irwin. "Alice Austen and Gertrude Tate: A Boston Marriage on Staten Island." *Historic House Trust Newsletter*, Fall 2010.

Farrell, Kelly. "Exposing the Soul: An Unexpected Encounter with Community-Based Interpretation." *Legacy: The Journal of the National Association of Interpretation*, February 2010, 20–23.

Faust, Drew Gilpin. *This Republic of Suffering: Death and the American Civil War*. New York: Knopf, 2008.

Feinberg, Leslie. *Transgender Warriors: Making History from Joan of Arc to RuPaul*. Boston: Beacon, 1996.

Ferentinos, Susan. "Lifting Our Skirts: Sharing the Sexual Past with Visitors." *Public History Commons: The Public Historian*, July 1, 2014. http://publichistorycommons.org/tph/.

———. "An Unpredictable Age: Sex, Consumption, and the Emergence of the American Teenager, 1900–1950." PhD diss., Indiana University, 2005.

Ferentinos, Susan, Stacia Kuceyeski, and Kenneth Turino. "Sex and Silences: Interpreting LGBT History." Panel presented at the American Alliance of Museums Annual Meeting, Seattle, 2014.

Foster, Thomas A. Introduction to *Long before Stonewall: Histories of Same-Sex Sexuality in Early America*, 1–16. New York: New York University Press, 2007.

———. *Sex and the Eighteenth-Century Man: Massachusetts and the History of Sexuality in America*. Boston: Beacon, 2006.

———. "The Sexual Abuse of Black Men under American Slavery." *Journal of the History of Sexuality* 30, no. 3 (September 2011): 445–64.

Foucault, Michel. *The History of Sexuality*. New York: Pantheon, 1978.

Frank, Nathaniel. "The President's Pleasant Surprise: How LGBT Advocates Ended Don't Ask, Don't Tell." "Special Issue on Evolution of Government Policy toward Homosexuality in the U.S. Military." *Journal of Homosexuality* 60, no. 2–3 (February 2013): 159–213.

Fraser, John, and Joe E. Heimlich. "Where Are We?" *Museums & Social Issues* 3, no. 1 (Spring 2008): 5–14.

Freedman, Estelle B. "'The Burning of Letters Continues': Elusive Identities and the Historical Construction of Sexuality." *Journal of Women's History* 9, no. 4 (Winter 1998): 181–200.

———. "'Uncontrolled Desires': The Response to the Sexual Psychopath, 1920–1960." In *Passion and Power: Sexuality in History*, edited by Kathy Peiss and Christina Simmons, 199–225. Philadelphia: Temple University Press, 1989.

Frost, Stuart. "Are Museums Doing Enough to Address LGBT History?" *Museums Journal* 111, no. 1 (January 2011): 19.

———. "Secret Museums: Hidden Histories of Sex and Sexuality." *Museums and Social Issues* 3, no. 1 (Spring 2008): 29–40.

Fur, Gunlög. "Weibe-Town and the Delawares-as-Women: Gender Crossing and Same-Sex Relations in Eighteenth-Century Northeastern Indian Culture." In *Long before Stonewall: Histories of Same-Sex Sexuality in Early America*, edited by Thomas A. Foster, 32–50. New York: New York University Press, 2007.

Gabriel, Paul. "Embracing Our Erotic Intelligence." *Museums & Social Issues* 3, no. 1 (April 1, 2008): 53–66.

———. "Why Grapple with Queer When You Can Fondle It? Embracing Our Erotic Intelligence." In *Gender, Sexuality and Museums: A Routledge Reader*, edited by Amy K. Levin, 71–79. New York: Routledge, 2010.

Gallo, Marcia M. "Different Daughters." *OAH Magazine of History* 20, no. 2 (March 1, 2006): 27–30.

———. *Different Daughters: A History of the Daughters of Bilitis and the Rise of the Lesbian Rights Movement*. New York: Carroll & Graf, 2006.

Gilfoyle, Timothy J. "Prostitutes in the Archives: Problems and Possibilities in Documenting the History of Sexuality." *American Archivist* 57, no. 3 (Summer 1994): 514–27.

Gitlin, Todd. *The Sixties: Years of Hope, Days of Rage*. Rev. trade ed. New York: Bantam, 1993.

"GLBT History Museum." *GLBT Historical Society*, 2014. http://www.glbthistory.org/museum/.

Godbeer, Richard. "'The Cry of Sodom': Discourse, Intercourse, and Desire in Colonial New England." *William and Mary Quarterly* 52, no. 2 (April 1, 1995): 259–86.

———. *The Overflowing of Friendship: Love between Men and the Creation of the American Republic*. Baltimore: Johns Hopkins University Press, 2009.

Goldman, Russell. "First Transgender Presidential Appointee Fears Beng Labeled 'Token.'" *ABC News*, January 5, 2010. http://abcnews.go.com/Politics/amanda-simpson-transgender-presidential-appointee-begins-work-commerce/story?id=9477161.

Gosselin, Viviane. "Civic Museography, Porous Narratives and the Choir Effect: Sex Talk in the City at the Museum of Vancouver." *THEMA. La revue des Musées de la civilisation*, 1 (March 24, 2014): 107–15.

Green, Emma. "This Tax Season: Total Chaos for Same-Sex Couples." *Atlantic.com*, April 2, 2014. http://www.theatlantic.com/business/archive/2014/04/this-tax-season-total-chaos-for-same-sex-couples/360033/.

Greenslit, Jana. "The Road to Revealing Queer: An Interview with Curator Erin Bailey, Part I." *Incluseum* (blog), March 5, 2014. http://incluseum.com/2014/03/05/the-road-to-revealing-queer-an-interview-with-curator-erin-bailey-part-i/.

———. "The Road to Revealing Queer: An Interview with Curator Erin Bailey, Part II." *Incluseum* (blog), March 14, 2014. http://incluseum.com/2014/03/14/the-road-to-revealing-queer-an-interview-with-curator-erin-bailey-part-ii/.

Griffiths, José-Marie, and Donald W. King. *Interconnections: The IMLS National Study on the Use of Libraries, Museums and the Internet; Conclusions Summary*. Washington, DC: Institute of Museums and Library Services, February 2008. http://interconnectionsreport.org/reports/ConclusionsSummaryFinalB.pdf.

Grinberg, Emanuella. "Wisconsin's Tammy Baldwin Is First Openly Gay Person Elected to Senate." *CNN*. Accessed April 10, 2014. http://www.cnn.com/2012/11/07/politics/wisconsin-tammy-baldwin-senate/index.html.

Gross, Larry. "The Past and the Future of Gay, Lesbian, Bisexual, and Transgender Studies." *Journal of Communication* 55, no. 3 (September 2005): 508–28.

Gustav-Wrathall, John D. *Take the Young Stranger by the Hand: Same-Sex Relations and the YMCA*. Chicago: University of Chicago Press, 1998.

Gutiérrez, Ramón A. "Warfare, Homosexuality, and Gender Status among American Indian Men in the Southwest." In *Long before Stonewall: Histories of Same-Sex Sexuality in Early America*, edited by Thomas A. Foster, 19–31. New York: New York University Press, 2007.

———. *When Jesus Came, the Corn Mothers Went Away: Marriage, Sexuality, and Power in New Mexico, 1500–1846*. Stanford, CA: Stanford University Press, 1991.

Gutterman, Lauren Jae. "OutHistory.org: An Experiment in LGBTQ Community History-Making." *Public Historian* 32, no. 4 (November 2010): 96–109.

Halperin, David M. *How to Do the History of Homosexuality*. Chicago: University of Chicago Press, 2002.

Hansen, Karen V. "'No *Kisses* Is Like Youres': An Erotic Friendship between Two African-American Women during the Mid-Nineteenth Century." *Gender & History* 7, no. 2 (August 1, 1995): 153–82.

Harden, Victoria Angela. *AIDS at 30: A History*. Washington, DC: Potomac, 2012.

Harris, Victoria. "Sex on the Margins: New Directions in the Historiography of Sexuality and Gender." *Historical Journal* 53, no. 4 (December 2010): 1085–1104.

Hatheway, Jay. *The Gilded Age Construction of Modern American Homophobia*. New York: Palgrave Macmillan, 2003.

Heimlich, Joe, and Judy Koke. "Gay and Lesbian Visitors and Cultural Institutions: Do They Come? Do They Care? A Pilot Study." *Museums & Social Issues* 3, no. 1 (April 1, 2008): 93–104.

Hinton, Gregory. "Out West." Keynote address, LGBTQ Alliance Luncheon, American Alliance of Museums, Seattle, May 18, 2014.

History Project. *Improper Bostonians: Lesbian and Gay History from the Puritans to Playland*. Boston: Beacon, 1998.

Horowitz, Helen Lefkowitz. *Attitudes toward Sex in Antebellum America: A Brief History with Documents*. New York: Palgrave Macmillan, 2006.

———. *Rereading Sex: Battles over Sexual Knowledge and Suppression in Nineteenth-Century America*. New York: Knopf, 2002.

Howard, John, ed. *Carryin' on in the Lesbian and Gay South*. New York: New York University Press, 1997.

———. *Men Like That: A Southern Queer History*. Chicago: University of Chicago Press, 1999.

How to Survive a Plague. Directed by David France. 2012. Orland Park, IL: MPI Home Video, 2013. DVD.

"It Gets Better Project | Give Hope to LGBT Youth." *It Gets Better*. Accessed April 22, 2014. http://www.itgetsbetter.org/.

Jabour, Anya. "Male Friendship and Masculinity in the Early National South: William Wirt and His Friends." *Journal of the Early Republic* 20, no. 1 (April 1, 2000): 83–111.

———. *Scarlett's Sisters: Young Women in the Old South*. Chapel Hill: University of North Carolina Press, 2007.

Jobin, David. Interview with Susan Ferentinos, May 20, 2014.

Johnson, David K. "The Boys of Fairy Town: Gay Male Culture on Chicago's Near North Side in the 1930s." In *Creating a Place for Ourselves: Lesbian, Gay, and Bisexual Community Histories*, edited by Brett Beemyn, 97–118. New York: Routledge, 1997.

———. *The Lavender Scare: The Cold War Persecution of Gays and Lesbians in the Federal Government*. Chicago: University of Chicago Press, 2004.

Johnson, Susan Lee. *Roaring Camp: The Social World of the California Gold Rush*. New York: Norton, 2000.

Kann, Mark E. *Taming Passion for the Public Good: Policing Sex in the Early Republic*. New York: New York University Press, 2013.

Katz, Jonathan. *Gay American History: Lesbians and Gay Men in the U.S.A.; A Documentary History*. Rev. ed. New York: Meridian, 1992.

———. *The Invention of Heterosexuality*. New York: Dutton, 1995.

———. *Love Stories: Sex between Men before Homosexuality*. Chicago: University of Chicago Press, 2001.

Katz, Jonathan D., and David C. Ward. *Hide/Seek: Difference and Desire in American Portraiture*. Washington, DC: Smithsonian Institution, 2010.

Kavanagh, Gaynor, ed. *Making Histories in Museums*. London: Leicester University Press, 1996.

Keen, Lisa. "A Year in Review." *Between the Lines*, January 2, 2014, 6–8.

Kendrick, Walter M. *The Secret Museum: Pornography in Modern Culture*. New York: Viking, 1987.

Kennedy, Elizabeth Lapovsky, and Madeline D. Davis. *Boots of Leather, Slippers of Gold: The History of a Lesbian Community*. New York: Routledge, 1993.

Kerr, Sue. "Pittsburgh Museum Faces Backlash for Supporting PrideFest, LGBTQ Community." *Gay Voices* (blog). *Huffington Post*, June 5, 2014. http://www.huffingtonpost.com/sue-kerr/pittsburgh-museum-faces-b_b_5452499.html.

Kinsey Institute. "Data from Alfred Kinsey's Studies." *Kinsey Institute for Research in Sex, Gender, and Reproduction*. Accessed April 3, 2014. http://www.kinseyinstitute.org/research/ak-data.html.

———. "Origin of the Institute." *Kinsey Institute for Research in Sex, Gender, and Reproduction*. Accessed June 2, 2014. http://www.kinseyinstitute.org/about/origins.html.

Kissack, Terence S. *Free Comrades: Anarchism and Homosexuality in the United States, 1895–1917*. Oakland: AK Press, 2008.

Kuceyeski, Stacia. "The Gay Ohio History Initiative as a Model for Collecting Institutions." *Museums & Social Issues* 3, no. 1 (April 1, 2008): 125–32.

———. Phone interview with Susan Ferentinos, April 3, 2014.

Kunzel, Regina G. *Criminal Intimacy: Prison and the Uneven History of Modern American Sexuality*. Chicago: University of Chicago Press, 2008.

Lee, Lisa Yun. "Peering into the Bedroom: Restorative Justice at the Jane Addams Hull House Museum." In *Routledge Companion to Museum Ethics: Redefining Ethics for the Twenty-First Century Museum*, edited by Janet Marstine, 174–88. New York: Routledge, 2011.

Lehner, Stephanie. "Becoming Visible: Mainstream Cultural Institutions and the Successful Presentation of LGBTQ History Exhibitions." MA thesis, State University of New York College at Oneonta, Cooperstown Graduate Program, 2008.

Lekus, Ian K. "Health Care, the AIDS Crisis, and the Politics of Community: The North Carolina Lesbian and Gay Health Project, 1982–1996." In *Modern American Queer History*, edited by Allida Mae Black, 227–52. Philadelphia: Temple University Press, 2001.

———. "The Long Sixties." *OAH Magazine of History* 20, no. 2 (March 1, 2006): 32–38.

"Leslie Lohman Museum of Gay and Lesbian Art." Accessed May 23, 2014. http://www.leslielohman.org/.

Levin, Amy K., ed. *Gender, Sexuality, and Museums: A Routledge Reader*. New York: Routledge, 2010.

Library of Congress, "'Creating the United States' to Close May 5"—News release, April 9, 2012. Accessed March 1, 2014. http://www.loc.gov/today/pr/2012/12-071.html.

Licht, Walter. *Industrializing America: The Nineteenth Century*. Baltimore: Johns Hopkins University Press, 1995.

Liptak, Adam. "Justices Extend Benefits to Gay Couples; Allow Same-Sex Marriages in California." *New York Times*, June 27, 2013, final edition.

Loftin, Craig M. *Masked Voices: Gay Men and Lesbians in Cold War America*. Albany: SUNY Press, 2012.

Lowrey, Annie. "Gay Marriages in All States Get Recognition from the IRS." *New York Times*, August 30, 2014.

Lowry, Thomas P. *The Story the Soldiers Wouldn't Tell: Sex in the Civil War*. Mechanicsburg, PA: Stackpole, 1994.

Lupkin, Paula. *Manhood Factories: YMCA Architecture and the Making of Modern Urban Culture*. Minneapolis: University of Minnesota Press, 2010.

Lyons, Clare A. "Mapping an Atlantic Sexual Culture: Homoeroticism in Eighteenth-Century Philadelphia." *William and Mary Quarterly* 60, no. 1 (January 1, 2003): 119–54.

———. *Sex among the Rabble: An Intimate History of Gender & Power in the Age of Revolution, Philadelphia, 1730–1830*. Chapel Hill: Omohundro Institute of Early American History and Culture, Williamsburg, Virginia / University of North Carolina Press, 2006.

Macleod, David I. *The Age of the Child: Children in America, 1890–1920*. New York: Twayne, 1998.

Marcus, Sharon. "Queer Theory for Everyone: A Review Essay." *Signs: Journal of Women in Culture & Society* 31, no. 1 (September 2005): 191–218.

"Marriage Equality Impact Map." *Out & About Nashville*, April 2014, 11.

Matrix Center for Digital Humanities and Social Sciences. "Oral History in the Digital Age." *Michigan State University*. Accessed May 23, 2014. http://ohda.matrix.msu.edu/.

May, Elaine Tyler. *Homeward Bound: American Families in the Cold War Era*. Rev. and updated ed. New York: Basic, 1999.

Mazumdar, Sucheta. "Beyond Bound Feet: Relocating Asian American Women." *OAH Magazine of History* 10, no. 4 (Summer 1996): 23–27.

McCarthy, Timothy Patrick. "Sizing Up Obama's GLBT Record." *Gay & Lesbian Review Worldwide*, October 9, 2012, 16–17.

McClellan, Michelle, Jonathan Farr, Andrea Rottmann, and April Slabosheski. "Henry Gerber House: Draft." National Historic Landmark nomination, University of Michigan Public History Initiative, National Park Service, 2014.

McElderry, Michael. *Finding Aid, Frank Kameny Papers*. Washington, DC: Library of Congress, 2008. http://lcweb2.loc.gov/service/mss/eadxmlmss/eadpdfmss/2009/ms009068.pdf.

McGarry, Molly, and Fred Wasserman. *Becoming Visible: An Illustrated History of Lesbian and Gay Life in Twentieth-Century America*. New York: Penguin Studio, 1998.

McIntyre, Darryl. "What to Collect? Museums and Lesbian, Gay, Bisexual and Transgender Collecting." *International Journal of Art & Design Education* 26, no. 1 (February 2007): 48–53.

Merriman, Nick, and Nima Poovaya-Smith. "Making Culturally Diverse Histories." In Gaynor Kavanagh, ed., *Making Histories in Museums*, edited by Gaynor Kavanagh, 176–87. London: Leicester University Press, 1996.

Mertens, Donna, John Fraser, and Joe Heimlich. "M or F? Gender, Identity, and the Transformative Research Paradigm." *Museums & Social Issues* 3, no. 1 (April 1, 2008): 81–92.

Metcalfe, Robin. *Queer Looking, Queer Acting: Lesbian and Gay Vernacular*. Halifax, NS: Mount Saint Vincent University Art Gallery, 1997.

Meyer, Leisa D. *Creating GI Jane: Sexuality and Power in the Women's Army Corps during World War II*. New York: Columbia University Press, 1996.

Meyerowitz, Joanne J. *How Sex Changed: A History of Transsexuality in the United States*. Cambridge, MA: Harvard University Press, 2002.

———. *Women Adrift: Independent Wage Earners in Chicago, 1880–1930*. Chicago: University of Chicago Press, 1988.

Milk. Directed by Gus Van Sant. 2008. Universal City, CA: Universal Studios Home Entertainment, 2009. DVD.

Miller, Heather Lee. "Sexologists Examine Lesbians and Prostitutes in the United States, 1840–1940." *NWSA Journal* 12, no. 3 (Fall 2000): 67–91.

Mills, Robert. "Queer Is Here? Lesbian, Gay, Bisexual and Transgender Histories and Public Culture." *History Workshop Journal*, no. 62 (October 1, 2006): 253–63.

———. "Theorizing the Queer Museum." *Museums & Social Issues* 3, no. 1 (April 1, 2008): 41–52.

Muller, Klaus. "Invisible Visitors: Museums and the Gay and Lesbian Community." *Museum News* 80, no. 5 (October 2001).

Mumford, Kevin J. *Interzones: Black/White Sex Districts in Chicago and New York in the Early Twentieth Century.* New York: Columbia University Press, 1997.

Murdoch, Joyce, and Deb Price. *Courting Justice: Gay Men and Lesbians v. the Supreme Court.* New York: Basic, 2001.

Murphy, Kevin D. "'Secure from All Intrusion': Heterotopia, Queer Space, and the Turn-of-the-Twentieth-Century American Resort." *Winterthur Portfolio* 43, no. 2/3 (Summer 2009): 185–228.

Murphy, Kevin P., Jason Ruiz, and David Serlin. "Editors' Introduction (Queer Transgressions Issue)." *Radical History Review*, no. 100 (Winter 2008): 1–9.

Murrin, John M. "'Things Fearful to Name': Bestiality in Colonial America." *Pennsylvania History* 65 (January 1, 1998): 8–43.

"Museum of Sex | NYC." Accessed May 23, 2014. http://museum.museumofsex.com/.

Neuman, Scott. "N. Dakota's Gay-Marriage Law Challenged; Wisc. Ban Struck Down." *The Two-Way* (blog), *NPR.org*, June 6, 2014. http://www.npr.org/blogs/thetwo-way/2014/06/06/319548157/north-dakotas-gay-marriage-ban-challenged-in-federal-court.

Newman, Sally. "The Archival Traces of Desire: Vernon Lee's Failed Sexuality and the Interpretation of Letters in Lesbian History." *Journal of the History of Sexuality* 14, no. 1/2 (January 2005): 51–75.

Newman, Toni. "President Barack Obama and Transgender Rights: The Real Deal." *Huffington Post*, April 12, 2012. http://www.huffingtonpost.com/toni-newman/obama-transgender-rights_b_1420542.html.

Newton, Esther. *Cherry Grove, Fire Island: Sixty Years in America's First Gay and Lesbian Town.* Boston: Beacon, 1993.

———. "The 'Fun Gay Ladies': Lesbians in Cherry Grove, 1936–1960." In *Creating a Place for Ourselves: Lesbian, Gay, and Bisexual Community Histories*, edited by Brett Beemyn, 145–64. New York: Routledge, 1997.

O'Keefe, Ed. "ENDA, Explained." *The Fix* (blog). *Washington Post*, November 4, 2013. http://www.washingtonpost.com/blogs/the-fix/wp/2013/11/04/what-is-the-employment-non-discrimination-act-enda/.

———. "Senate Votes to Ban Discrimination against Gay and Transgender Workers." *Washington Post*, November 7, 2013. http://www.washingtonpost.com/politics/senate-set-to-approve-gay-rights-bill/2013/11/07/05717e4a-47c1-11e3-a196-3544a03c2351_story.html.

ONE National Gay & Lesbian Archives, ONE Archives Gallery & Museum, University of Southern California, and Pacific Standard Time (Exhibition). *Cruising the Archive: Queer Art and Culture in Los Angeles, 1945–1980.* Edited by Ann Cvetkovich, David Frantz, and Mia Locks. Los Angeles: ONE National Gay & Lesbian Archives, 2011.

Oram, Alison. "Going on an Outing: The Historic House and Queer Public History." *Rethinking History* 15, no. 2 (June 2011): 189–207.

Ossewold, Jurriënne, and Paul Verstraeten. *Two of a Kind: A History of Gays and Lesbians in Holland.* Amsterdam: Amsterdams Historisch Museum, 1989.

"Out West at the Autry." *The Autry.* Accessed May 23, 2014. http://theautry.org/series/out-west.

Peiss, Kathy, and Christina Simmons. *Passion and Power: Sexuality in History.* Philadelphia: Temple University Press, 1989.

Peters, Jeremy W. "Decline and Fall of the 'H' Word." *New York Times*, March 21, 2014. http://www.nytimes.com/2014/03/23/fashion/gays-lesbians-the-term-homosexual.html.

Petry, Michael. "Hidden Histories: The Experience of Curating a Male Same-Sex Exhibition and the Problems Encountered." In *Gender, Sexuality, and Museums: A Routledge Reader*, edited by Amy K. Levin, 151–162. New York: Routledge, 2010.

Phillips, Edward. "Nazi Persecution of Homosexuals: The Curator's View." *Museums & Social Issues* 3, no. 1 (April 1, 2008): 105–14.

Plaster, Joey. "Imagined Conversations and Activist Lineages." *Radical History Review*, no. 113 (Spring 2012): 99–109.

"The Pop-Up Museum of Queer History." Accessed May 23, 2014. http://www.queermuseum.com/.

Potter, Claire Bond. "Taking Back Times Square." *Radical History Review*, no. 113 (Spring 2012): 67–80.

Preston, Julia. "Green Card Is Approved for Gay Men in Florida." *New York Times*, July 1, 2013, final edition.

"The Queer Ancestors Project." 2014. http://www.queerancestorsproject.org/.

"A Queer Timeline for Michigan/Ann Arbor/University of Michigan." Bentley Library, University of Michigan, 2013. http://bentley.umich.edu/exhibits/queer/timeline.pdf.

Rainey, Gertrude "Ma." "Sissy Blues." Paramount 12384-B, 1926.

Ramberg, Jenny. "'Are Queer Folk the People, Too?' Exhibit Review: National Constitution Center, Philadelphia, PA." *Museums & Social Issues* 3, no. 1 (April 1, 2008): 143–49.

Rand, Erica. *The Ellis Island Snow Globe*. Durham, NC: Duke University Press, 2005.

Reach Advisors. "Difficult Issues, Inclusive History." *Museum Audience Insight* (blog), July 8, 2008. http://reachadvisors.typepad.com/museum_audience_insight/2008/07/difficult-issues-inclusive-history.html.

Reis, Elizabeth. "Hermaphrodites and 'Same-Sex' Sex in Early America." In *Long before Stonewall: Histories of Same-Sex Sexuality in Early America*, edited by Thomas A. Foster, 144–63. New York: New York University Press, 2007.

Reynolds, Daniel. "John Boehner: 'No Way' ENDA Will Pass This Year." *Advocate.com*, January 30, 2014. Accessed April 22, 2014. http://www.advocate.com/politics/politicians/2014/01/30/john-boehner-no-way-enda-will-pass-year.

Reynolds, David S. *Walt Whitman*. New York: Oxford University Press, 2005.

Richards, David A. J. *The Sodomy Cases: Bowers v. Hardwick and Lawrence v. Texas*. Lawrence: University Press of Kansas, 2009.

Ridinger, Robert B. Marks. "Sister Fire: Representing the Legacies of Leatherwomen." In *Gender, Sexuality, and Museums: A Routledge Reader*, edited by Amy K. Levin, 172–81. New York: Routledge, 2010.

———. "Things Visible and Invisible: The Leather Archives and Museum." *Journal of Homosexuality* 43, no. 1 (March 2002): 1.

Rochman, Sue. "The Marrying Man." *Advocate*, April 8, 2008, 40–45.

Rosenzweig, Roy, and David Thelen. *The Presence of the Past: Popular Uses of History in American Life*. New York: Columbia University Press, 1998.

Rotundo, Anthony. "Romantic Friendship: Male Intimacy and Middle-Class Youth in the Northern United States, 1800–1900." *Journal of Social History* 23 (Fall 1989): 1–26.

Rubenstein, Maggi. "A Profile of the San Francisco Bisexual Center." *Journal of Homosexuality* 11, no. 1–2 (1985): 227–30.

Rupp, Leila J. *A Desired Past: A Short History of Same-Sex Love in America*. Chicago: University of Chicago Press, 1999.

———. "Romantic Friendships." In *Modern American Queer History*, edited by Allida Mae Black, 13–23. Philadelphia: Temple University Press, 2001.

———. "What's Queer Got to Do with It?" *Reviews in American History* 38, no. 2 (June 2010): 189–98.

Russo, Vito. *The Celluloid Closet: Homosexuality in the Movies*. Rev. ed. New York: Harper & Row, 1987.

Sager, Robin C. "The Multiple Metaphoric Civil Wars of Loreta Janeta Velazquez's 'The Woman in Battle.'" *Southern Quarterly* 48, no. 1 (Fall 2010): 27–45.

Sanders, James H., III. "The Museum's Silent Sexual Performance." *Museums & Social Issues* 3, no. 1 (Spring 2008): 15–25.

San Francisco Planning Department. "LGBT Historic Context Statement." *San Francisco Planning Department*. Accessed February 28, 2014. http://www.sf-planning.org/index.aspx?page=3673.

"Sara Josephine Baker: Public Health Pioneer." *OutHistory.org*. Accessed March 18, 2014. http://outhistory.org/exhibits/show/sara-josephine-baker/background.

Scalia, Antonin. *United States v. Windsor, Dissenting Opinion*, 2013. http://www.supremecourt.gov/opinions/12pdf/12-307_6j37.pdf.

Sedgwick, Eve Kosofsky. *Epistemology of the Closet*. Berkeley: University of California Press, 1990.

Shand-Tucci, Douglass. *Ralph Adams Cram: Life and Architecture. Volume I: Boston Bohemia, 1881–1900*. Amherst: University of Massachusetts Press, 1995.

Sides, Josh. *Erotic City: Sexual Revolutions and the Making of Modern San Francisco*. New York: Oxford University Press, 2009.

Simmons, Christina. "Modern Sexuality and the Myth of Victorian Repression." In *Passion and Power: Sexuality in History*, edited by Kathy Peiss and Christina Simmons, 157–77. Philadelphia: Temple University Press, 1989.

Simon, Nina. *The Participatory Museum*. Santa Cruz, CA: Museum 2.0, 2010.

A Single Man. Directed by Tom Ford. 2009. Culver City, CA: Sony Pictures Home Entertainment, 2010. DVD.

Sleeper, Henry Davis, A. Piatt Andrew, E. Parker Hayden, and Andrew L. Gray. *Beauport Chronicle: The Intimate Letters of Henry Davis Sleeper to Abram Piatt Andrew, Jr., 1906–1915*. Boston: Society for the Preservation of New England Antiquities, 1991.

Smith-Rosenberg, Carroll. "The Female World of Love and Ritual: Relations between Women in Nineteenth-Century America." *Signs: Journal of Women in Culture & Society* 1, no. 1 (1975): 1–29.

Somerville, Siobhan B. *Queering the Color Line: Race and the Invention of Homosexuality in American Culture*. Series Q. Durham, NC: Duke University Press, 2000.

Stein, Marc. *City of Sisterly and Brotherly Loves: Lesbian and Gay Philadelphia, 1945-1972*. Philadelphia: Temple University Press, 2004.

———, ed. *Encyclopedia of Lesbian, Gay, Bisexual, and Transgender History in America*. 3 vols. New York: Scribner / Thomson-Gale, 2004.

———. *Rethinking the Gay and Lesbian Movement*. New York: Routledge, 2012.

———. *Sexual Injustice: Supreme Court Decisions from Griswold to Roe*. Chapel Hill: University of North Carolina Press, 2010.

Steorn, Patrik. "Curating Queer Heritage: Queer Knowledge and Museum Practice." *Curator* 55, no. 3 (July 2012): 355–65.

"Stonewall National Museum and Archives." Accessed May 23, 2014. http://www.stonewallnationalmuseum.org/.

Stryker, Susan. *Gay by the Bay: A History of Queer Culture in the San Francisco Bay Area*. San Francisco: Chronicle, 1996.

———. *Transgender History*. Berkeley: Seal, 2008.

———. "Transgender History, Homonormativity, and Disciplinarity." *Radical History Review*, no. 100 (Winter 2008): 144–57.

Taylor, Tatum. "Undeniable Conjecture: Placing LGBT Heritage." Fitch Prize winning paper, Columbia University, 2011. http://preservationalumni.org/Default.aspx?pageId=785573.

Terry, Jennifer. *An American Obsession: Science, Medicine, and Homosexuality in Modern Society*. Chicago: University of Chicago Press, 1999.

"That's So Gay: Outing Early America." *Gay History in the Collections of the Library Company of Philadelphia*. Accessed May 30, 2014. http://www.gayatlcp.org/.

Thompson, Roger. *Sex in Middlesex: Popular Mores in a Massachusetts County, 1649–1699*. Amherst: University of Massachusetts Press, 1986.

Trexler, Richard C. *Sex and Conquest: Gendered Violence, Political Order, and the European Conquest of the Americas*. Cambridge: Polity, 1995.

Tseliou, Maria Anna. "Spotlight on Research—Subverting the Hetero-normative Museum." *Incluseum* (blog), April 11, 2013. http://incluseum.com/2013/04/11/spotlight-on-research-subverting-the-hetero-normative-museum/.

Tucker, Elizabeth. Phone interview with Susan Ferentinos, April 29, 2014.

Turino, Kenneth, and Susan Ferentinos. "Entering the Mainstream: Interpreting GLBT History." *AASLH History News*, Autumn 2012.

Tyburczy, Jennifer. "All Museums Are Sex Museums." *Radical History Review*, no. 113 (Spring 2012): 199–211.

US Census Bureau. "Historical Statistics of the United States." *Millenial Online Edition*, 2006. http://hsus.cambridge.org.ezproxy.lib.indiana.edu/HSUSWeb/index.do.

Vagnone, Frank D. "A Note from Franklin D. Vagnone, Executive Director." *Historic House Trust Newsletter*, Fall 2010.

Van Cleve, Stewart. *Land of 10,000 Loves: A History of Queer Minnesota*. Minneapolis: University of Minnesota Press, 2012.

Vanegas, Angela. "Representing Lesbians and Gay Men in British Social History Museums." In *Gender, Sexuality, and Museums: A Routledge Reader*, edited by Amy K. Levin, 163–71. New York: Routledge, 2010.

Verloo, Mieke. "Intersectional and Cross-Movement Politics and Policies: Reflections on Current Practices and Debates." *Signs* 38, no. 4 (June 1, 2013): 893–915.

Vicinus, Martha. "The History of Lesbian History." *Feminist Studies* 38, no. 3 (Fall 2012): 566–96.

Warner, Mary. "Fighting Homophobia in Stealth Mode." *AASLH Small Museums Online Community* (blog), June 1, 2012. http://blogs.aaslh.org/fighting-homophobia-in-stealth-mode/.

Weber, Andrew, and Brock Thompson. "Gay Rights and the Law: The Library of Congress Displays Gay Rights Documents." *In Custodia Legis: Law Librarians of Congress* (blog), Library of Congress, June 1, 2011. http://blogs.loc.gov/law/2011/06/gay-rights-and-the-law/.

Weeks, Jeffrey. *Sexuality*. 3rd ed. New York: Routledge, 2010.

Wesling, Meg. "The Unequal Promise of Marriage Equality." *American Quarterly* 66, no. 1 (March 2014): 171–79.

Wharton, Edith, and Ogden Codman Jr. *The Decoration of Houses*. New York: Scribner, 1897.

White, C. Todd. *Pre-Gay L.A.: A Social History of the Movement for Homosexual Rights*. Urbana: University of Illinois Press, 2009.

White House. "President Obama: It Gets Better." YouTube video, 3:07. Posted October 21, 2010. http://www.youtube.com/watch?v=geyAFbSDPVk&feature=youtube_gdata_player.

White, Kevin. *The First Sexual Revolution: Male Heterosexuality in Modern America*. New York: New York University Press, 1992.

Wilson, Fred, Paula Marincola, and Marjorie Schwartzer. "Mining the Museum Revisited: A Conversation." In *Letting Go? Sharing Historical Authority in a User-Generated World*, edited by Bill Adair, Benjamin Filene, and Laura Koloski, 230–41. Philadelphia: Pew Center for Arts & Heritage, 2011.

Woods, Carly S., Joshua P. Ewalt, and Sara J. Baker. "A Matter of Regionalism: Remembering Brandon Teena and Willa Cather at the Nebraska History Museum." *Quarterly Journal of Speech* 99, no. 3 (2013): 341–63.

Wrathall, John D. "Provenance as Text: Reading the Silences around Sexuality in Manuscript Collections." *Journal of American History* 79, no. 1 (June 1992): 165–78.

Yellis, Ken. "Concerning the Telling of Painful Tales: The Case of Masks of the Sacred Bush." *Curator* 55, no. 2 (April 2012): 139–51.

Young, Alfred F. *Masquerade: The Life and Times of Deborah Sampson, Continental Soldier*. New York: Knopf, 2004.

———. "A Modest Proposal: A Bill of Rights for American Museums." *Public Historian* 14, no. 3 (July 1, 1992): 67–75.

Index

abnormal. *See* norm: concept of
Acquired Immunodeficiency Syndrome. *See* AIDS
activism, LGBT:
    1960s radicalization of, 77-79
    1990s, 90-95
    AIDS. *See* AIDS: activism
    feminism. *See* feminism
    gay liberation, 66, 77-82, 85
    homophile movement, 66-70, 78
    lesbian, 67-68, 82, 90
    marriage equality. *See* marriage: same-sex
    military participation. 92-93, 96
    pride events. *See* LGBT pride events
ACT UP (AIDS Coalition to Unleash Power), 89-90
Addams, Jane, 11, 24, 26, 53;
    See also Jane Addams Hull-House Museum
adolescents. *See* youth
African American:
    association with sexual deviance (assumed), 39, 49-50, 57
    civil rights movement, 68, 76, 77, 92, 97
    education, 52
    feminists, 68, 82
    group, 36, 40, 50, 67, 82, 97
    individuals, 37, 60-61, 66, 68, 82, 100n32, 104
    neighborhoods, 60-61, 76, 93
    slavery. *See* slavery
    stereotypes of, 36, 39
    See also race
AIDS, 76, 86-90, 94;
    activism, 87-90, 92
    government response to, 88
    memory of, 3, 13, 91, 135, 164-65
    treatment, 86, 89-90, 92
AIDS/Brooklyn, 13

Alice Austen House, 113-14
Andrew, A. Piatt, 133
alternative labeling project. *See* Jane Addams Hull-House Museum
annual reminders (protests), 69
archives. *See* libraries and archives
Arkansas, 103
art:
    museums. *See* museums: art
    visual, 42, 110-111, 113, 116n8
    See also film; *Gay Liberation* (memorial); literature; music; television
Asian Americans, 40, 50, 67, 146;
    See also immigrants; race
Atlanta. *See* Atlanta History Center; John Q Collective
Atlanta History Center, 111-12, 155, 161
audiences. *See* museums: audiences
Austen, Alice, 113-14
Autry National Center of the American West, 15, 110, 161, 163;
    See also *Out West*
Azbug, Bella, 84

Bailey, Ann, 34
Baker, Sarah Josephine, 53
Baldwin, Tammy, 83
balls. *See* gender crossing: drag balls
Bamberger, Rose, 67
bars. *See* gathering places, LGBT
bathhouses. *See* gathering places, LGBT
Beauport, 132-35, 136
Becoming Visible: The Legacy of Stonewall, 15, 111, 113
Bello, Ada, 68
Bello, Maria, 104

197

Ben, Lisa. *See* Eyde, Edith
Benjamin, Harry 64
Bentley, Gladys, 60
berdache. *See* gender crossing: Two-Spirit
Bird, Merton L., 66
Bisexual Center, 145
bisexuality, 6, 21, 58, 60, 90, 104, 145-46
Blackwell, Emily, 53
Bonner, Cleo, 68
Boston, 50, 82;
    marriage. *See* marriage: Boston
    See also Boston Public Library; Historic New England;
Boston Public Library, 111
Bowers v. Hardwick, 88, 96
Bowman, Karl, 64
Briggs Initiative, 84, 90
Briggs, John, 84
Brooklyn Historical Society, 13
Brown, Addie, 37
Brown, Rita Mae, 82
Bryant, Anita, 84-85
Buchanan, Pat, 87
Buffalo Bill Center of the West, 163
Buford, Harry T., 42
butch-femme, 64, 90

California, 40, 66-67, 84, 90, 95, 97;
    See also Autry National Center of the American West; GLBT History Museum; Long Beach; Los Angeles; ONE Archives Gallery and Museum; *Out West*; Queer Ancestors Project; Rosie the Riveter/World War II National Historical Park; San Francisco
cataloging. *See* museums: collections
Cammermeyer, Margarethe, 92-93
Carpenter, Edward, 42, 56
Cashier, Albert, 42
Cather, Willa, 53
Cercle Hermaphroditis, 51
Chafee, John, 40
Chamberlain, Jason, 40
Chicago, 50, 56, 66, 76, 81, 124
    See also Chicago History Museum; International Museum of Surgical Sciences; Jane Addams Hull-House Museum; Leather Archives and Museum
Chicago History Museum, 112, 119-30, 161, 163, 165

Chicago Medical Society, 124
Christopher Street Liberation Day, 69, 81
Citizens Committee to Outlaw Entrapment, 67
Civil War, 41-42
Clark, Badger, 40
class, 27n9, 39-40, 53-54, 55;
    with sexual deviance (assumed), 25, 50, 51, 57, 59
    intersectionality with sexual orientation 7, 23, 89
    privilege, 33, 34-35
    stratification in US society, 35-36, 92
    working, 36, 54, 58-59, 61, 64
Cleveland, Rose, 53
Clinton, Bill, 93, 95
Codman Estate, 135-37, 157
Codman, Ogden, Jr., 135-37
Cold War, 62-65
college. *See* educational settings
colonial period, 29-34
Colorado, 93, 94
Columbia Hall, 50-51
Combahee River Collective, 82
Come Out!, 80
coming out, 60, 80, 91
Committee for Homosexual Freedom, 78
communism, 63, 66
Compton's Cafeteria Riot, 79
Comstock, Anthony, 44
Comstock Law, 44, 56-57, 67
Connecticut, 29, 31, 69
Congress, 62, 69, 92, 93, 95, 96, 104;
    LGBT candidates for, 81, 83
    See also names of specific laws and bills
Cooper, Gary, 133-34
controversy. *See* museums: controversy in
Corbin, Joan. *See* Elloree, Eve
Council on Religion and the Homosexual, 69, 78
courts. *See* legal cases
Cram, Ralph Adams, 136
Creating the United States, 155
cruising, 50-51, 83, 87, 152;
    See also sex: anonymous
Cullen, Countee, 61

Daley, Tom, 105
Daughters of Bilitis, 67-68, 95
Davis, Clive, 104
Day, F. Holland, 42

Defense of Marriage Act (DOMA), 95, 96-97
DeGrieck, Jerry, 84
Dewson, Molly, 24
Diagnostic and Statistical Manual of Mental Disorders. *See* mental illness, equation of LGBT identity with
difference:
    among LGBT people, 5-7, 23, 25-26, 162
    as a way to structure society, 7, 23, 34-35, 57, 123, 157
disco. *See* music
discrimination, employment, 61, 78, 94;
    civil servants' experience of, 62-63
    legal protection against, 104
    military, 62-63, 69
domestic partner benefits, 94-95
Don't Ask, Don't Tell (DADT). *See* military: Don't Ask, Don't Tell (DADT)
drag. *See* gender crossing: drag; gender crossing: drag balls
Drum, 78

Eakins, Thomas, 42
Eckstein, Ernestine, 68
economics, 35-36, 50, 53-54, 61, 83
educational settings:
    anti-LGBT politics and, 84, 93
    contemporary, 5, 91, 96, 125-27, 141-49
    history, 52-53, 84, 93
    See also gay-straight alliances
eighteenth century, 32-35, 36;
    See also colonial period; revolutionary period
Eisenhower, Dwight D., 63
Eiteljorg Museum of American Indians and Western Art, 163
elections. *See* politics
Ellis, Havelock, 56, 71-72n26
Elloree, Eve, 67
employment discrimination. *See* discrimination, employment
Employment Non-Discrimination Act (ENDA), 104
Enlightenment, 32-34
Equality Act of 1974, 84
Erickson, Reed, 141
erotica. *See* pornography
Etheridge, Melissa, 92
Executive Order 10450, 63
exhibits. *See names of individual exhibits*
Eyde, Edith, 66

Falwell, Jerry, 87
Feinstein, Dianne, 87
female impersonation. *See* gender crossing
feminism, 76, 80, 85;
    lesbians and, 59, 68, 82-83, 90, 145
    See also suffrage movement: women's
fetishism, 10, 56
Fields, Annie Adams, 137-39
film, 3, 60, 65, 91-92;
    actors, 88, 104
    museums and. *See* museums: film in
Florida, 31, 84-85;
    See also Stonewall National Museum and Archives
Foster, Jodie, 104
Frank, Barney, 83
Freud, Sigmund, 39, 56, 61
Friendship and Freedom, 66
frontier, 39-41

gathering places, LGBT, 50-51, 60-61, 78-79, 83, 87-88, 145
gay:
    bars. *See* gathering places, LGBT
    liberation. *See* activism, LGBT: gay liberation
    pride events. *See* LGBT pride events
    straight alliances, 91, 127, 143
Gay Academic Union, 129
Gay Activist Alliance, 81
Gay Liberation (memorial), 13-14
Gay Liberation Front, 80-81
Gay Men's Health Crisis (GMHC), 87
Gay Ohio History Initiative (GOHI), 13, 152
gender crossing, 51, 54, 64;
    drag, 40, 41, 64, 114
    drag balls, 51, 60, 69
    effeminacy in males, 33, 57-58
    frontier, 40, 41
    individuals, 34, 42
    inversion, 25, 55-56, 57
    See also medicine: medical definitions of same-sex sexual behavior and gender variance
    Two-Spirit, 30, 40, 146-47
    See also transgender
Georgia. *See* Atlanta History Center; John Q Collective
Gerber, Henry, 66
Gernreich, Rudi, 66
Gitting, Barbara, 68

GLBT Historical Society. *See* GLBT History Museum
GLBT History Museum, 110, 111, 112, 127, 129
Glide Urban Center, 78-79
Green, Tyler, 104
groups, LGBT. *See* organizations, LGBT
Gruber, James, 66

Harlem, 60-61, 93
hate crimes. *See* violence
Hawaii, 95
Hay, Harry, 66-67
Hays Code, 65
heroic friendship, 33-34, 36;
   See also romantic friendship
heteronormativity. *See* museums: as conveyors of cultural values
high school. *See* educational settings; youth
Hirschfeld, Magnus, 56, 64, 71-72n26
Historic House Trust of New York City, 113-14
Historic New England, 11, 130-39, 157, 161
historic sites. *See* Alice Austen House; Beauport; Codman Estate, Historic New England; Jane Addams Hull-House Museum; museums; Rosie the Riveter/ World War II Home Front National Historical Park; Sarah Orne Jewett House
History Project, 111, 135, 136, 137
historiography, 22-23, 27n3, 163-64;
   changing understandings, 22-23, 30, 36, 38
   disagreements over evidence, 30, 34, 39
Hodgers, Jennie, 42
Holder, Eric, 104
Hollingsworth v Perry, 97
Holocaust, memory of, 12, 87
Holocaust Memorial Museum. *See* United States Holocaust Memorial Museum
homelessness, 78-79, 128
homophile movement. *See* activism, LGBT: homophile movement
house museums. *See* Alice Austen House; Beauport; Codman Estate, Historic New England; Jane Addams Hull-House Museum; museums; Sarah Orne Jewett House
Hosmer, Harriet, 42
Hudson, Rock, 88
Hughes, Langston, 61
Hull, Bob, 66

Hull House. *See* Addams, Jane; Jane Addams Hull-House Museum

Idaho, 103
Illinois, 42, 50, 56, 66, 69, 81;
   See also Chicago History Museum; Illinois State Archives; International Museum of Surgical Sciences; Jane Adams Hull-House Museum, Leather Archives and Museum
Illinois State Archives, 124
immigrants, 40, 50, 58, 87-88, 103
Indiana, 60, 64, 103;
   See also Eiteljorg Museum of American Indians and Western Art
International Museum of Surgical Sciences, 124
intersex, 31
inversion. *See* gender-crossing: inversion
invisibility, LGBT, 11-15, 23-24, 61, 64, 113

Jane Addams Hull-House Museum, 11, 26, 129, 165
Janus Society, 77-78
Jay, Karla, 82
Jennings, Dale, 66-67
Jewett, Sarah Orne, 136-39
job discrimination. *See* discrimination, employment
John Q Collective, 110-11, 162
Jordan, Barbara, 100n32
Jorgensen, Christine, 64-65

Kameny, Frank, 69, 81, 83, 155
Kansas, 85, 95;
   See also Nelson-Atkins Museum of Art
Kennedy, Anthony, 93, 96
Kentucky, 94, 103, 104
Kertbeny, Karl Maria, 56
Kiernan, James G., 56
Kinsey, Alfred, 64-65
Kinsey Report, 64-65
Knights of the Clock, 66, 74n63
Koedt, Anne, 82
Kowalski, Sharon, 94
Kozachenko, Kathy, 84
Krafft-Ebing, Richard von, 56

The Ladder, 67
Lang, K.D., 92
language. *See* terminology

latinos:
    group, 39-41
    individuals, 42, 68, 69, 81-82
Lavender Menace, 82
Lavender University, 129
Lawrence, Louise, 68
Lawrence v. Texas, 95-96
laws, 51, 55, 62, 84, 92-97, 103;
    See also Briggs Initiative; Comstock Law; Defense of Marriage Act (DOMA); Employment Non-Discrimination Act; Equality Act of 1974; Measure 9; Proposition 8; sodomy (crime)
leather, 10;
    See also sadomasochism
Leather Archives and Museum, 112, 127
legal cases, 67, 89, 94-95, 103;
    colonial era, 29, 30-31
    Supreme Court, 67, 88, 93, 95-97, 103, 105
Lesbian Avengers, 90
Lesbian Resource Center, 145
lesbian sex wars. *See* sex: wars, lesbian
Leslie Lohman Museum of Gay and Lesbian Art, 110
Lewis, Edmonia, 42
LGBT pride events, 69, 81;
    See also Christopher Street Liberation Day
Liberty Bell protests. *See* annual reminders (protests)
libraries and archives, 111-12;
    See also Atlanta History Center; Boston Public Library; Illinois State Archives; Library Company of Philadelphia; Library of Congress; museums: collections; New York Public Library; Tretter Collection in GLBT Studies
Library Company of Philadelphia, 153-54
Library of Congress, 155
literature, 40, 42-43, 61, 65, 82;
    authors, 53, 61, 137-39
Long Beach (California), 51, 68
Lorde, Audre, 82
Los Angeles, 66-67, 76, 81, 86, 88;
    See also Autry National Center of the American West; ONE Archives Gallery and Museum; *Out West*
Lydston, G. Frank, 56
Lyon, Phyllis, 67-68, 95

magazines, LGBT. *See* periodicals, LGBT
Maine. *See* Historic New England; Sarah Orne Jewett House
male impersonation. *See* gender crossing
marriage:
    as a societal stabilizer, 30, 32, 33
    Boston, 53, 59, 61, 137-39
    heterosexual, 23, 27n9, 37, 52-54, 60, 62
    interracial, 40
    relationship to economics, 36, 53-54
    same-sex, 9-10, 67, 83, 93-97, 103, 128, 164
Martin, Del, 67-68, 95
Maryland, 94
Matlovich, Leonard, 92-93
Mattachine Society, 66-67, 69
Massachusetts, 50, 82, 83, 84, 95;
    See also Beauport; Boston Public Library; Codman Estate; Historic New England; History Project
McIlvenna, Tim, 78
McKay, Claude, 61
Measure 9, 93
medicine:
    access to medical care, 87-90, 92, 94
    field of, 55, 64, 87, 124
    medical decision making, 94, 96
    medical definitions of same-sex sexual behavior and gender variance, 6, 25, 29, 55-59, 64
    sex-reassignment, 6, 56, 64, 65, 81, 141
    See also AIDS; sexuality: studies of
Memory Flash, 162
mental illness, equation of LGBT identity with, 6, 56-57, 61-62, 81, 87;
    See also medicine: field of
methodology, 23-26
Metropolitan Community Church, 93-94
Mexican Americans. *See* Latinos
Miami, 84-85
Michigan, 76, 84, 103
military, 34, 42, 51, 62, 63, 92-93;
    Don't Ask, Don't Tell (DADT), 93, 96
    Screening for HIV, 88
Milk, Harvey, 84
Miller, Terry, 96
Miller, Wentworth, 104
Mining the Museum, 10
Minneapolis/ St. Paul, 84, 85, 145;
    See also Minnesota Historical Society; Tretter Collection in GLBT Studies

Minnesota, 84, 85, 94, 145;
See also Minnesota Historical Society; Morrison County (MN) Historical Society; Tretter Collection in GLBT Studies
Minnesota Historical Society, 11, 112, 141-49, 163
Missouri, 95
Morrison County (MN) Historical Society, 11
Moscone, George, 84
movies. See film
Museum of History and Industry (MOHAI), 12, 154, 161, 162
Museum of Sex, 110, 161, 162
Museum of Vancouver, 156, 161
museums:
   art, 110, 129, 161, 163
   as conveyors of cultural values, 10, 11-12, 157
   as facilitators, 10, 11
   as sites of public dialogue, 9-11
   audiences, 11, 12-15, 124-28, 135
   collections, 12-13, 112-13, 124, 136
   controversy in, 10-11, 113, 116n8, 127
   exhibits. See names of individual exhibits
   film in, 123-24, 127, 128-29
   inclusive interpretation, 11-15, 124-25, 155-56, 166
   LGBT communities and, 113, 124-28, 133-35, 152, 162-63
   partners, 124, 129 135, 137, 141-49, 162-63
   sexual content in, 12, 112-13, 127, 135, 156-57
   staff, 121-23, 133-35, 148-49, 152, 161
   tours. See tours
   visitor studies, 11, 12, 128
   See also Atlanta History Center; Autry National Center of the American West; Brooklyn Historical Society; Buffalo Bill Center of the West, Chicago History Museum; Eiteljorg Museum of American Indians and Western Art; GLBT History Museum; historic sites; International Museum of Surgical Sciences; Jane Addams Hull-House Museum; Leather Archives and Museum; Leslie Lohman Museum of Gay and Lesbian Art; libraries and archives; Minnesota Historical Society; Morrison County (MN) Historical Society; Museum of History and Industry; Museum of Sex; Museum of Vancouver; National Constitution Center; National Museum of American History; National Museum of Fine Arts (Sweden); Nelson-Atkins Museum of Art; ONE Archives Gallery and Museum; Pop-Up Museum of Queer History; Rosie the Riveter/ World War II Home Front National Historical Park; Stonewall National Museum and Archives; ToonSeum, tours, United State Holocaust Memorial Museum
music, 60-61, 83, 92, 104

National Constitution Center, 113, 155-56
National Gay and Lesbian Task Force, 81
National Museum of American History, 166
National Museum of Fine Arts (Sweden), 161
National Organization of Women (NOW), 82
National Park Service. See National Register of Historic Places; Rosie the Riveter/National World War II Home Front National Historical Park
National Register of Historic Places, 75
Native Americans, 30, 32, 39-41, 146-47
Navratilova, Martina, 145
Nazi Persecution of Homosexuals, 1933-1945, 12-13
Nebraska, 92;
   See also Nebraska Historical Society
Nebraska Historical Society, 155-56
Nelson-Atkins Museum of Art, 129
New Jersey, 76
New Mexico, 95
Newport Naval Training Station, 51
New York (state), 31, 61, 84, 95, 96;
   See also Alice Austen House; Brooklyn Historical Society; *Gay Liberation* (memorial); Historic House Trust of New York City; Leslie Lohman Museum of Gay and Lesbian Art; Museum of Sex; New York City; New York Public Library; Pop-Up Museum of Queer History
New York City, 50-51, 60-61, 66, 78, 93;
   AIDS and, 87-89
   Stonewall riots and their legacy, 79-82
   See also Alice Austen House; Brooklyn Historical Society; *Gay Liberation* (memorial); Historic House Trust of New York City; Leslie Lohman Museum of Gay and Lesbian Art; Museum of Sex; New York Public Library; Pop-Up Museum of Queer History

New York Public Library, 15, 111, 113
Newsom, Gavin, 95
newspapers, LGBT. *See* periodicals, LGBT
nineteenth century, 35-44, 49-59
Nobilette, M. K., 104
Noble, Elaine, 84
nonmonogamy, 10, 83, 152
norm, concept of, 7, 57;
    See also difference: as a way to structure society

Obama, Barack, 93, 96, 104
Ohio Historical Society. *See* Ohio History
    Connection
Ohio History Connection, 13, 152
Oklahoma, 95, 103
ONE, 67
ONE Archives Gallery and Museum, 110, 112
ONE v. Olesen, 67
Oral history, 111, 112, 116n13, 133, 155, 162
Oregon, 50-51, 85, 93, 95, 103
organizations, LGBT, 51, 66-69, 77-82, 87,
    89-90, 129
Outhistory.org, 145, 165
Out in Chicago, 112, 119-30, 162, 163, 165
Out West, 15, 110, 152, 161, 163

Page, Ellen, 104
parenting, 61-62, 94
Parents and Friends of Lesbians and Gays
    (PFLAG), 91, 121
Paresis Hall. *See* Columbia Hall
partners. *See* domestic partner benefits; museums:
    partners
Paul, Alice, 24
Pennsylvania, 32, 69, 77-78, 103;
    See also Library Company of Philadelphia;
    National Constitution Center; ToonSeum
periodicals, LGBT, 66-68, 78, 80, 135
Philadelphia, 62, 69, 77-78;
    See also Library Company of Philadelphia;
    National Constitution Center
police treatment, 51, 66-67, 69, 78-79, 81-82;
    See also laws
politics, 76, 84, 92-97;
    anti-LGBT, 84-88, 92-97
    LGBT candidates and elected officials, 69, 81,
    83-84
    See also activism, LGBT; African American: civil
    rights movement; Congress; feminism; laws;
    social reform; suffrage movement: women's

polyamory. *See* nonmonogamy
Popov, Traian, 103
Pop-Up Museum of Queer History, 110, 111
pornography, 77-78, 90, 136, 157;
    See also Comstock Law
Portland (Oregon), 51, 95
Primus, Rebecca, 37
Prince, Virginia, 68
Progressive Era 49-54
Proposition 6. *See* Briggs Initiative
Proposition 8, 97
psychology. *See* medicine, field of; mental illness,
    equation of LGBT identity with
Public Faces/ Private Lives: Boston's Lesbian and
    Gay History, 111, 135
public opinion, 9-10, 87, 91, 96;
    See also museums: visitor studies

queer:
    studies, 7
    use of the term. *See* terminology
Queer Ancestors Project, 110
Queer Nation, 90
Queering the Museum, 162
    See also *Revealing Queer*

race, 34-35, 39-41, 55, 64, 92;
    assumptions about sexual deviance and, 39, 51,
    57
    intersectionality with sexual orientation, 7, 23,
    82, 87, 89, 92
Radicalesbians. *See* Lavender Menace
Rainey, Ma, 60-61
Reagan, Ronald, 86, 88
Reid, Ann Carll, 67
religion, 10, 29-31, 34, 87, 93, 104; social reform
    and, 44, 85
    See also Council on Religion and the
    Homosexual
Religious Right. *See* politics: anti-LGBT
research. *See* historiography; methodology
Revealing Queer, 12, 154, 162
revolutionary period, 34-35
Rhode Island, 51
romantic friendship, 25, 36-39, 41, 53;
    See also heroic friendship
Romer v. Evans, 93, 96
Rosie the Riveter/National World War II Home
    Front National Historical Park, 11, 161, 165
Rowland, Chuck, 66

sadomasochism, 90, 56, 152;
    See also leather
Saint Paul. See Minneapolis/ St. Paul
Salt Lake City, 61
Sam, Michael, 105
same-sex:
    environments, 25, 31-32, 40-41, 44, 50, 51-52
    marriage. See marriage: same-sex
    See also military; separate spheres
Sampson, Deborah, 34
San Francisco, 69, 81, 84, 90, 95, 145;
    AIDS and, 87-88
    lesbians, 61, 67
    See also GLBT History Museum; Queer Ancestors Project
San Francisco AIDS Foundation, 87
San Francisco Public Health Department, 78, 87-88
Sarah Orne Jewett House, 136-39
Sargent, John Singer, 42
Sarria, José, 69
Savage, Dan, 96
Save Our Children, 85, 90
Scalia, Antonin, 103
schools. See educational settings; youth
Schroeder, Patricia, 93
science. See medicine: field of
Seattle, 84;
    See also Museum of History and Industry (MOHAI)
secrecy. See invisibility, LGBT
Sension, Nicholas, 29
separate spheres, 36
seventeenth century. See colonial period
sex:
    anonymous, 51, 78, 83, 87
    change. See medicine: sex reassignment
    reassignment. See medicine: sex reassignment
    segregation. See same-sex environments
    wars, lesbian, 90
sexology. See medicine; sexuality: studies of
Sex Talk in the City, 156, 161, 162
sexuality:
    in museum exhibitions. See museums: sexual content in
    insight to be gained from studying, 7, 23, 123, 157
    social construction of, 7, 22-23
    studies of, 52, 60, 64-65
Shepard, Matthew, 92

Silverman, Mervyn, 87
Simpson, Amanda, 96
Simpson, Evangeline, 53
slavery, 31-32; 34-35, 36, 39;
    See also African American
Sleeper, Henry Davis, 11, 24, 132-35, 136
Smith, Barbara, 82
Smith, Bessie, 60
Smith, Mary Rozet, 26, 53;
    See also Jane Addams Hull-House Museum
Smithsonian. See National Museum of American History
Snake Pit, 81
social reform, 44, 50, 53
Society for Human Rights, 66
Society for Individual Rights, 69
sodomy (crime), 29, 30-31, 32, 51, 88;
    military and, 42
    repeal of sodomy laws, 69, 95-96
sources, historical, 22, 23-24, 36, 39, 57, 133;
    See also methodology
sports, 105, 145
stakeholders, input, 5, 124-29, 151-52, 162
Stevens, Konrad, 66
Stonewall National Museum and Archives, 110, 112, 157
Stonewall riots, 79-80;
    context for, 75-79
    legacy, 80-82
Street Transvestite Action Coalition (STAR), 81
Studds, Gerry, 83
subcultures, creation of LGBT 25-26, 29-30, 33, 50-51, 61, 83
suffrage movement, women's, 53, 59
Summer History Immersion Program (SHIP). See Minnesota Historical Society
Supreme Court. See legal cases: Supreme Court
sustainability of LGBT interpretation, 128-30, 165-66
Symonds, John Addington, 42, 56

Tate, Gertrude, 113-14
Teena, Brandon, 92
teens. See youth
television, 91, 145
Tennessee, 103
Tequila, Tila, 146
terminology, 5-7, 25-26, 153-54, 163, 164
Texas, 94, 95, 100n32, 103;
    See also *Lawrence v. Texas*

That's So Gay: Outing Early America, 153-54
Third World AIDS Advisory Task Force (TWAATF), 87
Thomas, M. Carey, 24, 53
Thompson, Karen, 94
Thurman, Wallace, 61
Tobin, Kay, 68
ToonSeum, 165
tours, 113, 129, 133-39, 161
transgender, 56, 64, 78-79, 90, 92, 96, 104;
    definitions, 6, 81
    individuals, 65, 68, 96
    interpretation in museums, 11, 152
    neglect within LGBT politics, 6, 21, 81, 83, 104
    See also gender crossing; medicine: medical definitions of same-sex sexual behavior and gender variance; medicine: sex-reassignment
Transvestia, 68
Trent, Djaun, 104
Tretter Collection in GLBT Studies, 141-49
Trout, Benjamin, 51
twentieth century, 49-70, 75-95;
    1910s, 51, 53, 56
    1920s, 51, 56, 59-61, 66, 76, 93
    1930s, 51, 56, 61-62, 64
    1940s, 62-65, 66
    1950s, 62-68
    1960s, 51, 59, 62-64, 68-70, 75-80, 82, 93
    1970s, 59, 62, 77, 80-85, 94
    1980s, 83, 84, 86-90, 94
    1990s, 5, 83, 90-95, 153
twenty-first century, 57-58, 81, 83, 95-97, 103-5
Two-Spirit. *See* gender crossing: Two-Spirit

Ulrichs, Karl Heinrich, 55-56
United States Holocaust Memorial Museum, 12-13
United States v. Windsor, 96-97, 103, 105
university. *See* educational settings
University of Minnesota. *See* Tretter Collection in GLBT Studies
Unspoken Past: Atlanta's Lesbian and Gay History, 1940-1970, 111-12, 155
urbanization, 36, 42-43, 50-52, 70n3
Utah, 61, 103

Vanguard, 79
Van Waters, Miriam, 24

Velazquez, Loreta Janeta, 42
Vermont, 95
Vice Versa, 66
video. *See* film
Vinales, Alfredo Diego, 81-82
violence, 76, 84, 92, 96, 127-28;
    sexual, 30, 39, 90
Virginia, 31, 103
visitors. *See* museums: audiences; museums: visitor studies
visual art. *See* art, visual

Washington, DC, 62, 69, 81, 83-84, 103;
    See also Library of Congress; National Museum of American History; National Register of Historic Places; United States Holocaust Memorial Museum
Washington (state), 84;
    See also Museum of History and Industry (MOHAI)
Wechsler, Nancy, 84
We the People: The Nebraska Viewpoint, 155-56
White, Byron, 88
White, Dan, 84
White Night Riots, 84
Whitman, Walt, 42-43
Whitney, Anne, 42
Wilkinson, Jemima, 34
Windsor, Edith, 96-97
Wisconsin, 83, 103
Wittman, Carl, 77
Wolf, Irma. *See* Reid, Ann Carll
women's movement. *See* feminism; suffrage movement, women's
World War II, 56, 62
working classes. *See* class: working
Wyoming, 92, 152;
    See also Buffalo Bill Center of the West

YMCA (Young Men's Christian Association), 44, 51
Young, Darren, 105
youth:
    homosexual development in, 56, 61-62
    LGBT, 78-79, 96
    museums and, 12, 125-27, 141-49
    nineteenth century, 31, 33, 44, 50
    twentieth century, 31, 33, 44, 50
    See also educational settings; gay: straight alliances

About the Authors

Susan Ferentinos is a public history researcher, writer, and consultant based in Bloomington, Indiana, where she specializes in historical project management and using the past to create community. She has lectured widely on the topic of interpreting LGBT history and recently served on the planning team for the National Park Service Women's History Initiative. Ferentinos holds a PhD in US history with a focus on the history of gender and sexuality and a Master of Library Science with a concentration in special collections, both from Indiana University. She has served on the board of the National Collaborative for Women's History Sites and on the Leadership Development Committee of the American Association for State and Local History.

Jill Austin joined the Chicago History Museum as a curator in 2005 after having worked in public history at the Detroit Historical Museum. She got her start in museum education twenty years ago while completing an MA in the history of art and architecture at the University of Pittsburgh. She is currently developing an immersive gallery experience, *Chicago by the Numbers*, in which visitors can use numbers as tools to approach Chicago history, and continues to lead program development of the yearly "Out at CHM" series.

Jennifer Brier is director of the Program in Gender and Women's Studies at the University of Illinois at Chicago, where she is also an associate professor of history. She specializes in US gay and lesbian history, the history of sexuality and gender, and public history. Brier is the author of *Infectious Ideas: U.S. Political Response to the AIDS Crisis* (2009, reissued in paperback in 2011). She is currently at work on an innovative public history project called *History Moves*, a community-curated mobile gallery that will provide a space for Chicago-based community organizers and activists to share their histories with a wide audience.

Kyle Parsons is a diversity outreach specialist with the Minnesota Historical Society, where he works with community outreach programs such as the Museum Fellows Programs, National History Day in Minnesota, and the Summer History Immersion Program. His target audiences are high school and college students, especially those from communities that are traditionally underrepresented in the museum field.

Kenneth C. Turino is manager of community engagement and exhibitions at Historic New England based in Boston, Massachusetts. He oversees Historic New England's community engagement programs throughout all six New England states and the organization's traveling exhibition program. He created and directs the Program in New England Studies, an intensive one-week course of study on New England architecture and material culture. An adjunct professor in the Tufts University Museum Studies Program, he teaches courses on exhibition development and revitalizing historic house museums. Turino is on the Council of the American Association for State and Local History and sits on AASLH's Historic House Committee.

Stewart Van Cleve wrote *Land of 10,000 Loves: A History of Queer Minnesota* (2012) while working as the assistant curator of the Jean-Nickolaus Tretter Collection in GLBT Studies at the University of Minnesota. In 2013, he completed the Master of Urban Studies program at Portland State University's Toulan School of Urban Studies and Planning. He is currently pursuing his second master's degree in library and information science at St. Catherine University.